This book—one in the four-volume set, Global Governance and the Quest for Justice—focuses on the international and regional organisations that represent the key players in the evolving global order.

The papers in this collection seek to map the real world of global governance—exploring who governs and how, what the leading international and regional organisations claim to do and what they actually do—as well as assessing the gap between the ideal of constitutionalised global governance and the actuality of governance under globalisation. The contributors discuss what it would mean for global governance to aspire to Rule of Law standards of transparency, accountability and participation together with categorical respect for human rights.

In this collection, the perspective of modern public lawyers is systematically applied to the governance deficit associated with globalisation and to its institutional correction in pursuit of a legitimate regime of global governance.

Global Governance and the Quest for Justice

Volume I: International and Regional Organisations
Edited by Douglas Lewis

Volume II: Corporate Governance
Edited by Sorcha Macleod and John Parkinson

Volume III: Civil Society
Edited by Peter Odell and Chris Willett

Volume IV: Human Rights
Edited by Roger Brownsword

Global Governance and the Quest for Justice

Volume I: International and Regional Organisations

Edited by
DOUGLAS LEWIS

Douglas Lewis is
Professor of Public Law at the
University of Sheffield

·HART·
PUBLISHING

OXFORD AND PORTLAND, OREGON
2006

Published in North America (US and Canada) by
Hart Publishing
c/o International Specialized Book Services
5804 NE Hassalo Street
Portland, Oregon
97213-3644
USA
Tel: +1 503 287 3093 or toll-free: (1) 800 944 6190
Fax: +1 503 280 8832
E-mail: orders@isbs.com
Web Site: www.isbs.com

Hart Publishing, Salter's Boatyard, Folly Bridge, Abingdon Rd,
Oxford, OX1 4LB Telephone: +44 (0)1865 245533
Fax: +44 (0)1865 794882
email: mail@hartpub.co.uk
WEBSITE: http//:www.hartpub.co.uk

British Library Cataloguing in Publication Data
Data Available

ISBN-13: 978-1-84113-408-6 (paperback)
ISBN-10: 1-84113-408-2 (paperback)

Typeset by Compuscript Ltd, Shannon
Printed and bound in Great Britain by
Biddles Ltd, King's Lynn, Norfolk

Contents

Preface   vii
List of Contributors   xi

Editor's Introduction: International and Regional Organisations
Douglas Lewis   xiii

1   Global Governance and the Search for Justice
    Douglas Lewis   1

2   The Fight Against Global Terrorism—How Can the Law
    Respond to 'New' Terrorism?
    Fergal Davis   21

3   Is the European Central Bank a Case for Institutional
    Adaptation to the Challenges of Globalisation? Implications
    for the European Union's Democratic Legitimacy
    Paulo Vila Maior   39

4   The Globalisation of International Justice
    John Merrills   69

5   The Security Council and the Challenges of Collective
    Security in the Twenty-First Century: What Role for
    African Regional Organisations?
    Ademola Abass   91

6   WTO Law and Environmental Standards: Lessons from
    the TRIPS Agreement?
    Peter Rott   113

7   Legal Fetishism and the Contradictions of the GATS
    Jane Kelsey   133

8   The Legal Protection of Biotechnological Material:
    Concord in Discord
    Margaret Llewelyn   151

9   CARICOM and the Role of Regional Organisations in
    the Global Legal Order
    Richard Kirkham   177

10 Globalisation and Global Justice in Competition Law
    Kim Marshall   199

11 From Constitutions to Constitutionalism: A Constitutional
    Approach for Global Governance
    Miguel Poiares Maduro   227

Preface

L AW, AS LON Fuller famously remarked, orders social life by 'subjecting human conduct to the governance of rules';[1] but, as he also remarked, law is not just about *order*, it is about the establishment of a *just* order.[2] Law, formal as well as informal, hard or soft, high or low, purports to set (just) standards and to provide the framework for the (fair) resolution of disputes. Legal rules, of course, are not the only mechanisms for channelling behaviour—market prices, for example, may be as prohibitive as the rules of the criminal code—but it is a truism that it is society's need for effective and legitimate governance that offers the raison d'etre for law.

Fifty years ago, the legal imagination centred on governance within and by the nation state. The municipal legal system was the paradigm; its architecture (especially its division of the public from the private) cleanlined; its organisation hierarchical; its modus operandi (even if Austin had over-stated the coercive character of law) largely one of command and control; and its authority unquestioned.[3] Beyond the boundaries of local legal systems, the first seeds of regional and global governance had been sown but it was to be some time before they would begin to flower. If anyone ruled the world, it was the governments of nation states.

Fifty years on, the landscape of legal governance looks very different. To be sure, the municipal legal system remains an important landmark. However, governance within the nation state no longer respects a simple division of the public and the private; in many cases, hierarchical organisation has given way to more complex regulatory networks; each particular regulatory space is characterised by its own distinctive regime of governance and stakeholding; command and control is no longer viewed as the principal regulatory response; and, confronted with various crises of legitimacy, nation states have sought to retain public confidence by aspiring to more responsive forms of governance.[4]

---

[1] Lon L Fuller, *The Morality of Law* (New Haven, Yale University Press, 1969) at 96.
[2] Lon L Fuller, 'Positivism and Fidelity to Law—A Reply to Professor Hart' (1957–58) 71 *Harvard Law Review* 630.
[3] Cf HLA Hart, *The Concept of Law* (Oxford, Clarendon Press, 1961).
[4] See eg Julia Black, 'De-centring Regulation: Understanding the Role of Regulation and Self-Regulation in a 'Post-Regulatory' World' (2001) 54 *Current Legal Problems* 103; Norman Douglas Lewis, *Choice and the Legal Order: Rising Above Politics* (London, Butterworths, 1996); Philippe Nonet and Philip Selznick, *Law and Society in Transition: Toward Responsive Law* (New York, Harper & Row, 1978); and Gunther Teubner, 'Substantive and Reflexive Elements in Modern Law' (1983) 17 *Law and Society Review* 239, and 'After Legal Instrumentalism? Strategic Models of Post-Regulatory Law' in Gunther Teubner (ed), *Dilemmas of Law in the Welfare State* (Berlin, Walter de Gruyter, 1986) 299.

At the same time that local governance has grown more complex and difficult to map, the world beyond the nation state has moved on. Not only has regional governance developed rapidly (in Europe, to the point at which a Constitution for the enlarged Union is under debate), but manifold international agencies whose brief is global governance are now operating to regulate fields that are, in some cases, narrow and specialised but, in other cases, broad and general. If mapping municipal law has become more challenging, this applies *a fortiori* to governance at the regional or global level where the regulatory players and processes may be considerably less transparent. Moreover, these zones of governance— the local, the regional, and the global—do not operate independently of one another. Accordingly, any account of governance in the Twenty-First Century must be in some sense an account of global governance because the activities of global regulators impinge on the activities of those who purport to govern in both local and regional zones.

To a considerable extent, global governance has grown alongside the activities of organisations whose predominant concerns have been international security and the promotion of respect for human rights. However, it has been the push towards a globalised economy that has perhaps exerted the greater influence—that is to say, 'globalisation' has served to accelerate both the actuality, and our perception, of global governance. With the lowering of barriers to trade and the making of new markets (traditional as well as electronic), the processes of integration and harmonisation have been set in motion and the governance activities of bodies such as the IMF, the World Bank and the WTO have assumed a much higher profile.[5] If nation states still rule the world, their grip on the reins of governance seems much less secure.

Against this background, *Global Governance and the Quest for Justice* is a four-volume set addressing the legal and ethical deficits associated with the current round of 'globalisation' and discussing the building blocks for modes of global governance that respect the demands of legality and justice. To put this another way, this set explores the tension between the order that is being instated by the governance that comes with globalisation (the reality, as it were, of globalised governance) and the aspiration of a just world order represented by the ideal of global governance.[6]

Each volume focuses on one of four key concerns arising from globalised governance, namely: whether the leading international and regional organisations are sufficiently constitutionalised,[7] whether transnational

---

[5] See eg, Joseph Stiglitz, *Globalization and its Discontents* (London, Penguin, Allen Lane, 2002). For an account that is less focused on the economy, see Boaventura de Sousa Santos, *Toward a New Legal Common Sense* 2nd edn (London, Butterworths, 2002).

[6] Compare the central themes of George Monbiot, *The Age of Consent* (London, Flamingo, 2003).

[7] Douglas Lewis (ed), *International and Regional Organisations*. (Oxford, Hart, 2005).

corporations are sufficiently accountable,[8] whether the distinctive interests of civil society are sufficiently respected[9] and whether human rights are given due protection.[10] If the pathology of globalised governance involves a lack of institutional transparency and accountability, the ability of the more powerful players to act outside the rules and to immunise themselves against responsibility, a yawning democratic deficit, and a neglect of human rights, environmental integrity and cultural identity, then this might be a new world order but it falls a long way short of the ideal of global governance.

In the opening years of the Twenty-First Century, the prospects for legitimate and effective governance—that is to say, for lawful governance—are not overwhelmingly good. Local governance, even in the best-run regimes, has its own problems with regard to the effectiveness and legitimacy of its regulatory measures; regionalisation does not always ease these difficulties; and globalised governance accentuates the contrast between the power of those who are unaccountable and the relative powerlessness of those who are accountable. Yet, in every sense, global governance surely is *the* project for the coming generation of lawyers.[11] If the papers in these volumes set in train a sustained, focused and forward-looking debate about the co-ordination of governance in pursuit of our best conception of an ordered and just global community, then they will have served their purpose—and, if law plays its part in setting the framework for the elaboration and application of such global governance, then its purpose, too, will have been fulfilled.

Roger Brownsword and Douglas Lewis
Sheffield, January 2004

---

[8] Sorcha Macleod and John Parkinson (eds), *Corporate Governance*.
[9] Peter Odell and Chris Willett (eds), *Civil Society*.
[10] Roger Brownsword (ed), *Human Rights*.
[11] Cf Douglas Lewis, 'Law and Globalisation: An Opportunity for Europe and its Partners and Their Legal Scholars' (2002) 8 *European Public Law* 219.

List of Contributors

Ademola Abass, Reader in Law, University of Reading

Fergal Davis, Lecturer, Faculty of Law, University of Sheffield

Jane Kelsey, Professor, School of Law, University of Auckland, NZ

Richard Kirkham, Lecturer, Faculty of Law, University of Sheffield

Douglas Lewis, Professor of Public Law, Faculty of Law, University of Sheffield

Margaret Llewelyn, Reader in Intellectual Property Law, Faculty of Law, University of Sheffield

Miguel Maduro, Professor, Law School, Universidade Nova de Lisboa, Portugal

Paulo Vila Maior, Reader, Universidade Fernando Pessoa, Porto, Portugal

Kim Marshall, Senior Lecturer in Law, School of Law, University of Westminster

John Merrills, Professor of International Law, Faculty of Law, University of Sheffield

Peter Rott, Junior Professor of Private Law, University of Bremen, Germany

Editor's Introduction

IN TERMS OF global governance most immediate concentration could be expected to be on the international and regional organisations since, inter alia, they wear, perhaps unlike global corporations, the mantle of legitimacy. As will become increasingly clear from consolidating the arguments presented in the four volumes there is a great deal more to the *realpolitik* of global governance than these, relatively, transparent organisations. Nevertheless they represent the obvious starting point for any effective analysis of the 'new world order'. This is on account of both their own centrality in the scheme of things and the networks of relationships in which they are involved with other actors on the world stage.

It is perhaps natural to give centrality to the United Nations in any treatment of global governance, even though its effectiveness is so heavily dependent on power structures and political accommodations. However, it is obvious that bodies such as the World Trade Organisation (WTO) and the World Bank (the Bank) and regional organisations, perhaps in particular the European Union, must be accorded a prominent status. This volume, like the others in the series, is not intended to be encyclopaedic but to give some indication of the influence of a few of the central actors. So much has been written and so much is known about both the UN itself and the European Union that little attention is given here to their basic structures and tasks. Rather we have concentrated on how they and other 'legitimate' organisations influence and are influenced by the ebb and flow of global activity.

Both the 'bookend' chapters by Lewis and Maduro attempt an overview of the problematics and the desiderata of global governance and both are concerned to inject elements of legitimacy and democratic reform into the debate. The intervening chapters are, relatively speaking, discrete in describing the phenomenology of international and regional organisations.

Davis addresses the significance of the International Criminal Court with particular reference to the war on terror, an issue that is timely, to say the least.

Vila Major's chosen subject is the European Central Bank, a body that thus far has been largely colonised by economists. His concern is primarily its legitimacy in acting as a guarantor of the Community's political 'tablets', although that, of course, has to be viewed in terms of its effectiveness in enhancing price stability.

Merrills addresses the globalisation of international justice through three case studies. He argues that international litigation is blooming, will continue to bloom and must be viewed against the background of larger political and democratic expectations.

Abass's contribution is particularly novel, as well as being informative and controversial. It is an analysis of the role of African regional organisations, and in particular their relationships with the UN, in the field of promoting and stabilising collective security.

For present purposes the contributions of both Rott and Kelsey can be addressed together. They deal respectively with 'TRIPs' and 'GATs', those bodies of international commercial and trade law which are becoming increasingly important in a world of globalised free trade. There are large arguments concerning the democratic legitimacy of these bodies and the degree of fairness which they either promote or inhibit.

Margaret Llewelyn discusses TRIPS (the Agreement on Trade Related Aspects of Intellectual Property Rights) with special attention to the legal protection of biotechnological material, while Richard Kirkham discusses the role of regional organisations in the global legal order with special reference to CARICOM, the Caribbean Community and Common Market. The following essay is Kim Marshall's Globalisation and Global Justice in Competition Law.

As already indicated, Maduro seeks to pull together various strands of global behaviour and asks how far they can be poured into the mould of international democratic expectations. He thereby kick-starts a debate which will become increasingly crucial as time goes by.

Unfortunately, we have not been able to include the 'paper' delivered by Dr Ko-Yung Tung, the former Vice-President and General Counsel of the World Bank. Nevertheless Dr Tung delivered a spirited defence of the contribution of the Bank to global human development. As is well known, the Bank has had many critics over the years who have condemned the Bank's policy of 'conditionality'; that is to say, attaching conditions to loans which dictate the shape of economic policy in the borrowing countries. Such conditions have traditionally been associated with 'Chicago' economics which, it is claimed, advance the interests of the developed world rather than those of the developing countries. In recent years, Dr Tung argued, such conditions have been replaced by those which insist on good 'governance' which seek to enhance democratic principles and the independence of the judiciary. There is clearly the need for continued scholarly attention to the operations of the Bank but it is clear that it remains a crucial player in the global economy and will remain so for the foreseeable future.

1

Global Governance and the Search for Justice

DOUGLAS LEWIS

T
HERE HAS BEEN much talk of globalisation in recent years and I shall not burden you with restating what has been eloquently expressed elsewhere.[1] The burden of the argument for most of us is that since globalisation has occurred in a substantially unplanned fashion without anything closely resembling the Philadelphian Constitutional Convention seeking to order the principles and the institutions for governing the global order, then legitimacy assumes a crucial importance. For the constitutional lawyer legitimacy reads across to the ancient virtues of openness, consultation, participation and accountability. These are, as we would now argue, subsumed by or a vital part of the human rights package; the core of being human needs institutional expression for each global citizen to engage in self-discovery and to flower and flourish.

This poses a dilemma. There are many who are anti-globalisation, insisting that globalisation is the enemy of the local, of diversity, of community; that it places the bounty of the planet in a few, unrepresentative hands and therefore disenfranchises the mass of humanity. Others argue that globalisation is simply the result of global citizens doing business with each other; communing in other words. This produces an increase in opportunities—in essence of freedom—and breeds cross-cultural understanding. Does the lawyer need to take sides in these disputes or can she simply ply her trade wherever the opportunity arises to turn a penny? Well, there are clearly those who do the latter as the complexity of TRIPS, GATS, European competition law and so on increase and abound. International arbitration assumes an ever-growing importance and so, in a 'black letter' way, so to speak, lawyers are already active in the game. The constitutional lawyer, on the other hand,—the institutional and moral philosopher—has to take sides; not in terms of whether globalisation is a

---

[1] See eg, David Held, *Global Transformations: Politics, Economics and Culture,* (Polity 1999); Titus Alexander, *Unravelling Global Apartheid,* (Polity 1996). Noreena Hertz, *The Silent Takeover: Global Capitalism and the Death of Democracy,* (Heinemann 2001).

good or a bad thing, but whether it satisfies the democratic dictates at the larger level that we have come to demand at the level of nation states. To oversimplify in order to make a point, are the principles underpinning the OECD operating effectively at the global level? If so fine; if not, then constitutional lawyers in particular have a lot of work to do.

De Santos's work is the market leader among legal theorists in the field of globalisation[2] but there has been relatively little juristic work aimed at project-building thus far.[3] The *Global Accountability Project*, sponsored by the One World Trust, is the first and so far the only attempt to draw up a taxonomy of openness and accountability along a range of global players, from TNCs, through IGOs to civil society. At the point of writing, however, it is only a pilot project whose value is limited by the size of its sample. Interestingly, I was the only lawyer represented on its oversight board. Nevertheless the whole project team have been speaking the language of the constitutional lawyer, the logic of the enterprise being to outline nothing less than a 'global constitution'. The two axes forming the hub of the research project were access to information and member control. Eighteen organisations were examined to assess their overall accountability record and the results were unsurprisingly mixed. However, one of the most valuable achievements of the research, which is ongoing, was to provide a taxonomy of good practice in accountability.

What I am offering here is essentially a theoretical overview of the law and globalisation, or at least making an attempt at a charting exercise. I shall argue that what is needed is for us to go back to the role and trade of the constitutional lawyer in order to bring on board the 'black letter' lawyers who operate on the global stage so as to persuade them to contextualise their craft. It is a kind of plea for a globalised socio-legal studies leap with a constitutional lawyer's underpinning.

Thirty years ago a gap was opening up between old and new attitudes to constitutional/public law. The Old was sticking doggedly to the 'new' law of judicial review, while the New was extending the range into the world of public administration itself, to quangos and what was to become the New Public Management. Others had tilled those particular fields before but from the discipline of the political scientist or public administrator and not from the discipline of the public lawyer.[4] We are at a similar juncture in relation to globalisation. I recently had a conversation with a High Court judge, specialising in judicial review, when I spoke of my interest in globalisation, of the role of the World Bank, the IMF, the WTO,

---

[2] See eg Boaventura de Santos, *Toward a New Common Sense: Science and Politics in Paradigmatic Transition* (1995).

[3] For a rudimentary outline of the arguments see the present author, *Law and Governance: The Old meets the New*, (Cavendish Publishers 2001) Chapter 10, 'Governance and Globalisation: The Next Frontier.

[4] One of the landmarks of the new public law was Tony Prosser's *Nationalised Industries and Public Control*, (Blackwell 1986).

NGOs and the like and was dismayed to hear him ask what this all had to do with law. My feelings were of a slightly more than mild exasperation.

Back in 1986 Ian Harden and I wrote what was then a radical book on the British Constitution, partly in response to those who would frequently claim that we did not, or perhaps still do not, have a constitution as such.[5] In it, we argued that there is in a settled society always a constitution, even if sometimes you have to look hard to uncover it. These were not original sentiments since they can be found in the work of Eugen Ehrlich, Karl Llewellyn and even Talcot Parsons.[6] Indeed one of Llewellyn's celebrated law jobs was 'the Say', which translated from his somewhat tortuous Anglo-German literary style in effect means 'the constitution of groups'. Who has the Say in deciding what is what, although he largely neglected the central issue of legitimacy.

Llewellyn also remarked that power will always be exercised somewhere by someone since nature abhors a vacuum. Part of the job of the constitutional lawyer is to trace the sources of such power and then to ask if they are exercised with full moral authority. Some of these issues are actively pursued in the sister volume on globalisation and human rights. But to return to the 'new' public law; what its proponents argued was that things like the New Public Management and 'quangos' needed to be married to the principles underlying the Glorious Revolution in order to test the legitimacy of their operations. Were they operating according to canons of openness and accountability,—according in effect to the principles of the 'ideal speech' situation. After the development of the industrial revolution it became necessary to ask similar questions about what some began to call the 'private fiefdoms'; with the global growth of Trans National Corporations, (and see the accompanying volume dedicated to corporate governance) the concerns are becoming increasingly acute.

Now globalisation,—or at least its extent—has crept up on us, just as the Party system in the UK emerged somewhere around the time of the Tamworth Manifesto which parasited on the royal prerogative which means that the principles of the Revolution had to be reapplied in changing circumstances. However the globalisation phenomenon is hugely more complex than even the most complex of national systems and so the task of constitutionalising it fairly daunting. Even so, a start has to be made somewhere.

To repeat; the immediate need is to map out the 'constitution', which means in the first instance that we ask who is wielding the power. Then

---

[5] Ian Harden and Norman Lewis, *The Noble Lie: the British Constitution and the Rule of Law*, (Century Hutchinson 1986).

[6] See eg, Norman Lewis, 'Towards a Sociology of Public Administration', (1981) 32 *Northern Ireland Legal Quarterly*, pp 89–105. For example, Ehrlich famously remarked that marriage existed before Family 'Law'.

we must ask whether such power is being wielded legitimately. This is an inordinately difficult exercise. To take but one example; the United Nations. If we could cede legitimacy to one organisation at the global level presumably it would be it, but of course there is a need to look deeper—not least at the politics behind the UN and its relationships with other agencies and configurations. At the time of writing the Second Gulf war has thrown everything into confusion but the likely outcome is that the UN will, in one way or another, be reformed. It should be stressed, however, that the humanitarian aspects of its work will remain largely unchanged.

The influence of the UN is hard to gauge. The outside world tends to look almost exclusively at the Security Council while of course the many and varied agencies of the UN pursue tireless work, much of which is never registered in the developed world. Furthermore it hosted a range of high-profile conferences during the 1990s, some of which were more successful than others. The main conferences related to the environment (Rio 1992), human rights (Vienna 1993), population issues (Cairo 1994), social development (Copenhagen 1995) gender equality (Beijing 1995) and cities' and shelter issues (Istanbul 1996).

All these were significant in both the breadth of their coverage and the depth of their proposed solutions. They, for the most part, produced lasting and generally positive outcomes. Under the glare of publicity, governments felt compelled to agree to a number of commitments across the board. The final consensus documents were not legally binding but nevertheless provided a road-map of key priorities and areas for immediate action. The five-year reviews have not been particularly noteworthy and the ten-year reviews are only now beginning to come in. UNCTAD and UNEP have been relatively disappointing in their impact and a deal of hard work will be needed to breathe life back into them. UNEP, for example, networks extensively—with such bodies as the World Council for Sustainable Development, World Resources Institute together with representatives of the business community. Even so, progress has been slow and there is thus far no sign of the establishment of a UN Environmental Agency, let alone a UN Environmental Court.

There is an official view, however, that things are getting better on the sustainable development front through pressure being brought on the WTO from a number of different quarters. The WTO Ministerial meeting at Doha in November 2001 launched new liberalisation negotiations—the Doha Development Agenda (DDA). The aim is to conclude these by 2005 with an interim checkpoint at the WTO's 5th Ministerial meeting in Cancun in September 2003. The Declaration does hold out some seeds for hope in relation to SHE issues and sustainable development, recognising that no country should be prevented from taking measures in these fields provided that it is not a disguised form of discrimination against other members. More interestingly paragraph 31 says

With a view to enhancing the mutual supportiveness of trade and environment, we agree to negotiations, without prejudicing their outcome, on:

(i)   the relationship between existing WTO rules and specific trade obligations set out in multilateral environmental agreements (MEAs).

(ii) procedures for the regular information exchange between MEA secretariats and the relevant WTO committees, and the criteria for the granting of observer status;

Para 32 says

We instruct the Committee on Trade and Environment ... to give particular attention to:

(i)   the effect of environmental measures on market access ...

So in a sense there is all to play for but since these are largely voluntary measures, they will need to be closely monitored.[7]

Let us take another example; the WTO. Clearly it is important for lawyers to know about TRIPS but I think it is much more important to know about the WTO; in particular how it operates. Although the official version is that the WTO belongs to its members and that it has to act unanimously, the reality, as most serious students will know, is that it is the 'green room' meetings which matter. This involves a handful of the most powerful nations producing an agenda on a take it or leave it basis for the remainder. This may be improving since, at Doha, it was said that there were no green room discussions without a high proportion of representation from the African nations.[8] The United States Federal law has addressed these problems at the national level ever since the first FDR presidency. The administrative law of the United States is probably the most advanced in the world, particularly in respect of the Administrative Procedure Act's requirements for rule-making, for fair procedures, for restraints on ex parte activities and for Government in the Sunshine. I am often surprised at the lack of constitutional enterprise by EU lawyers who seem not to have addressed the issue of an APA for the Union, let alone for those bodies with whom it has to deal. Given the enormous influence of the WTO it is high time that it should be institutionally legitimated, to say nothing of examining its operational activities in the light of the three generations of human rights. On 14 November 2002 an 'invitation only'

---

[7] Note that the ILO established in February 2002 a World Commission on the Social Dimension of Globalisation which is engaged in a wide-ranging dialogue with international organisations, governments, social partners and other stakeholders on the wider issues of globalisation. It is expected to report towards the end of 2003.

[8] See *Implementation of PIU Report: 'Rights of Exchange: Social, Health, Environmental and Trade Objectives on the Global Stage,'* 3rd Report DTI, December 2002.

mini- ministerial of the WTO was held in Sydney. It was said to be a private 'unofficial' meeting of 25 WTO members to discuss the most contentious issues currently facing the membership; TRIPS and health, Market Access and the 'Singapore issues'. This caused 150 NGOs to issue a statement which criticised the WTO for a failure 'to adhere to democratic principles'.[9] Interestingly the UK government is now committed to greater openness in these matters.[10] Furthermore the UK government has made considerable progress in providing for transparency in terms of early de-restriction of WTO documents. The government also meets religiously with NGO representatives to discuss a wide range of SHE (social, health and environment) issues, although so far there is no formal provision for the involvement of NGOs in the deliberations of the WTO itself.

Let me dwell a little longer on the WTO. There is, as I have argued elsewhere, a good case for claiming that its Disputes Panel is the Supreme Court of the New World Order. Where GATT provisions have been disregarded the Panel's rulings are effectively enforceable. Contrast this with the weak sanctions attaching to breach of most of the multilateral environmental agreements on labour and social conventions. This need not have been the case. When trade issues and liberalisation were first being discussed at the end of the Second World War it was proposed that an International Trade Organisation should be established with a much wider remit than that now possessed by the WTO. Where there was a conflict between trade issues and human rights issues it was proposed that an appeal should lie from the ITO to the International Court of Justice at the Hague. This, however, did not find favour with the Americans and consequently the idea was still-born. If human rights conventions are to be taken seriously the proposal should be urgently re-examined. At the moment the WTO is clearly in the box seat and does not look favourably on the establishment of another juristic forum which might challenge its ascendancy.[11]

In fact, there is a remarkable story to be told about why the WTO and Bretton Woods organisations have seized the initiative from the UN, whose powers are remarkably stronger than is generally believed. With the US contributing 25 per cent of the UN budget, it may be expected that it will continue to call the tune in its own perceived interests. In which case, the answer may be to devise an alternative funding formula. The fact of the matter is that any serious reading of the UN Charter reveals that the area of 'economic security' is assigned to the General Assembly and the Economic and Social Council (ECOSOC), a matter drowned out by the *de*

---

[9] www.corpwatch.org/bulletins/PBDjsp?articleid=4855.
[10] The most recent follow-up to *Rights of Exchange—Rights of Exchange: Social, Health and Trade Objectives on the Global Stage*, 3rd Report DTI December 2002 is the authority for what follows.
[11] See DTI PIU Report 2002.

facto prominence of the other international governmental organisations.[12] Sadly, in 1997 the G7 seemed to be rowing in the opposite direction. Many sensible reform suggestions lie on the table but they are insufficiently publicised, with the result that no real bandwagon has begun to roll to re-establish the moral authority of the UN.

Historically, the public/private divide has been judiciously maintained; the public sphere is subject to constitutional restraints, the private free from state control. Historically, that was a libertarian position easily justified. These days when the private sector can no longer be equated with the butcher's shop on the corner of the high street the picture is radically transformed. Even at the national level, company law has been intruding for over a hundred years, but given the enormous power and influence yielded by the TNCs in the global village attention must be turned to their regulation.

It is scarcely satisfactory that shareholder interests alone should constitute the only legitimate concern, even at the level of the nation state, as witness the concern of the EU that its member states should ensure that the interests of workers are not overlooked in an increasing range of circumstances. When we consider that the influence of the TNCs is such that it makes life and death decisions in countries far away from the place where they are registered then the anxieties become that much more acute. This is why both the EU, the OECD and the UN have all attempted to persuade TNCs to adopt voluntary codes of conduct covering at least SHE issues. These matters have been developed elsewhere.[13]

Of course, even at the national level tasks formerly performed by the state sector have, in recent years, increasingly been farmed out to the private sector (and indeed to the 'third' or voluntary sector). This has thrown up considerable problems of openness and accountability.[14]

The position adopted here is that the need for both openness and accountability to interested and affected publics ought to be determined by reference to protecting the fundamental interests of citizens, and not by reference to the provenance or structural characteristics of the institution wielding influence over the lives of a wide range of constituencies.[15] This ought to be the case at both the national, regional and global levels.

Naturally, company law requirements vary considerably from country to country and from regional bloc to regional bloc and only by examining such legislation (and practice) individually can a proper picture be painted.

---

[12] See, eg, *For a Strong and Democratic United Nations*, South Centre, Geneva 1997.

[13] See Douglas Lewis and Sorcha MacLeod, 'Transnational Corporations: Influence and Responsibility' (2004) *Global Social Policy*, 77–97.

[14] See, eg, *The Private World of Government*, Douglas Lewis and Jeffrey Goh, Occasional Papers, Centre for Socio-Legal Studies, University of Sheffield, UK 1998.

[15] See *Structural Pluralism and the Right to Information*, Alasdair Roberts, Working Paper 15, School of Policy Studies, Queens University, Canada, 2001.

It is worth repeating, however often it is remarked, that 29 of the world's biggest economic entities are multinational corporations; this according to UNCTAD. The field is led by EXON which is larger than all but 44 national economies.[16] Its estimated value is about the same size as the economy of Pakistan and larger than Peru's, while Daimler-Chrysler, General Electric and Toyota are all comparable in size to the economy of Nigeria. In addition, foreign direct investment does and will continue to outstrip by far development aid. It is inconceivable that the international, public, to say nothing of the company lawyer, should be unconcerned about this state of affairs.

Back at the national level, jurisdictions vary substantially in their willingness to cause the private sector to disclose, for example, information. Many governments now recognise a citizen's right to access and correct personal information collected by private firms. This narrow piercing of corporate privacy is defended as a method of discouraging unfair treatment and unjustified intrusions into personal privacy, and is now permitted under data protection laws adopted throughout the EU and, eg Canada. Some nations have also recognised broader rights of access to information held by private organisations. South Africa's Promotion of Access to Information Act, adopted in 2002, implements a guarantee in its 1996 Constitution that citizens will have a right of access to information held by another person 'that is required for the exercise or protection of any rights'. It appears that the courts are likely to be liberal in defining the range of rights whose imperilment would warrant breaching corporate secrecy.[17] Famously, of course, it was a South African court which forced the giant pharmaceutical companies, fighting to protect their drug prices, to reveal closely guarded secrets of their business practices, including pricing policies.[18]

There are other requirements on non-government actors to disclose information. These are too numerous and diverse to specify here but, for example, health professionals in private practice have a duty to disclose information about a serious danger of violence by one person against another. Commercial enterprises have an obligation to provide their workers with information about the release of toxic chemicals by their facilities. Private employers also frequently have an obligation to provide their workers with information about hazardous materials used in their workplace, and manufacturers have an obligation to provide consumers with information about hazards posed by defective products. Health and safety is an area where generally there are heavy duties of disclosure.[19] It

---

[16] See *The Financial Times*, 13 August 2002.

[17] See Gideon Pimstone, 'Going quietly about their business: Access to corporate information and the open democracy bill', *South African Journal of Human Rights*, 15.1, 2–24.

[18] See eg, *The Guardian*, London 8 March 2001.

[19] See eg, Tom Tietenburg and David Wheeler, *Empowering the community: information strategies for pollution control*, Waterville, Maine: Colby College, Department of Economics.

has been obvious then, for many years, that 'the public interest' must be protected from the self-interested activities of the private sector. It is a natural extension that the world community seeks to rein in the activities of TNCs in certain respects, given their enormous influence. The only question is how best this is to be achieved; through voluntary codes or regulation; at the regional or international level and the like. This is where the work of the scholar needs increasingly to be concentrated.

In fact there is heightened academic interest in what is usually termed Corporate Social Responsibility (CSR). Given their far-reaching influence in a globalised market-place, TNCs are being pressed to honour human rights, including the social, economic and environmental. In order to deliver on these expectations disclosure of their practices and procedures is being demanded more and more frequently.

Recent years have seen a proliferation of self-regulatory measures which expose what was previously confidential information. TNCs as diverse as IKEA, Kmart, Levi Strauss, Phillips and Shell have produced codes of conduct detailing workers' rights, environmental policies and ethical standards adhered to by the company wherever it operates[20] The OECD Guidelines are probably the best-known principles governing the activities of TNCs in the social and environmental sphere, although the Global Compact at the United Nations website[21] is also important. However the practice is less encouraging. A Report in 2001 indicated that nearly a half of the UK's largest companies have rejected government requests to disclose information about their environmental and social performance. A survey of the top 200 quoted companies found that 97 do not disclose any information on these issues whatsoever. Even so, a series of socially responsible investment indicators known as FTSEE4Good was launched in July 2001 by FTSE International, a joint venture between the Financial Times and the London Stock Exchange.[22] These issues are taken up in greater detail in the corporate governance volume. However, what is important is that serious work is being conducted in this area—perhaps more so than with IGOs.

When we talk of civil society, most think of NGOs, of which there are many thousands around the world; some international in scope like Oxfam, Friends of the Earth and the like, but many more operating at the local level. Some are involved in development work, others in exposing inequalities and injustice in the developing world and yet others in advocacy. Again, important academic work is being conducted in this area, although there are still huge gaps in our knowledge and, once more, little research and analysis by the legal community.

---

[20] See eg, Roger Blainpain (ed) *Multinational Enterprises and the Social Challenges of the XXlst Century*, Amsterdam, Kluwer 2000.

[21] www.globalcompact.org

[22] See *The Financial Times*, 25 June 2001.

First of all it should be said that 20 per cent of all aid to developing countries is now channelled by or through NGOs. The problem of generalisation here, of course, is that the range, size, scope and function is so broad as to be meaningless. Even so, several issues are worth highlighting.

Some of the largest, internationally based NGOs, Save the Children, Amnesty, Friends of the Earth and the like are fairly well-exposed. A great deal of information about them is available about their workings and a large number of reports and publications emanate from them. Their websites provide a mass of information for the interested observer.

Beyond that, the picture is more confused. There is a discernible movement towards urging greater transparency as an indicator of an organisation's effectiveness. By necessity, more and more filtering of information about an organisation's activities is taking place. The result is that any public statement about the organisation's work with its clients is often substantially edited and may be a partial representation of what is occurring on the ground. Until recently, the possibility of donors to these organisations (and others) gaining access to the lower level documentation and accounts of what was taking place in the organisation's work with its clients was very limited. The main opportunity was during field visits to the site of an organisation's work. However, with the global expansion of access to the internet the technical constraints on public access to field reports of aid organisation's achievements are rapidly being removed. At the very least it should now be possible for many northern donor NGOs to allow the annual progress reports of their southern partner organisations to be publicly monitored by placing those reports directly on to the Web. Where those partners themselves have access to the internet, they in turn could place reports from their own offices directly on to it.[23]

The evaluation of NGO activities is closely associated with the amount of information provided.[24] A great deal of recent work has become available which gives specific attention to assessing performance and the management of information.[25] Most of the impact studies so far have come to the conclusion that, in spite of a growing interest in evaluation, there is still a lack of reliable evidence on the impact of NGO development projects and programmes.[26] One World Trust stated:

[23] See www.mande.co.uk/archives

[24] See *The Impact of NGO Development Projects*, Overseas Development Institute, 1996, www.odi.org.uk.

[25] See eg *Striking a Balance: A Guide to Enhancing the Effectiveness of NGO Organisations in International Development*. A Fowler, (Earthscan, London 1997) and *Informational Management for Development Organisations*, M Power, (Oxfam 1999).

[26] *Searching for Impact and Methods: NGO Evaluation Synthesis Study. A Report produced for the OECD/DAC Expert Group on Evaluation.* RC Riddell and others. Department for International Development Corporation, Ministry of Foreign Affairs, Helsinki, 1997. www.valt.helsinki. fi/ids/ngo.

... NGOs come close to the bottom in the access to information dimension. What is surprising is that they often fail to provide the information likely to be of sufficient use to stakeholders. how they are spending their money and how well they have been achieving their aims. Less than half of the NGOs within this study publish an annual report online and only the IFRC and Oxfam International provide financial information within their annual reports.[27]

Happily, most of the large bilateral aid agencies are now making their evaluation reports publicly accessible on a global scale via the internet.[28] A small number of NGOs have done the same. The next step forward in transparency would be for those organisations to place their annual progress reports in the public domain as well via the internet. Another step forward, already taken by organisations such as Christian Aid is to provide hypertext links to their own southern partner NGO web sites, allowing outsiders more direct access to documented accounts of aid funded activities written by those closer to the action.

Many NGOs have performed valuable work in acting as gadflies to change global priorities and even to support unpopular but misunderstood causes. However, they have their critics. For example, a huge amount of the aid being sent to Africa is effectively controlled by NGOs which have been criticised for being under-regulated, being at cross-purposes with each other, insufficiently accountable and even helping to promote corruption.[29] The point is often made that since 40 percent of NGOs total income is from official sources they are often a front for government policies. Some NGOs have been (at least partially) funded by TNCs which looks like a form of capture. It is also clear that NGOs do not always have the same interests. Within the NGO world north and south can seem to have what look like neo-colonial relationships. In Eastern Europe NGOs are heavily associated with the importation of Western norms for political and economic life and are resented accordingly. One way and another some in-depth analysis of the pros and cons of NGO activities should be undertaken; preferably by the UN.

Networking and partnerships are a vital element of what is generally termed New Public Management. I have argued elsewhere[30] that, valuable though these may be, there can be problems about overall ownership and therefore of accountability. For example, alliances between companies and NGOs attract varying degrees of enthusiasm. While companies can gain kudos, advice, market intelligence and a better understanding of the risks to their reputation, the benefits are less immediately obvious for

---

[27] P 6, The research also found that all of the groups studied limit access to information about their decision-making processes.

[28] See www.mande.co.uk/sources.htm.

[29] See letters page, *The Guardian*, 1 July 2002.

[30] *Law and Governance: the Old meets the New*, Ch. 10.

pressure groups, whose reputation depends on being trusted as independent critics.[31]

On the global scale the same observations can be made in spades. Networks are sometimes relatively open and transparent and, at other times, extremely shadowy. Many development projects are of the former variety whereby IGOs, national governments and NGOs work together to advance development aims. A good example is furnished by the World Bank's Comprehensive Development Frameworks.

> Greater poverty reduction requires stronger partnerships at country level. This is one of the key principles of the Comprehensive Development Framework and is, therefore, also essential for the Poverty Reduction Strategy Papers. It calls for country governments to reach out to all partners to ensure their individual contributions are taken on board, and achieve the highest development impact at the lowest possible cost. It reflects experience that coordination, genuine consultation, support for country ownership, trust and transparency all promote aid effectiveness.[32]

The CDF is said to be a long-term holistic approach to development which recognises the importance of macro-economic fundamentals, but which gives equal weight to the institutional, structural and social underpinnings of a robust market economy. It emphasises strong partnerships among governments, donors, civil society, the private sector and other actors. Most important, it claims, is that the borrowing country is in the box seat, both owning and driving the development agenda, with the Bank and other partners each defining their support in the respective business plans. This is mirrored in the European Union where good governance is now part of development assistance. Better governance involves more transparency, more accountability and more popular participation in the decisions that count.

It is clear that, for the Bank to walk down this particular road, it will need to walk away from its past, since it has not always spoken the language of inclusion:

> It is worth noting that throughout the 1980s and most of the 1990s there were a very large number of cases before the ILO Committee on Freedom of Association and Committee of Experts concerning breaches of Conventions 87 and 98 resulting from reforms implemented as part of structural adjustment and stabilisation programmes. Frequently the defence in these cases rested on the fact that they were implementing conditions demanded by the IMF and the World Bank.[33]

---

[31] See Working from a Shared Platform, *Financial Times* 29 November 2002.

[32] *Country-Led Partnership: With Whom and for What?* World Bank 2000.

[33] ICFTU, 'Transforming the Global Economy: a Stocktaking of Trade Union Action with International and Regional Institutions', Draft Report ICFTU, Brussels 2001.

Considerable criticism of both the Bank and the IMF are not hard to find. However, perhaps the most telling is that of the UN which has demanded that decisions about how to manage globalisation must be made more democratic. Criticism has been made about the disproportionate influence of the Big Five, the lack of clout by developing nations and the lack of transparency of institutional behaviour.[34] Amongst the most damaging criticisms of the Bretton Woods institutions in recent years are those levelled in relation to the corrupt and incompetent privatisations in Russia and some other countries in transition.[35]

The International Confederation of Free Trade Unions (ICFTU) both jointly and severally has done good work in recent years in seeking to map out global power configurations but its scope for independent scholarly disclosures is limited. Whether the Bank has changed or whether its critics' counter-claims are well-founded, it is not possible to say at this time. Networks are constantly being created to push both common and single causes. Their legitimacy at this juncture is tenuous. And they will necessarily line up from time to time with some of the big players in circumstances where there may or may not be capture. Someone needs to take the lead in pulling together a well-resourced and independent research team operating under the auspices of a body which enjoys a large measure of international moral authority.

Networks can be a genuine good, in particular in terms of what we might call 'added value'. However, there is too little sunshine cast on some of the most important of them. For example, we know far too little about even the relationships formed by the European Commission, while of course the EU is one of the bigger players on the global stage. Just one example must suffice for present purposes. I have spoken of this phenomenon on numerous previous occasions, but that is because it is too important to ignore. I refer to the Transatlantic Business Dialogue (TABD) and its connections both with the European Commission and the US government.

TABD describes itself as a 'unique business-driven process helping to shape US-EU economic policy issues'. To repeat what I have said elsewhere; 'if you can shape that axis then you are a big player in anybody's league'.[36]

Since 1995, the TABD has offered a political framework for enhanced cooperation between the transatlantic business community and the governments of the European Union and the US. It is an informal process whereby European and US companies develop joint US-EU policy recommendations for action by the European Commission and US Administration, as well as for the US Congress and European Parliament.[37]

[34] UN Annual Survey 2002, *Deepening Democracy in a Fragmented World.*
[35] See eg, Joseph Stiglitz, *Globalization and its Discontents*, Penguin 2002.
[36] See 'Law and Globalisation: an Opportunity for Europe.', above pp 227–9
[37] www.tabd.com.

TABD was launched in Seville in 1995 at a conference attended by EU and US company chief executives, but led by the European Commissioners for trade and industry and the US Secretary of Commerce. TABD's main aim is to boost transatlantic trade and investment opportunities with special emphasis on the removal of unwanted regulation and the harmonisation of regulatory procedures which are deemed to be necessary. Its joint recommendations are communicated to senior US and European officials who, in turn, work with business to develop effective policy with the ultimate goal of benefiting both economies through improved competitiveness. There is nothing especially secretive about the existence of TABD or the fact that its recommendations heavily inform the GATT agenda and the annual trade rounds. But once more, although it makes its recommendations publicly available, its meetings with the influential are inevitably *ex parte* with no minutes being publicly available.[38]

This represents only one aspect of one network but it is interesting that even the largely social-democratic European Union has no real 'access' laws such as those which exist in US Federal law to expose the inner workings of government to wider publics.

At this point a word should be said about the influence of regional groupings, including the EU. The study of the EU has been an academic industry for many years and yet lawyers, at least, have concentrated on the more rather than the less obvious aspects of its workings; the dignified rather than the working elements of the constitution, so to speak. We now know a little more about the secrecy of the EU than we used to do, but still little about its consultation procedures: the designation and nature of its 'partners'—those who most influence its agenda. There is still a great deal of work to be done in this area and it is probably necessary to adopt a two-pronged, reinforcing, research approach; the Commission outwards and pressure groups inwards. A team research effort is what is required. However, one point about the EU is worth making in order to indicate how far it has to go in order to make the world order a fairer place. The Common Agricultural Policy is rightly condemned for its impact on the third world but one statistic paints the starkest of pictures:

> At a time when a fifth of the world's population lives on a dollar a day, the average cow in the EU receives a $2.20 daily handout from Brussels.[39]

The secrecy of the EU is most stark and, at times, alarming. For example, only the fact of documents being leaked to the press exposed the fact

---

[38] It is also strongly believed that the food industry has infiltrated the World Health Organisation, just as the tobacco industry has done. See *The Guardian* 9 January 2003.

[39] Larry Elliott, *The Guardian* 30 October 2002.

that the Union recently demanded full-scale privatisation of public monopolies across the world as its price for dismantling the CAP in recent discussions with the WTO.[40]

However, too few lawyers know much about other regional blocs or groupings and their influence actual and potential on IGOs, TNCs, NGOs and the 'hybrids'. We know even less about how the blocs inter-react.[41] One thing which becomes apparent as we examine the New World Order (NWO) more closely is that the networks which are so ubiquitous range between those which have fairly formal working relationships and those which are issue-based. Thus, there is a certain amount of what lawyers call 'forum-shopping' from one issue to another. If some interest is losing out in a particular forum it may be encouraged to jump ship, and re-form and re-engage in a different setting or forum. In any study of these phenomena the increasing influence of regional blocs will need to be better understood. The potential for blocs coming together on particular issues to bring pressure on seemingly indomitable forces is growing and will continue to grow.

Some argue that, just as the state plays an intermediate and autonomous role between social forces shaped by productive forces and a world order that is created and defined by a particular configuration of power, so regionalism plays a similar role within globalisation.[42] Polyani had earlier referred to the concept of a regionalised world order.[43] This is not the place to discuss the dialectics of regionalism in the developing world but it is probably accurate to say that the present wave of regional cooperation seeks to avoid regional protectionism/isolation in favour of seeking to manipulate the terms of participation in the global economy. Let us return to the EU for a moment.

All external trade policy issues for EU members are conducted at the EU level—in practice by the Commission. Competence on SHE issues, on the other hand, is vested partly in the EU and partly in the individual member states. Many standards and regulations are determined at the EU level, especially those concerning the safety and environmental performance of products. This stems mainly from the additional EU competence in developing and enforcing the EU internal market. In practical terms, this means that the EU role in relation to environmental standards is more significant than in health and labour standards. It also means that, even where there is discretion for member states, the latter need to follow EU

---

[40] *The Guardian*, 17 April 2002.

[41] It is worth noting, for example, that the EU grants trade preferences to seventy-eight African, Caribbean and Pacific states.

[42] Robert Cox, 'Social forces, states and world orders: Beyond international relations theory', (1981) 10 *Millennium* 141.

[43] See Bjorn Hettne, 'Introduction: the international political economy of transformation', in Bjorn Hettne (ed.), *International Political Economy: Understanding Global Disorder*, (Zed Books, New Jersey 2003) p 19.

treaty provisions, for example in relation to notification of proposed new SHE standards.[44]

However, added to this is that both the UK, for example, and the EU itself will also seek to strike accords with others over common interests. For instance, Egypt and the European Union took a significant step towards setting up a free trade area in manufactured goods in June 2001 by signing an association agreement that had been the subject of difficult negotiations for more than five years. Although the agreement is heavily focused on economic ties, it also includes a human rights clause.[45] We shall see that the EU is also strongly engaged in inter-regional debate and discussion, a matter not as closely followed by scholars as it might be.

There are many who see the EU as the world's most successful social democratic project[46] and as such a potentially civilising influence across the globe, inter alia because of its internal programme, because of the human rights conditionality imposed on some of its economic arrangements, because of its greater commitment to human development in the South than some other geopolitical forces. As such, it can be expected to engage in a number of linkages which nudge us towards a fairer global system even in the absence of blanket coverage by multilateral conventions. Even so, there are those who believe that the great European dream has been subverted by TNCs and their umbrella organisations, as witness, they would argue, the effect of the European Round Table of Industrialists (ERT) on the EU's approach to enlargement, which could do to central Europe what many of the WTO's rules have done for the South. Documents presented to the EU would allow some of the largest TNCs to resist pressure from non-European competitors.[47] The trouble with journalistic perceptions is that they may not be thorough, reliable or sufficiently well researched. Make a gesture and move on. We need more than this. We need to open up the whole process to democratic scrutiny, and this will not happen in the absence of detailed, grinding work informed by assumedly shared democratic insights using the tools of public and international law with which we are, or should be, all familiar. There are those within the Union who have recognised the need for such developments. For example, in July 2001 the President of the European Commission issued a White Paper on Governance which called for the policy-making process to be opened up in an attempt to get regional bodies, trade unions and NGOs involved in the Union.[48] For the time being,

---

[44] See n 8 *Rights of Exchange*, p 19.

[45] See *Financial Times*, 26 June 2001.

[46] The EU is the world's largest aid donor. However it's development programme has been heavily criticised by the UK Secretary of State for International Development, Clare Short. She insists that the Millennium Development Goals are poorly targeted. *The Guardian* 29 June 2002.

[47] George Monbiot, 'Stealing Europe', *The Guardian*, 20 June 2001.

[48] See *The Guardian*, 26 July 2001.

however, this vision has been overtaken by the Convention on the Future of the Union chaired by Giscard D'Estaing. It is to be hoped that this document will spark a much livelier debate on the future of the accountability of the Union in its many dealings.

As ever, some sort of map-chart would represent a starting-point. Leaving the EU aside, most are familiar with NAFTA, although its workings are not sufficiently broadcast. MERCOSUR, the common market of the Southern Cone, CARICOM, the Caribbean common market, APEC, the Asia-Pacific cooperation forum, ASEAN, the East Asian free trade zone, the OAU, the South African Development Community and the East African Community are simply the most prominent.[49] Other regional arrangements, such as the Free Trade Area of the Americas, are well advanced on the drawing board. COMESA, the Common Market for eastern and southern Africa is perhaps worth a special mention. The problem of Western aid being funnelled into sleaze and corruption is well documented by COMESA which appears to provide a welcome antidote through its Court of Justice which is modelled on the ECJ. It has recently been used by a private company to challenge alleged corruption by the Kenyan government in the hope that success would represent a spur to inward investment. At the very least, the case ensured that, through the discovery of documents, much information would enter the public domain which would otherwise be sheltered.[50] Not only is not enough known about many of these regional organisations' operation and influence,[51] but, even more intriguingly, their interactions with each other are potentially enormously important.[52]

The negotiations between SADC and the EU during the 1990s have been well charted,[53] but other notable alliances include ASEM (the EU's heads of state, the President of the EU Commission and the leaders of ten Asian nations), ASEF, the Asia-Europe Foundation, the Summit of the Americas, the ASEAN regional forum (involving the US and Australia) etc. Trade union alliance with a host of bodies and organisations are also coming to change the face not only of labour but of global coalitions

---

[49] For a useful summary of some of their activities see ICFTU, see, n 25. In 1994 the IMF listed sixty-eight regional economic arrangements.

[50] See *Financial Times*, 1 August 2001.

[51] There is also some evidence that the IMF and the World Bank support regional integration among developing countries as a means of advancing neoliberal economic orthodoxy. Anthoni van Nieukerk and Gary van Staden, *Southern Africa at the Crossroads: Prospects for the Political Economy of the Region*, (SAHA, Johannesburg 1991). Formerly, the Bretton Woods institutions feared that regional integration could act as a kind of trade union opposition to their policies. One way or another, there is clearly strength in numbers.

[52] The New Africa Initiative, a kind of Marshall Plan for Africa, has recently reported receiving promises of support from the European Union, *The Guardian*, 24 October 2001.

[53] South African Department of Foreign Affairs, *South African Foreign Policy Discussion Document*, Department of Foreign Affairs, Pretoria, 1996. The South African Parliament also forged an alliance with factions of the EU Parliament to lobby the EU on SADC's behalf.

generally. As well as the fact that the charting exercise has hardly begun, we know relatively little about how this web of alliances and networks operate; how far institutionally, how far informally and with what degree of pluralistic input and what degree of transparency.

A few more issues are worth mentioning. The first relates to NAFTA which was only accepted by President Clinton with the addition of supplementary and labour agreements. This is interesting in itself, quite apart from the Treaty being accompanied by two trade-related dispute settlement mechanisms. It can be argued that this represents the first international labour agreement linked to a trade treaty although it has to be said that the labour unions' assessment of its effectiveness is less sanguine[54] Nonetheless it may contain the germs of some useful developments.[55]

A second phenomenon is worth observing. Interest is now growing in regional arrangements to provide collective defence mechanisms against systemic failures and instability and regional currencies are increasingly seen as a viable alternative to dollarisation. The European experience has been held up as a model for regional arrangements, which probably require the inclusion of a major reserve-currency and it will continue to assume a key role for this purpose. In Asia initiatives involving developing countries and Japan could constitute an important step towards closer regional monetary integration.[56]

In fact there are now so many regional and regional/national linkages which vary from Free Trade Agreements (FTAs) through to ,say, the East African Economic Community, complete with its own court system based on the ECJ, that a veritable melange of political and legal entities are appearing all over the NWO.

There is a growing tendency to write the influence of national governments out of the equation under the NWO. This is a mistake. It is also part of a general tendency towards reductionism. As is made clear in *Rights of Exchange*, there is no solution, but rather solutions. For instance, speaking of SHE issues the document states:

> when there are no significant spillover effects and the SHE issue is national
> in source and scope, national level instruments ... and voluntary instru-
> ments are the relevant policy options;

[54] ICFTU see above n 33, pp 62–63.

[55] The proposed Free Trade Agreement for the Americas has been the subject of much disagreement and at the time of writing agreement on its essentials had still not been reached. See eg *Financial Times*, 7 August 2002.

[56] See Rubens Ricupero, 'Developing Countries and Reform of the International Financial System, *South Letter* No.37 p 18, Geneva (2002).

[57] See n 26 p 53.

when there are transboundary spillover effects, multilateral agreements are the best option: a decision then has to be made about whether trade or non-trade instruments (or a combined package) are most appropriate;

if multilateral instruments cannot be negotiated or are ineffective, then voluntary initiatives and national level (externally focused) instruments are the second-best options.[57]

Other examples of, eg UK activity in seeking to influence the global agenda includes working with the ILO to support the efforts of the World Commission on the Social Dimension of Globalisation, pressuring the European Commission for a 'strategic stocktake' between the Commission and member states on the interaction between trade and SHE objectives, bringing together and commissioning research in social and environmental areas, and active encouragement of the Commission to promote global sustainability building on synergies with the Doha, Monterrey and WSSD processes.[58]

Added to this, national governments can have a positive influence on global events, can fail to be facilitative, or can be obstructionist, either severally or jointly. Examples of each are, for instance, the UK's announcement in 2002 that it was to raise African aid to £I Billion year, Blair's 'Marshall plan' for the world's poorest continent,[59] individual nation's failure to defend the environment down to the US efforts to block cheap drug deals for poor countries[60] and even to block human, environmental and freedom of information rights from being enshrined in the earth summit's plan of action to protect multinational companies from litigation and protests by the poor.[61]

It would also be wrong to underestimate the influence of individual governments in relation both to TNCs, NGOs, IGOs and other foreign governmental players. What is perhaps particularly disturbing in a UK setting is not so much the lack of governmental clout, but the arrangements whereby the UK Parliament and other national constituencies are excluded from voice in the decisions arrived at. This has always been a problem for UK constitutional law, but given the range of networks in which governments now operate, it cannot be seriously doubted that the executive (and an increasingly concentrated one at that) is far too dominant an influence. Parliament has traditionally been relatively powerless in the field of foreign affairs but the executive now plays away much more

---

[58] *Implementation of PIU Report, 'Rights of Exchange: Social, Health, Environmental and Trade Objectives on the Global Stage'*, 3rd Report DTI December 2002. It is worth noting that the document reinforces the belief that the primary responsibility for dialogue with civil society lies at the national level of each of the WTO member governments.

[59] See *The Guardian*, 25 June 2002.

[60] See *The Guardian*, 21 December 2002.

[61] *The Guardian*, 30 August 2002.

extensively than in the traditional areas of 'dignified' international relations.

With perhaps the exception of the WTO, the major IGOs have been underplayed in this brief introduction.[62] Some are, understandably, much more visible than others but there is quite an alphabet soup of them out there and their mutual interactions need to be much better understood than is currently the case. However, as I should have indicated by now, the global order is a pretty crowded stage and the actors many and varied. Constitutionalising or reconstitutionalising the world order is beginning to sound, even to political pragmatists, like an idea whose time has come. The One World Trust has done and is continuing to do valuable work in this field but it needs to be buttressed by a larger international panel of scholars who can spare the time to work on the ground. To repeat something which I have said elsewhere:

> What should be realized is that global politics is always ultimately expressed through some form of law, be it hard or soft, formal or informal. What is now needed is that the new politics must be based on reformed institutions and new rules based on hard evidence of the role and function of influential forces. This represents a challenge to all lawyers and the whole academic community.[63]

---

[62] The OECD, in particular, faces a critical time in its history. European and NATO enlargement have put increasing pressure on it to tackle its own enlargement. The fall of the Berlin Wall forced an initial reappraisal of the OECD's role and the need to transform it into a new international organisation setting standards and creating values for the entire world. What role should be seen, for example, for Russia, China, Brazil and India? See *Financial Times*, 3 March 2003.

[63] See Lewis, (2000) 8 *European Public Law* p 239.

2

The Fight Against Global Terrorism— How Can the Law Respond to 'New' Terrorism?

FERGAL DAVIS *

Terrorism is not new and neither are anti-terrorism measures, however, it is contended that the threat of global terror, with it ability to cross borders and attack in any number of locations, requires a concerted response from the international community. This article will examine two legislative responses to the threat of global terror. These are; the possibility of utilising the new International Criminal Court (ICC) in the war on terror; and the possibility of adapting the 'Proscription' approach from domestic law. The utility of these approaches will be considered in the context of the 'new' emerging threat of a less organised, less centralised form of terrorism. Consideration will be given to the developments in the Al-Qaeda network since 2001 and the trends in world terrorism which have been identified. Following such an examination it will be obvious that the ICC and the proscription model are inadequate to deal with this new form of non-group group. The need for a working definition of terrorism will be considered in light of the preceding arguments. The difficulties associated with such a mission are clear, however, defining terrorism is the only logical, consistent and acceptable approach.

INTRODUCTION

CROSS BORDER, INTERNATIONAL terrorism, requires a cross border solution. Nation States need to cooperate if they are to tackle a threat from within and without their own jurisdiction. This premise is central to this article, while some may argue in favour of domestic responses this article will focus on the global approach to a global phenomenon. Domestic law will, obviously, have a role to play but that role can be discussed elsewhere. The purpose of this article is to consider the best possible international approach to the problem of international

* Centre for Socio-Legal Studies, Faculty of Law, University of Sheffield. The author is very grateful to Prof. D. Lewis of the Centre for Socio-Legal Studies and Dr. G. Hogan, School of Law, TCD for their help and assistance. All opinions and errors are my own.

terrorism. To that end consideration will be given to the International Criminal Court (ICC) and the 'Proscription' model. Both approaches have been suggested as a suitable means of executing the war on terror. Both approaches will be considered in light of the emerging threat of 'new' terrorism. 'New' terrorism essentially involves a shift in style from organised groups to decentralised support networks. These networks are already a significant feature of the terrorist landscape and neither the ICC nor Proscription is well placed to fight them. As such an alternative is required. The only possible approach, capable of facing down both the new threat and the old traditional terrorist threat is a definitional approach. This article will analyse the nature of 'new' terrorism and outline some of the reasons behind the rejection of the ICC and Proscription. Consideration will then be given to the advantages and disadvantages of a definitional approach.

In attempting to fulfil such a brief it will not be possible to examine any one of the issues in the depth they deserve. The concept of decentralised terrorism is the subject of many books in its own right and the ICC has formed the basis for more than one PhD thesis. This article hopes to draw these issues together and place them on the same page. As such it is both ambitious and limited.

THE 'NEW' TERRORISM

The nature of terrorism is fundamentally changing; therefore, before any evaluation of the various responses to the terrorist threat is possible it is first necessary to consider the nature of the 'new' terrorism. In order to understand the 'new' threat it is important that consideration is given to the 'old' threat.[1] The distinguishing feature of the old terrorists was their level of organisation. Classically, terrorist groups were organised in a cell structure.

> The cell has many variants, but the essential principle is simple and effective. Each is part of a hierarchy and is responsible to a single point of contact above. Within each cell, which is typically three to ten persons, a member may not even know all his or her compatriots ... The result is an organization which can act decisively and quickly. Also such an organization cannot easily be 'rolled up' by security forces ...[2]

From the point of view of the terrorist organisation such a structure has many advantages; from the point of view of the lawmaker the important factor is that such a group is organised. The cell structure demands organisation; it requires a leadership to direct the various cells who then

---

[1] The phrases 'old' and 'new' are not entirely accurate but they shall be employed for the sake of convenience.

[2] Harmon C., *Terrorism Today*, (London, Frank Cass Publications, 2000), p 98.

operate independently but often toward a common purpose. The Irish Republican Army (IRA) for example is organised into a strict cell structure under the leadership of the Army Council.[3] As a result it is possible to target the organisation as a unit. The legislative tool of proscription will be considered in this context later. The 'new' terrorism lacks the organisation of groups like the IRA. A shift has occurred and a new threat has emerged as a result of that shift. A significant development in recent years is the increased '... involvement in terrorism by non-government groups, individuals and, often, 'non-group-groups' of individuals who come together for the purpose of committing a terrorist act and then separate'.[4] It is this shift away from organised terrorist groups with identifiable names and cell structures towards a more post-modern terrorism that needs to be considered and legislated for. A number of groups and non-groups will be examined in order to illustrate this new terrorism before consideration will turn to the necessary responses to it.

The most infamous terrorist group operating in the world today is undoubtedly Al-Qaeda, however the nature of Al-Qaeda is disputed. Al-Qaeda suicide hijackers carried out the infamous attacks on the World Trade Centre, New York City, the Pentagon Washington DC and Shanksville Pennsylvania on 11 September 2001; it directed the attack on the USS Cole in the port of Aden, Yemen on 12 December 2000 and conducted the US Embassy bombings in Nairobi, Kenya and Tanzania in August 1998.[5] That Al-Qaeda carried out these attacks is relatively undisputed, however, the nature of the group is the source of some considerable debate. It has been suggested that there are essentially two Al-Qaeda's, the pre and post 2001 models. According to this theory 'Al-Qaeda remains a useful term to describe bin Laden, his close associates and the infrastructure created in Afghanistan between 1996 and 2001' however that organisation was effectively demolished by the invasion of Afghanistan and the removal of the Taliban.[6] The State Department, however, is of the opinion that 'Al-Qaeda has cells worldwide', it recognises that the organisation was based in Afghanistan until its removal and states that it has since 'dispersed in small groups across South Asia, Southeast Asia, and the Middle East'.[7] While it appears clear that the group was an organisation before the overthrow of the Taliban, it does not appear to have retained that organisational structure. Burke argues that Al-Qaeda should be conceived of 'as an ideology, an agenda and a way of

[3] United States Dept. of State, *Patterns of Global Terrorism 2002*, (Dept of State Publication, April 2003), Appendix C, p 135, hereinafter *Patterns of Global Terrorism 2002*.
[4] Anderson 'International Terrorism & International Cooperation' in *Countering Suicide Terrorism: An International Conference*, (Herzilya, The Interdisciplinary Center, 2001), p 52.
[5] See n 3, p 119.
[6] Burke, 'Al-Qaeda—a meaningless label' *The Observer*, January 12 2003, <http://www.observer.co.uk/Print/0,38584581540,00.html> accessed 20 April 2003.
[7] See n 3, p 119.

seeing the world...'[8] The conception of Al-Qaeda in these terms is supported by a review of the history of the group. Osama bin Ladin developed an organised resistance movement in Afghanistan with the aim of repelling the invading forces of the Soviet Union. To that end he was involved in the establishment of the Maktab-al-Khidarnat (MAK) group which set up an organised conscription service and brought Muslims to Afghanistan for training and fighting. By 1988, bin Ladin split from MAK and formed Al-Qaeda. By 1998 bin Ladin had announced the formation of a new group the 'Islamic World Front for the struggle against the Jews and the Crusaders'. This organisation can accurately be described as an umbrella group for Islamic Extremists.[9] It is clear from this development that Al-Qaeda began life as an organised militia, MAK, and grew into a terrorist organisation based in Afghanistan. The World Front allowed Al-Qaeda to develop further into 'a multi-national support group which funds and orchestrates the activities of Islamic militants worldwide'.[10] It is in this sense that Al-Qaeda is an ideology or agenda.

It might appear that the lack of an organised structure would weaken a terrorist group, however, that is not the case. An examination of Al-Qaeda activities before and after 2001 should allow a greater understanding of the threat posed by 'new' terrorism. In late 1999 Mohammed al-Tubaiti travelled to Afghanistan and requested a 'martyrdom mission' from Al-Qaeda. Al-Turbaiti was told to come back when he had his own plan and that it would then be evaluated. He went to Morocco and recruited individuals to his cause, he returned to Afghanistan and presented his scheme at which point he was given money and sent back to Morocco.[11] The story of Mohammed Al-Turbaiti illustrates an important point; even before Al-Qaeda was expelled from Afghanistan the organisation operated by providing support, facilitating the activities of others. The removal of its Afghan base has increased the need for Al-Qaeda to operate in such a fashion. The group Jemaah Islamiah (JI) provides a more than adequate example of the post-Afghanistan model. JI was responsible for the Bali bombings on 12 October 2002.[12] It has been described as a 'regional Islamic militant network linked to al-Qa'eda'.[13] The use of the phrase 'network' when referring to JI is interesting since it implicitly recognises that the group is not quite an organisation. The State Department notes that 'along with raising its own funds, the JI receives

---

[8] Burke, 'Terror's Myriad Faces', *The Observer*, May 18 2003, <http://www.guardian.co.uk/Print/0,3858,4671444,00.html> accessed 19 May 2003.

[9] www.ict.org.il accessed 25 September 2003.

[10] *Ibid.*

[11] Burke, 'Terror's Myriad Faces', *The Observer*, May 18 2003, <http://www.guardian.co.uk/Print/0,3858,4671444,00.html> accessed 19 May 2003.

[12] See n 3, p 110.

[13] Spillius, 'Bali Bomber Greets Death Sentence With Thumbs-Up', *The Daily Telegraph*, August 8 2003, p 1.

money and logistic assistance from Middle Eastern and South Asian contacts, NGOs, and other groups, including al-Qaeda'.[14] It seems obvious that Al-Qaeda is continuing to play a role in international terrorism but that its new role is more in the field of consultancy and logistics. This development has not reduced its deadly capability.

When considering this new form of deconstructed terrorist organisation it would be unwise to overstate the novelty of the approach. Terrorist organisations have a long history of cooperation and support for each other. The arrest of Niall Connolly, Martin McCauley and Jim Monaghan in Bogota on 11 August, 2001, suggested a link between the IRA and FARC;[15] prior to that the Japanese Red Army, (JRA) had carried out a number of actions on behalf or in support of other groups.[16] The outstanding feature of the new threat is not just the willingness to share information and logistical support, but rather it is the loosening of organisational ties. An examination of domestic terrorism in the US should help to further explain the significance of this development. The 'Freedom Club' posted parcel bombs which maimed and murdered scientists and others whom the Freedom Club accused of damaging the environment. The significant factor is that the Freedom Club as a terrorist organisation consisted of one member, Theodore Kaczynski.[17] If Al-Qaeda is operating as an ideology other ideologies are using the internet to spread their message. The American neo-fascist Milton John Kleim Jr has suggested that 'USENET offers enormous opportunity for the Aryan resistance to disseminate our message ...'[18] It seems logical to suggest that neo-fascist terrorists would be willing to share logistical information with other, like-minded, individuals. Harmon notes that

> organizationally, the classic cell structure and hierarchy still predominate, but so too flourish their opposites, found in the American militias, ecoterrorists, or autonomous Islamic extremist groups where, decentralisation may be the prized key.[19]

Terrorism has significantly altered since the Vietnam War when the North Vietnamese organised and controlled the National Liberation Front for South Vietnam.[20] Although cell based organisations continue to exist and even dominate the terrorist landscape a new breed of group has emerged. Al-Qaeda is no longer an organisation in the usual sense and has grown

---

[14] See n 3, p 111.
[15] Stanage, 'Justice Denied', *Magill*, August 2003, p 26.
[16] See n 3, p 137.
[17] Harmon, See n 2, p 10.
[18] *Ibid*, p 49.
[19] See n 2, p 124.
[20] See n 2, p 58.

into a consultancy group. The activities of JI provide a chilling illustration of how effective this terrorist outsourcing can be. The American experience of Kaczynski acting as a lone terrorist amply illustrate the ability of a lone individual to wreak havoc. The American militias and neo-fascists willingness to share information allows for a new decentralised form of terrorism which requires a new approach in terms of law enforcement.

'NEW' TERRORISM & THE ICC

The Rome Statute of the International Criminal Court received its necessary 60th ratification on 11 April 2002 and came into force on 1 July of that year.[21] The Statute and Court it creates are undoubtedly a significant achievement in the field of International Humanitarian Law (IHL). It has been suggested that the International Criminal Court (ICC) could prove to be useful tool in the fight against terrorism, after all surely an International Criminal Court would be best placed to try crimes of International Terrorism. This approach is simplistic and unhelpful.

Article 5 of the Rome Statute provides that the ICC has jurisdiction over four crimes; namely, Genocide, Crimes against Humanity, War Crimes, and the Crime of Aggression. Article 5.2 states that 'the Court shall exercise jurisdiction over the crime of aggression once a provision is adopted ... defining the crime ...',[22] as such the crime of aggression will not be considered for the purposes of this work. Genocide, as defined by Article 6, involves acts 'committed with intent to destroy, in whole or in part, a national, ethnical, racial or religious group'. The Army for the Liberation of Rwanda was formed from the army of the Rwandan Hutu regime which carried out the genocidal massacres of 1994.[23] The definition of genocide is clearly applicable to such an organisation, however, genocide requires a high standard of proof and many if not most terrorist groups would fall short of any such definition. For example, although the IRA was engaged in a sectarian conflict with Protestant Paramilitaries it would be difficult to argue that its aim was the destruction of the Protestant peoples of Northern Ireland. Similarly, IRA bomb attacks in Britain, such as the Warrington bombing, were designed to further the political end of a United Ireland through the use of violence not to destroy in whole or in part the British people. Furthermore, the attacks of 11 September 2001 were undoubtedly acts of terrorism but they do not appear to have been intended to destroy any one ethnical, racial or

---

[21] <http://untreaty.un.org/ENGLISH/bible/englishinternetbible/partl/chapterVIII/treaty10.asp> accessed 14 October 2003.

[22] The Rome Statute of the International Criminal Court, Article 5.2, see <http://www.un.org/law/icc/statute/99_corr/cstatute.htm> accessed 1 October 2001.

[23] See n 3, p 129.

religious group, rather they were designed to kill and provoke terror. Genocide as a term has been reserved for events such as the Holocaust, the actions of the Khmer Rouge in Cambodia, the Hutu massacres in Rwanda etc. Terrorists may commit genocide but the crime of genocide will only be applicable in a minority of cases, therefore if the ICC is to play a role in combating international terrorism more serious consideration needs to be given to the Courts jurisdiction over other offences.

The law relating to the commission of War Crimes is set out in the four Geneva Conventions of 1949, their Additional Protocols of 1977 and Customary International Law. The definition of War Crimes contained in Article 8 of the Rome Statute refers to these sources of law. War Crimes are capable of being committed in two distinct circumstances, international armed conflicts and armed conflicts not of an international character. The law relating to international armed conflicts is set down in the four Geneva Conventions. Article 2 Common to the four Geneva Conventions states clearly that 'the present Convention shall apply to all cases of declared war or of any other armed conflict which may arise between two or more of the High Contracting Parties, even if the state of war is not recognised by one of them'. Although such a conflict does not necessarily have to be declared it does require an international dimension. Article 2 is unambiguous in demanding that an international armed conflict requires at least two state parties, as such it would be unlikely that it has jurisdiction over non-state parties such as terrorist groups. Naturally, a terrorist group which was controlled by a State might satisfy the requirements, for example the National Liberation Front for South Vietnam appears to have been controlled by the North Vietnamese.[24] However, for the sake of convenience this article will focus on conflicts not of an international character. This approach is adopted for two reasons; firstly, conflicts involving terrorists will not satisfy the requirements of Article 2; secondly, it is generally accepted that most conflicts in the world today are of a non-international character.[25]

The law of war is surprisingly thin on the ground when it comes to regulating conflicts of a non-international character. The general provisions are to be found in Article 3, Common to the four Geneva Conventions. This provisions sets out the minimum levels expected of parties to a 'conflict not of an international character'. Common Article 3 protects those not involved in hostilities from the following:

(a) violence to life and person, in particular murder of all kinds, mutilation, cruel treatment and torture;

(b) taking hostages;

---

[24] Harmon, See n 2, 58.
[25] Jelena Pejic 'Article 1 F(a): The Notion of International Crimes', (2000) 12 *International Journal of Refugee Law, Special Supplementary Issue on Exclusion*, 13.

    (c)   outrages upon personal dignity, in particular humiliating and degrad-
        ing treatment;

    (d)   the passing of sentences and carrying out of executions without previ-
        ous judgment pronounced by a regularly constituted court ...

Terrorists have clearly breached these standards. Common Article 3 is
supplemented by Additional Protocol II to the Geneva Conventions. This
Additional Protocol II refers to conflicts occurring

> in the territory of a High Contracting Party between its armed forces and
> dissident armed forces or other organized armed groups which, under
> responsible command, exercise such control over a part of a territory as to
> enable them to carry out sustained and concerted military operations and to
> implement this Protocol.

While it is obvious that these provisions could be applied, in some cir-
cumstances, to a terrorist group they only apply in the territory of a High
Contracting Party. Importantly, it appears that terrorists could be tried for
Grave Breaches of Common Article 3 and, where applicable, Additional
Protocol II.

Unfortunately the Geneva Conventions and their Additional Protocols
are not as useful in the war on terror as they might at first appear. The
Appeals Chamber of the International Criminal Tribunal for the Former
Yugoslavia (ICTY) stated in the *Tadic* case that for the purposes of
Common Article 3 'an armed conflict exists wherever there is ... protracted armed violence between governmental authorities and organized
armed groups or between such groups within a State'.[26] International
Committee of the Red Cross (ICRC) commentary on Common Article 3
states that the dissident forces must have 'an organized military force, an
authority responsible for its acts, acting within a determinate territory
and having the means of respecting and ensuring the respect for the
Convention'.[27] These criteria exclude most terrorist organisations, the
territorial requirement alone is fulfilled by only a handful of terrorist
organisations. The threat of 'new' terrorism, discussed earlier, specifically
avoids having an organised military force with an authority responsible
for its acts. Arguably, an organised terrorist group with a cell structure
and leadership, such as the IRA or Abu Nidal Organisation would fulfil
these criteria but the 'Islamic World Front for the struggle against the Jews
and the Crusaders' would not. It has been said that the purpose of these
criteria is to distinguish armed conflict from 'mere acts of banditry or

---

[26] ICTY Decision on the Defence Motion for Interlocutory Appeal on Jurisdiction, 2
October 1995, para 70, *The Tadic Case*.
[27] *The Prosecutor v Akeyesu*, Case No ICTR–96–4–T, para 619.

unorganised and short-lived insurrection'.[28] There is some truth in this view, however, in essence the enforcement of IHL requires symmetry and reciprocity.

> In traditional 'symmetrical' warfare, the warring states adhere to the conventional model of a uniformed military distinct from their civilian population. They are concerned with maintaining their reputation for 'playing by the rules', knowing that violating the rules of war today may lead a present or future opponent to violate the same rules tomorrow.[29]

The Conventions require symmetry, that is why they refer to organised forces, and terrorists are asymmetrical. The more symmetrical a terrorist organisation is, that is the more organised it is and the more it resembles a formal army, the more likely it is that it will be covered by IHL. Unfortunately, the trend, as we have seen, is away from symmetrical forces and toward decentralised unstructured non-groups which fall beyond the definitions of IHL.

The ICC has jurisdiction over four crimes and so far three are unsuitable. The crime of aggression is undefined and inoperable, genocide only applies in very limited circumstances and War Crimes may present the opportunity for prosecuting some groups but are on the whole inadequate since most terrorist groups do not control set territory. Furthermore, as terrorist groups become increasingly asymmetrical they become increasingly less susceptible to IHL. The fourth and final category of offence over which the ICC has jurisdiction is Crimes Against Humanity.

Crimes Against Humanity, as a concept, predate the Rome Statute and the ICC, however the definition of Crimes Against Humanity contained in Article 7 of the Statute is comprehensive and will surely become the authoritative definition.[30] Article 7 is a list of prohibited actions, ranging from murder, extermination and enslavement to enforced disappearance and apartheid. These actions are deemed to be crimes against humanity when they are 'committed as part of a widespread or systematic attack directed against any civilian population, with knowledge of the attack'.[31] Terrorist organisations are incapable of committing some of these offences, for example the crime of apartheid is defined as 'inhumane acts ... committed in the context of an institutionalised regime of systematic oppression and domination of one racial group over any other racial group ...',[32] but

---

[28] *Ibid.*

[29] Radlauer, 'War Crimes & Gentleman's Agreements', April, 2003, <http://www.ict.org. il/articles/articledet.cfm?articleid+479> accessed 28 April 2003.

[30] Robertson, Crimes Against Humanity: the struggle for global justice, (London, Allen Lane, 1999) p 310.

[31] Article 7.1 The Rome Statute of the International Criminal Court.

[32] Article 7.2 (h) The Rome Statute of the International Criminal Court.

many of the other offences have been committed by terrorists. In this context it is possible to view the targeting of civilian aircraft and civilian targets such as the World Trade Centre or British shopping precincts as crimes against humanity. Since terrorists, by their nature, target civilians the offences covered by the phrase 'crimes against humanity' appear suitable.

The difficulty in pursuing terrorists under the banner of crimes against humanity arises when we examine the need for 'widespread or systematic' attacks. In *Akeyesu* the International Criminal Tribunal for Rwanda (ICTR) provided an excellent definition of the phrase.

> The concept of 'widespread' may be defined as massive, frequent, large scale action, carried out collectively with considerable seriousness and directed against a multiplicity of victims. The concept of 'systematic' may be defined as thoroughly organised and following a regular pattern on the basis of a common policy involving substantial public or private resources. There is no requirement that this policy must be adopted formally as the policy of a state. There must however be some kind of preconceived plan or policy.[33]

The need for massive, frequent, large scale action may be problematic. The events of 11 September 2001 might fulfil such criteria, given the coordination of the attacks on New York and Washington. Those attacks could also be said to fulfil the criteria necessary for a 'systematic' attack, since they were clearly thoroughly organised following a regular pattern with a common policy. Robertson points to the bombings of US embassies in Kenya and Tanzania in 1998 and states that, these multiple acts of murder were part of a systematic attack against a civilian population pursuant to an organizational policy to commit such attacks ...' therefore they were crimes against humanity.[34] Al-Qaeda has committed crimes against humanity.

The acts referred to occurred before the development of the 'new' Al-Qaeda. The transnational terrorist consultancy, which has been referred to as an ideology, could not be said to possess the necessary organisation to commit crimes against humanity. The 'Islamic World Front for the struggle against the Jews and the Crusaders' certainly has a common policy and substantial resources. They operate to a preconceived plan, their actions and those of the groups, such as JI that, they support follow a pattern. The issue is do these groups possess the organisation? Do they act collectively? It is difficult to see how the Freedom Club, a one man terrorist organisation,[35] could be viewed as acting collectively. If the ICC to is to have jurisdiction over terrorists then 'crimes against humanity' offer the

---

[33] *The Prosecutor v Akeyesu*, Case No ICTR–96–4–T, para 580.
[34] Robertson, See n 30 above, p 311.
[35] Harmon, See n 2, p 10.

best option for prosecutions. This category does not require an armed conflict. It avoids the unusually high standard of genocide. It does not require state power. Unfortunately, crimes against humanity can only be committed as part of a collective. The development of non-group groups and the move away from organised structures puts pressure upon this definition. Neo-nazis on the web have a common policy, but it is stretching the concept of collectivity to breaking point to suggest that a neo-nazi terrorist acting alone, but with strategic support from likeminded individuals who have never met, could be said to have acted in a thoroughly organised manner. As terrorism develops it will move further away from the current definition of crimes against humanity. The ICC, therefore, is not well placed to tackle the terrorist threat at present and will become increasingly less able to fulfil that role.

PROSCRIPTION

The ICC is a recent development which some heralded as a possible weapon in the war on terror. The weaknesses of the ICC in this context have been identified, as a result attention will now turn to a more traditional domestic approach to fighting terror. National legislators have often utilised proscription in their attempts to disrupt terrorists. Examples of this approach include the Republic of Ireland's Offences Against the State Act, 1939 and the UK's Terrorism Act 2000. Proscription is simply a legislative tool whereby certain organisations are named as terrorist. This approach assists in disrupting terrorists groups since mere membership of a proscribed group is a criminal offence and fundraising on behalf of or advertising and supporting a terrorist group can be criminalised. As a method of fighting terrorism proscription has a number of limitations.

Proscription involves the naming of groups as terrorist, it is, by its very nature reactive. The US had not frozen the assets of JI, nor had the United Nations Security Council named it as a terrorist group, until after the Bali bombing. [36] Other examples of delay in naming groups also exist. The Alex Boncayao Brigade (ABB) is said to have been formed in the mid-1980's following a split from the Communist Party of the Philippines, however it was not added to the US Terrorist Exclusion list until December 2001, despite the fact that it is believed to have been involved in the murder of Colonel James Rowe of the US Army in 1989.[37] Proscription leads to unpredictable results with some groups being proscribed and others being ignored. It is also self evident that before a group can be named as terrorist it must first have done something to merit the

---

[36] 'Australia Unveils Anti-Terror Plans' <http://bbc.co.uk/1/hi/world/asia-pacific/2356017.stm> accessed 24 October 2002.
[37] See n 3, p 127.

title. This is not a fatal weakness in the proscription model since, once identified, it can be used to bring the full weight of the law down upon an organisation.

A second problem associated with the proscription approach is that it can lead to farcical results. A brief review of proscribed organisations serves to highlight the difficulties. The Schedule to the Terrorism Act, includes the organisation Saor Éire (Free Ireland), this organisation first appeared in the 1930's in Ireland. Saor Éire was a leftwing, militant organisation and it does not appear to have been very successful during the 1930's. Its greatest achievement was the level of alarm it inspired in the Religious and Political Hierarchies in Ireland at the time, which viewed it with a deep suspicion.[38] The title has been 'occasionally used since that time by various Republican factions'.[39] Despite the fact that the title has fallen out of use it would be unwise to de-proscribe the organisation since that would facilitate its use in the future. Republican groups in Ireland are keen to maintain a form of historical legitimacy; hence the various factions utilising varieties of the name Irish Republican Army.[40] It appears ridiculous to maintain the proscription of this defunct movement, once seen as communistic and hell bent upon the perversion of Irish youth, but it would be unwise to remove its name from the Schedule. Once an organisation is proscribed any alteration of that status would be seen as legitimising it. On the other hand an organisation can avoid proscription by simply changing its name. The South African group People Against Gangsterism and Drugs (PAGAD) uses a series of front names including Muslims Against Global Oppression and Muslims Against Illegitimate Leaders.[41] Hizballah employs a similar tactic.[42] A further difficulty with the proscription approach is a result of its very nature. It is not always possible to gain agreement on which groups should be named. The refrain of 'one man's terrorist is another man's freedom fighter' is used to justify the actions of some groups. It might have been difficult for some to admit that the ANC was a terrorist organisation, during its period of opposition to the apartheid regime, even though its has been suggested that that group was responsible for crimes against humanity.[43] The main difficulty associated with the proscription approach, however, is not that it is reactive or that it can lead to ridiculous outcomes but rather that it does not

---

[38] See Joint Pastoral issued by his Eminence Cardinal Macrory, and the Archbishops & Bishops of Ireland (October, 1931) and Summary of Opening Statement made by the President in Dail Eireann, ON 14th OCTOBER, 1931, Dept. of an Taoiseach, file S 2267.

[39] Walker, *Blackstone's Guide ot the Anti-Terrorism Legislation*, (Oxford, 2002), p 39.

[40] Old, Official, Provisional, Real and Continuity are all prefixes to the term IRA.

[41] See n 5, p 141.

[42] Hizballah is also known as Islamic Jihad, Revolutionary Justice Organization, Organization of the Oppressed on Earth and Islamic Jihad for the Liberation of Palestine. See *Patterns of Global Terrorism 2002*, p 108.

[43] Robertson, See n 30 above, p 311.

take account of the developments associated with 'new' terrorism. One can only proscribe an organisation if an organisation exists to be proscribed.

DEFINING TERRORISM

The weakness of IHL is that it is based on an assumption of symmetry, it requires terrorist groups to resemble, as closely as possible, the structures of a regular army. Phrases such as collectivity and control predominate. Similarly the traditional legislative approach of proscription requires an organisation to exist so that it can be named. If the nature of terrorism were to fundamentally shift great swathes of anti-terror legislation would become useless. A different approach is required. Rather than attempting to twist the definition of crimes against humanity it would be better to define terrorism as an international crime. Such a move would avoid the difficulties associated with proscription, since rather than naming a group it would be possible to judge any act against the definition. This approach would cover traditional terrorist groups and new non-group groups and individuals. Such an approach would truly criminalise terrorism. At a domestic level legislation does define terrorism as well as naming terrorist groups. S1 of the Terrorism Act, 2000, goes to great lengths to define terrorism based on the nature of the activity. The fight against international terrorism requires an international definition of terrorism.

Unfortunately, the project of defining terrorism faces a series of serious, and possibly insurmountable, difficulties. In a survey of leading academics 109 alternative definitions of terrorism were proposed.[44] Forging international agreement on what constitutes terrorism has proved to be extremely difficult, indeed the Rome Conference rejected jurisdiction over the specific crime of terrorism,[45] having failed to agree on a definition for the crime of aggression it was probably wise to leave the crime of terrorism to another day. Ganor identifies a number of methods which can be employed to distinguish the actions of a group from terrorism. In 1986 President Hafez el-Assad of Syria stated that his government had always opposed terrorism 'but terrorism is one thing and a national struggle against occupation is another'.[46] Salah Khalef of the group Black September, which carried out the attack on the Munich Olympics in 1972, differentiated between terrorism, which he said he was opposed to, and revolutionary violence, which was said to be acceptable.[47] The problem

---

[44] Ganor, 'Defining Terrorism: Is One Man's Terrorist Another Man's Freedom Fighter?' <http://www.ict.org.il/articles/define.htm> accessed 28 April 2003.
[45] Robertson, p 311.
[46] Ganor, See n 44.
[47] *Ibid.*

with such an approach is that it seeks to justify the actions of the revolutionary or the national liberator by distinguishing those actions from the terrorist. Any attempt to distinguish between national liberation and terrorism is doomed to fail. The issue involved is too emotive and political, it would be impossible to reach an agrrement, just as it is difficult to gain international agreement on which groups are terrorist under the proscription model. The best approach is to ignore this debate, the best approach is to define terrorism in objective terms.

The Institute for Counter Terrorism has proposed the following definition 'terrorism is the intentional use of, or threat to use violence against civilians or against civilian targets, in order to attain political aims'. The definition is based on three elements, namely, identifying the essence of the activity; recognising that the aim of the activity is political and explicitly noting that the targets of terrorists are civilians.[48] This approach has a number of key advantages. This definition pulls the rug from under those who seek to justify terrorist actions. It is not possible to justify the use or threat of violence against a civilian population, even in the context of national liberation. Rather than criminalising the name, as with proscription, this approach criminalises the act. It is obvious to any lawyer that such an approach is preferable to all others. This model does not criminalise those engaged in struggles for national liberation, rather it criminalises those movements for national liberation who employ terrorist techniques. The definitional model would cover existing 'old' terrorist groups as well as the 'new' terrorists. Furthermore it avoids the difficulties associated with proscription. Finally, defining terrorism as a crime removes the necessity to twist existing definitions of War Crimes or Crimes Against Humanity.

The difficulties associated with any such project are political and not legal. Along with proscribing organisations domestic legislation has already provided definitions of terrorism. Definition is possible, however the reluctance of some states to engage in a process of defining terrorism has to be recognised. The 1979 Convention against hostage taking should have been a relatively uncontroversial measure. Hostage taking is clearly an attack on civilians, by its very nature, it involves a substantial economic cost and is, one would assume, opposed by the majority of states. However, a clause was included in the convention on hostage taking stating that it would not apply in armed conflicts 'in which people are fighting against colonial domination and alien occupation and against racist regimes in the exercise of their right to self determination'.[49] It is unacceptable to suggest that hostage taking is ever legitimate, it is prohibited

---

[48] See n 44.

[49] 'Israel seeks international support for a treaty against suicide bombers' *Haaretz* <http://www.haaretzdaily.com/hasen/objects/pages/Print/ArticleEn.jhtml?itemNo=2691 41> accessed 5 March 2003.

by the Laws of War and it should be viewed as an illegitimate tactic, even when employed against a racist regime. If a similar clause were to be inserted into a definition of terrorism it would entirely undermine the project, worse again it would legitimise the targeting of civilians in some circumstances. In short, it would be better to have no definition of terrorism than to have one which allowed for some terrorism.

There are two important developments which may facilitate attempts to define terrorism. Firstly, international terrorism is a cross border phenomenon, similar to piracy, aircraft hijacking etc. Universal jurisdiction against pirates has been explained as follows,

> it is an offence against the law of nations; and as the scene of the pirate's operations is the high seas, which it is not the right or duty of any nation to police, he is denied the protection of the flag which he may carry and is treated as an outlaw—as the enemy of mankind—*hostis humanis generis*— whom any nation may in the interests of all capture and punish.[50]

Piracy is committed on the high seas, beyond the jurisdiction of any one state, however, were it to be committed within the jurisdiction of a state it would be a crime simpliciter. In order to ensure that the pirate cannot evade justice simply by remaining beyond any one states jurisdiction the nations of the world employed the concept of universal jurisdiction allowing any one state to prosecute the pirate. Similarly, terrorist actions are crimes simpliciter when they are carried out within any given state, however tackling the international terrorist requires more than just domestic law since international terrorists form international networks and cross borders etc. As such it is in the interests of all that any nation can prosecute terrorists rather than allowing terrorists evade justice by avoiding any one states jurisdiction. Piracy provides the precedent.

The second significant factor is the 'war on terror'. The difficulties associated with any attempt to define terrorism are political. By bringing forward a reasonable definition of terrorism, such as the above proposal, it becomes increasingly difficult for nations to object. President George W Bush Jr stated that 'every nation, in every region, now has a decision to make. Either you are with us, or you are with the terrorists'.[51] This is a strong statement but in effect it means very little. A reasonable definition of terrorism, which cannot be opposed on principled grounds, would force states to nail their colours to the mast, ever aware that you are either with us or with the terrorists. The precedent of piracy is available, but

---

[50] *The Lotus Case (France v Turkey)* (1927) PCIJ Ser. A, no 10. See Robertson, see n 30 above, p 220.

[51] President Bush, *Address to a Joint Session of Congress & the American People*, 20 September, 2001.   <http://www.whitehouse.gov/news/releases/2001/09/print/20010920-8.html> accessed 14 October 2003.

more importantly any state unwilling to ratify such a treaty would have to argue that it is acceptable to use violence or the threat of violence against civilians in the pursuit of a political end.

CONCLUSIONS

This article has examined a number of possible responses to terrorism. The ICC is unsuitable because the crimes over which it has jurisdiction do not adequately cover the offences committed by terrorists. Utilising the ICC involves twisting the ordinary meaning of Crimes Against Humanity and is therefore unacceptable. Proscription has been the traditional approach of legislators seeking to criminalise terrorist activities. This approach can lead to farcical results and is not wholly satisfactory when tackling traditional terror groups. The development is Al-Qaeda as a franchise or support network can be seen as the beginnings of a new form of international terrorism. These new non-group groups are not amenable to prosecution before the ICC due to their lack of organisation. As a non-group such terrorists are also capable of avoiding proscription. New terrorism requires a new response.

Having considered the key contenders it is clear that the only satisfactory response to terrorism, the only response capable of acting in a cross border fashion and of tackling both the old and the new, the existing and the future terrorist threat is the definitional model. Defining terrorism as an international crime criminalises the activity and as such avoids all discussion of the merits of a groups cause. This approach has a precedent in the form of piracy and has the ability to adapt to the changing nature of terrorism. Vitally, a definitional approach forces countries to justify their opposition. A reasonable, objective definition of terrorism is unopposable unless you are willing to state that there are circumstances where it is acceptable to target civilians. This approach allows severe diplomatic pressure to be brought to bear on states. Unfortunately it is highly unlikely that the definitional model will be pursued. The current regime in the United States has shown a distinct lack of interest in international law. President Bush has informed the UN of its intention not to become a party to the Rome Statute[52] and it does seem likely that it will alter its opinion in order to secure a definition of terrorism. In the context of the war on terror the Bush Whitehouse might choose to pursue this approach but it is unlikely. A further possibility would involve those countries which have ratified the Rome Statute amending it to include a crime of terrorism. Such an approach would be welcome but it is impossible to comment further since the viability of the ICC as an institution is not, at

---

[52] <http://untreaty.un.org/ENGLISH/bible/englishinternetbible/partl/chapterVIII/treaty10.asp> accessed 14 October 2003.

present, entirely clear. A final option would involve multilateral agreements between interested nations. Under such a model likeminded nations, such as NATO, the Commonwealth, NAFTA, the EU etc could pursue a policy of introducing coordinated legislation with a common definition of international terrorism. The obvious downside of such an approach is its lack of coherence. In the end defining terrorism is the only viable option in the long term, it is a policy which must be pursued, sooner, rather than later.

3

Is the European Central Bank a Case for Institutional Adaptation to the Challenges of Globalisation? Implications for European Union's Democratic Legitimacy

PAULO VILA MAIOR

Paper presented to the 'Global Governance and the Search for Justice Conference', University of Sheffield, 29 April—1 May, 2003. Fundação Calouste Gulbenkian (Lisbon, Portugal) provided the author with research funding.

ABSTRACT

The paper focus on the constitutional implications derived from the specific nature of the European Central Bank (ECB) for the would-be polity formation in the European Union (EU). The emphasis is placed on the alleged absence of democratic legitimacy and the intertwined weak pattern of accountability the ECB shows. My argument tries to challenge the reasoning supporting this conventional criticism. Maybe the ECB is not so undemocratic; maybe the institutional arrangements for its accountability are not to be so harshly criticised. The denial of the conventional criticism relies on the specific nature of the supranational polity that is emerging, for which Economic and Monetary Union (and the ECB by large) plays a prominent role. The reasons for this alternative interpretation are twofold. One depicts the specific nature of the European integration process, and the inherent changes to the traditional vision of sovereignty, democracy and accountability. The other challenges the way member states themselves are currently unable to satisfy the requirements of democratic legitimacy and accountability for reasons related to a decay of parliamentary democracies and for the diminished ability nation states have to be the central agents of decision-making in a world of increased economic interdependence. Therefore the ECB may be in possession of sufficient democratic legitimacy (and thus the claims of limited accountability fall apart) if one assess its performance as being the guarantee for price stability as the main political-economic outcome the supranational bank can afford to the European citizens.

1 INTRODUCTION

WITH THE TREATY on the European Union (TEU) the process of European integration undergone a profound material transformation with the establishment of Economic and Monetary Union (EMU). An additional change took place in the institutional arena, where a supranational central bank was created (from the beginning of EMU stage three onwards) to deal with monetary policy. The relationship of material with institutional arenas of transformation provided scholars on European integration with a rich terrain for discussion.

Economists focused on the macroeconomic implications associated with monetary union, concentrating on the political-economic model that was chosen for EMU and debating the feasibility of EMU's operational details for the future. Political scientists' centre of attention was more on the political connotations of EMU, notably on the issue of democratic legitimacy and the inherent consequences for the EU as an emerging polity, as well as for the structure of the nation-state in the EU. The debate is rich and the author's intention is to feed this debate with some inputs that depart from the conventional wisdom concerning how democratic the European Central Bank (ECB) is.

The next section raises the nature of the problem linked with EMU, the ECB as a powerful body and the main questions that arise in the face of such political-economy model underpinning monetary integration in Europe. These are the questions I will address in the fourth and final section, trying to bring useful insights from political science that cast some light on an alternative framework for assessing how democratic the ECB can be (if it can be democratic at all). In the third section the arguments laid down in the literature supporting the existing democratic legitimacy and accountability within the ECB will be highlighted.

2 THE PROBLEM AND THE MAIN QUESTIONS

There is a problem linked to the existence of the ECB when the critical literature is reviewed: the limited (for some absent) democratic legitimacy this new institution is associated with. Considering the ECB is the most visible institutional support of EMU, it is important to trace back to its origins and ask whether the decision to launch EMU was the main cause for the precise institutional characterisation of the ECB that is so deeply criticised by several scholars. That is, acknowledging the ECB possesses certain features that are subject of contention both for politicians and academics, it is unquestionable that a problem comes to the surface: *the ECB is not anchored to the traditional notion of democratic legitimacy.* As such, detractors raise several doubts on how the ECB is legitimate to produce a policy outcome that affects the public by and large for items that are relevant for their welfare. Let us focus on the source of this problem, briefly reviewing the main characters that give the mask for EMU's political economic-model.

A careful look at EMU paves the way for two important conclusions on the impact of monetary union: the precise meaning EMU has, and its constitutional (from where derive important sequels for the whole process of European integration). EMU was created as an outstanding roadmap for a political-economic orthodoxy that is akin to the monetarist school (Begg and Hodson 2000: 1, and Dyson 2002a: 2). The main elements constituting the monetarist-led conception of EMU are price stability as the sacred macroeconomic goal attached to EMU (Taylor 2000: 185), the prominence monetary policy has to achieve such goal (Dyson 2000a: 27), a secondary role for fiscal policy, and a clear separation of competences between the monetary authority (the ECB) and fiscal authorities (national governments).

The latter aspect means that monetary policy is subject to a full centralisation process of policy-making, in the sense that the ECB is endowed with exclusive competences to act on monetary policy. On the fiscal policy terrain decentralisation is the keyword. National governments keep on being the sole authorities with competences to chose fiscal policy preferences and instruments. Nevertheless, this competence is somewhat blurred for the prominence attached to monetary policy and the high priority related to price stability: fiscal policy is subordinated to monetary policy and to the pursuit of price stability; furthermore, national competences on fiscal policy are limited by the subsequent implementation of the Stability and Growth Pact with its ceilings upon deficits that constraint national governments' ability to use fiscal policy instruments to alleviate certain macroeconomic problems that temporarily affect them.

The relation between monetary and fiscal policy in EMU is the instructive evidence of the philosophy underneath monetary integration in the EU. Not only exclusive competences on monetary policy were assigned to the ECB, a newly supranational body; but, importantly, the ECB was afforded with considerable independence *vis-à-vis* political authorities (both at national and supranational levels). The mentioned picture is instructive of the clear separation of functions that EMU brought to the forefront in macroeconomic policy, adding elements of uniqueness for the mixed framework of analysis and the implication that stems from it:

— On an unprecedented way, a supranational entity made a separation of responsibilities on two of the most important aspects of economic policy (monetary and fiscal policy, both being ascribed to different layers in economic policy-making, respectively the ECB and national governments);

— Moreover, the roadmap for price stability forced the architects of EMU to select monetary policy as the privileged instrument to achieve low levels of inflation, downgrading the importance of fiscal policy—indeed opening the window for receiving the influence of monetarism and rejecting the Keynesian-led economic policy (McKay 1996: 9–10, McNamara 1999: 456, Pollack 2000: 276, and Crouch 2002: 281);

— And, thirdly, as an innovation on the institutional domain the ECB was empowered with considerable independence.

The innovation is straightforward when the historical observation of member states' practice is illustrative of the absence of political independence, or at least of limited independence, enjoyed by central banks. The exception was Germany, where the Bundesbank indeed was afforded with considerable guarantees of independence. The innovation also rests on the supranational arena. Here again, imprinting the sense of uniqueness that goes hand in hand with European integration, the creation of the ECB was a mirror of unprecedented political independence (Dyson 2002b: 358–9). Considering the Federal Reserve of the United States and the Bundesbank as the reference points for independent central banking, the ECB is even most independent (Harden 1993: 153, and Dyson 1994: 150). In this context, the ECB went far beyond what was already stated as the reasonable confines of central bank independence, deepening the limits towards a new dimension that wasn't acknowledged anywhere.

The extended political independence the ECB was endowed with raises the main source of concern to those who voiced against how the supranational central bank is structured. Contrary to other examples of great central bank independence, the ECB is reported as having excessive independence and limited accountability and transparency. Critics argue the ECB is independent from elected politicians, thus being unaccountable. If national and supranational central bankers are unaccountable, they lack democratic legitimacy (Verdun 1998: 107–8, Begg and Green 1998: 7, Crowley and Rowley 1998: 24, and Moran 2002: 276). The reasoning standing on the conventional literature that urges against the existing EMU institutional set up leads me to raise the first two research questions:

i) Is the ECB unaccountable to elected politicians?

ii) If the ECB is held as unaccountable, another question is whether this is a source of an undemocratically legitimate supranational central bank. The source of the problem runs as follows: it is possible the ECB is unaccountable; what follows is whether this is enough to reach the conclusion that the ECB is not democratic. The alternative is to investigate whether the scarce accountability the ECB has prevented the institution from being democratically legitimate at all, or if it only puts in jeopardy its democratic legitimacy without saying the ECB is undemocratic at all? This second question raises a matter of degree—that is, the ECB lacking democratic legitimacy, or the ECB not performing well in terms of democratic legitimacy?

Apart from the conceptual meaning of EMU, now it is important to observe what implications emerge from EMU. The relevance attached to EMU for the overall process of European integration, notably for how deeply it was responsible for a redefinition of the European integration project, is already noticeable. EMU was constitutionalised through the Treaty of Maastricht, and further developed a deeply rooted constitutional dimension for European integration in what concerns the position of the EU regarding how economic policy is run.

In this sense, EMU had an intertwined effect of being subject to constitutionalisation and leaving more constitutional seeds that deepened European integration. EMU was conceptualised as a macroeconomic template for the EU and for its member states: a template geared towards price stability, thus leaving behind other macroeconomic objectives (growth and employment). There is no unanimity among the literature on how this constitutional effect is so steady: some argue price stability is indeed the only goal the ECB seeks through monetary policy (McNamara 2001: 169, and Amtenbrink 2002: 150), while others claim that albeit this is the guiding light that serves for the ECB to shape monetary policy other goals are secondary, but attainable (among them employment and sustainable growth) (Begg and Green 1998: 4, Cukierman 2001: 40–75, and Dyson 2002a: 22).

Aside this discussion, what is important is to reflect on the macroeconomic priority that was scheduled by the framers of monetary union in Europe. It is undisputable the fight against inflation is the central worry. The next step is to proceed to the implications coming from the option of price stability, and the noticeable neglect of other goals such as growth and employment. That substantial option can impact on citizens' daily welfare, as well as non-governmental and governmental institutions that face constraints in their preferences when they are presented with a political-economic roadmap for macroeconomic stability based on low inflation.

The relevance is accrued when one find important evidence, from recent past experience in the majority of EU member states, that inflation was not the highest priority in terms of macroeconomic policy. Following a pro-Keynesian economic policy, the maintenance of a certain rate of unemployment, together with pre-defined targets of economic growth, were the yardsticks that inspired these member states' economic policies. Here again member states that run against this tendency were the minority, Germany being the outstanding and most successful example (Heisenberg 1998: 263–77).

Therefore a vast majority of member states (here encompassing both governmental authorities, non-governmental bodies, firms and individuals) was forced to change perceptions of how policy-making was adjusted to a new template for economic policy. Accordingly behaviours had also to adapt to the new reality. When I pay attention to the constitutional dimension anchored in this macroeconomic transformation, the purpose is to emphasise how a new perception of macroeconomic dynamics, being a reason for strong individual or collective adaptation, meant room for changing habits and reversed priorities about specific outcomes assigned to economic policy. This behavioural change is equated to constitutional change, in the sense that the structures member states were used to exploit were subject of substantial transformation, being replaced by other structures to which all the above-mentioned actors were invited to accommodate.

Another constitutional implication accruing from EMU was the recognition that economics started reigning over politics[1]. Several indications feed this conclusion. Firstly, as a structural dominant force, the recognition that price stability was assumed as the main objective for economic policy. What is at stake is the overall consequence for the decision-making process (both in the mere economic arena and the broad political decision-making sphere) that derives from the prioritisation of price stability. As it was previously highlighted, price stability was a reflection of monetarist dominance as a paradigm for macroeconomic policy.

Another crucial aspect of this school of economic thought was the prominence attached to monetary policy, and the awareness that officials responsible for monetary policy should be as much independent as possible. Here lies the crucial feature underpinning the divorce between economics and politics—to be accurate, how macroeconomic policy greatly emancipated from the overall process of political decision-making (Shapiro and Hacker-Córdon 1999: 3). This bestowed the general perception that politicians are insensitive to account for medium-to long-term objectives that are coherent and sustainable. Politicians run after short-term incentives associated with their re-election. As such politicians don't care for inflation and the overall stabilisation of the macroeconomic conditions, and can jeopardise these goals (Cukierman 2001: 40–75, and Baimbridge, Burkitt and Whyman 1999: 19).

The arguments presented give the intellectual case for transforming the essence of economic policy. Despite being a political phenomenon—in the

---

[1] This is the diagnosis made by Stastny (2002), although this assessment is made in general terms, without looking specifically to EMU. In this sense there is some similarity with the claim that the state has evolved towards a category of 'market-state' (Bobbitt 2002: 213–43). Against this perception Boyer (2000: 26), asserting EMU is a political project, and Moran (2002: 259) viewing monetary union as a new system of governance that is emerging, thus imprinting a political connotation to the European integration process.

sense that economic policy is a product of the state, or supranational, institutions—the fact is that economic policy was stripped out of politicians' influences. This happened at least in the most prominent sphere of overall economic policy (monetary policy). Now monetary policy was devoted to professionals, acting with absolute independence from elected officials. Considering:

— These professional networks (Peterson and O'Toole 2001: 302) are constituted by individuals showing strong interests in performing independently from politicians;

— These professionals are tied together by strong links that accrue from a common perception of how the issues they are entitled to solve should be decided;

— Central bankers are not elected and were afforded with enhanced political independence, being able to avoid pressures exercised by elected politicians.

The overall picture standing from these considerations is the new balance of power within the member states and even within the EU itself. A three-fold dimension has to be observed.

— Firstly, central bankers (national and supranational, both acting through the ECB Governing Council) are powerful enough to interfere with national governments' preferences for economic policy. Changes in interest rates, and the remaining instruments available to the ECB, can offset any plan of a national government to frustrate the inflation target previously defined by the ECB. The obvious implication is how a supranational sphere can impact on national governments' policies and options that have economic effects. The supranational sphere grows in ascendancy over the national sphere.

— Secondly, there is a political implication that cannot be underestimated: non-elected officials (central bankers) have the strength and the means to impose strong constraints to elected politicians that still possess some economic competences at the national level, and literally blown the outcomes desired by the latter. At least apparently, some redistribution of power within the EU meant that formally a de-democratisation occurred.

— Thirdly, another political implication closes this circular line of reasoning: indeed economics reigns over politics, since professional economists empowered with political-economic competences can constrain the freedom politicians still have (through fiscal policy) to define their own priorities and preferences in terms of available outcomes.

The picture presented also produces important consequences on the nature of the decision-making process related with economic policy. Non-political bodies were substantially empowered *vis-à-vis* elected officials. This is another way to express how economics has grown in ascendancy over politics, notably for the reflection this phenomenon accounts. Since politicians acknowledged the powerful role played by international financial markets, even upon the freedom politicians themselves have to undertake the decisions they would like to implement without that market-led constraint, they were forced to realise how economic policy should be subject of enhanced expertise and thus de-politicised (Shapiro and Hacker-Córdon 1999: 3).

Professional economists, when acting in a truly independent supranational central bank, are well equipped to interpret the signals markets express and best suited to implement a monetary policy that matches markets' preferences. This is a clear indication of how powerful the forces operating in the environment of globalised markets are. Several authors provide persuasive accounts of how meaningless it would be an alternative scenario where national politicians would stubbornly insist in getting out of reach of the economic interdependence that affects the whole world (Underhill 2002: 37). Instead, globalisation forced national politicians to be aware of how impotent they are to go against the tide of economic interdependence. EMU is also seen in this context as an answer to the challenges from an increasingly globalised world where markets commanded politics, and politics react to markets. This can be seen as another expression of the dominance of economics over politics.

The tendency for economics' experts being empowered was spatially located on a twofold dimension: in the supranational arena with the creation of the ECB endowed with strong powers and a belt of independence preventing politicians' interferences; and in the national sphere, by granting the same belt of political independence to national central bankers, at the same time that finance ministers were empowered in the domestic correlation of powers among ministers (Dyson 2000b: 646). In a word, all the aspects that have been described amount to a bureaucratisation of economic policy-making—and to the extent that economics assumed a central role for the whole process of policy-making, the same conclusion infects the process used by public powers to undertake decisions. Here conventional notions of state-centric democratic legitimacy must come to the surface in order to evaluate whether the move towards bureaucratised politics is satisfactory.

So EMU is responsible for a deep constitutional change—both in the European integration process and in member states' domestic political structures. In the context of European integration it deepened the process of supranational European integration (Cameron 1998: 189). Issues like the single currency, a supranational monetary policy, the subordination of national fiscal policies to the centralised monetary policy, the constitutional change determined by a different policy orthodoxy inherent to the firm commitment to price stability—all this suggests the steps taken for feeding the supranational texture of European integration.

Probably more important are the implications for statehood. Here the transformations member states were forced to accommodate to (the abdication of formal monetary sovereignty, the loss of national currencies, and the external constraint (Dyson 2002b: 658) embedded in the commitment for price stability, something akin to tying their own hands to externally induced discipline)[2] provide external evidence of how 'life changed' after EMU was launched. Not that changes meant a 'revolution', because in the ongoing process of macroeconomic convergence dictated by the imperative to follow German leadership in the years of the European Monetary System (EMS) the remaining member states were used to run after Germany's policy orientations. The change came in the formal sense, forcing member states to amend their own constitutions and, to a lower level, accommodating low politics procedures to the requirements inherent to the political-economic model dominating EMU.

Summing up, EMU heavily impacted on the daily life of individuals, corporations and decision-making bodies at the national level. EMU empowered non-elected officials on the supranational arena (and even on the national sphere, as it is shown by the enhanced role national central bankers have). The reason for inquiry is whether there is an imbalance that directs the EU (through EMU and its institutional settlement) towards a worrying scenario of limited—if not absent—democratic legitimacy. Indeed change in the process of European integration was sharp and thrilling. The launch of monetary union imprinted a challenge not least for conventional standards of national sovereignty; the means chosen to make such change operational, especially the characters of the institutional architecture of EMU, were far removed from traditional concerns of state-centric democratic legitimacy. The imbalance is striking: deep change without encompassing, in its outcome, the procedures of democratic legitimacy that citizens were used to observe at the national level. From this scenario two other questions must be addressed:

i) EMU accentuated the (alleged) democratic deficit of the EU?

ii) Should EMU be interpreted as a necessary answer to worldwide tensions from globalisation, thus accepting the underestimation of popular claims? Are markets more powerful than individuals? Hence, are markets the alternative site for assessing the democratic

---

[2] To a non-conventional approach, see McNamara (1999: 466): her suggestion is that EMU means a powerful external constraint to member states, since they were pushed to a necessary adaptation to the challenges stemming from globalisation. According to the author, this is instructive enough to reject the mere accommodation of member states to a neo-liberal agenda; something more powerful happened—the need to adjust to globalisation.

legitimacy of those organisational answers to its challenges—and not anymore the individual as source of democratic legitimacy?

3 THE LITERATURE SUPPORTING ECB'S DEMOCRATIC LEGITIMACY AND ACCOUNTABILITY

It is important to critically reflect on the arguments that urge against the ECB for being scarcely accountably (if not unaccountable at all) and undemocratic. Firstly, to consider the ECB as a non-genuine supranational institution arguing with the over-representation of national central bankers (Welfens 1996: 37–8, Buiter 1999: 192, and Eijffinger and de Haan 2000: 33–4) misrepresents the reality and ignores the specific context of central banking. More important than the national affiliations within the Governing Council is to acknowledge how central bankers constitute a powerful epistemic community where supranational interests, and notably the objectives that match central bankers' own ideological creeds, are achieved (Verdun 1999: 323). Central bankers provided several manifestations of how national-independent they are: above their national interests central bankers have a sit on the Governing Council of the ECB to contribute for a monetary policy strategy that matches supranational interests and goes in line with their professional patterns of economic rationality. Accordingly, they are prepared to be immune to pressures bolstered by national governments.

To this purpose it is interesting to depict the distinction between electoral and non-electoral accountability (Keohane and Nye Jr, 2001: 12–4). The former comprises the conventional means of political control, referring back to transparency, domestic accountability, and legislative control; non-electoral accountability goes away from this standard and encompasses other means to provide non-political accountability—through markets and through epistemic communities. Concerning the latter, Keohane and Nye Jr (2001: 13) argue the powerfulness associated to accountability made through epistemic communities derives from (...) *professional ethic standards* (that) *can be used to hold adversaries accountable.*

The application of this conclusion to the context of European central banking provides straightforward results, since central bankers are expected to speak a language and behave according to certain professional standards that are commonsense to other experts outside the ECB. As such supranational and national central bankers become subjects of tight accountability on the face of the purposes they are committed to, the language they express, and the outcomes provided by monetary policy. Other experts can put under stress the way monetary policy is being run and such yardsticks will easily ascertain the results from it. Relying on Keohane and Nye Jr's conceptualisation, it is expected that a powerful seed of non-electoral accountability can be related with the ECB.

Secondly, when the critical literature stresses the ECB is not account-able enough and suggests it should be hold accountable to the European Parliament (Butt Phillip 2002: 43–4) they fall into a conceptual trap when the specific context of European integration is considered. Indeed some authors claim that empowering the European Parliament would be a mis-take, especially when the constraints of European integration are acknowledged and the EU institutional balance is highlighted. Following one author's persuasive analysis (Schmidt 2001: 340), two powerful rea-sons prevent the European Parliament from being empowered in the overall EU institutional balance.

— Firstly, such solution would erode the salutary intergovernmental basis upon which the EU relies. For Schmidt this is not a corruption of the supranational template of European integration; on the con-trary, to rely on this intergovernmental basis is to provide a strong linkage between the EU as polity and democratic legitimacy (Laffan 1998: 330–1). Supranational institutions are not able to provide such element; only the intergovernmental actors that intervene in the ongoing development of European integration are democratically legitimised to do it. And when they feed relevant changes to European integration they grant the democratic foundation for anchoring the EU and its institutions on democratic legitimacy.

— Secondly, the increasing belt of democratic legitimacy associated to the European Parliament does not compensate the possible erosion of the intergovernmental basis. This institution is absent in sub-stantive democratic legitimacy for its inability to speak on behalf of the European people, just because there isn't such a thing (Weiler 1999, with his 'no-demos' thesis).

Turning specifically to the claims that the ECB is neither democratically legitimate nor accountable (Anderson 1997: 130, de Grauwe 1997: 181–2, and Underhill 2002: 46), some authors present a different approach reject-ing the conventional criticism the supranational central bank faces. The starting point is the 'transmission belt theory'. According to this theoretical model, supranational institutions' legitimacy is derived from the democrat-ic legitimacy owned by national institutions—the ones that created supra-national institutions and empowered them with certain competences (Majone 2001: 260, and Menon and Weatherill 2002: 118). This constitutes an indirect form of democratic legitimacy, the only available instrument devised to accept a non-conventional, non state-centric notion of democrat-ic legitimacy to supranational institutions, because these cannot be seen through the lens of statehood. Moreover, if the big moments that created and developed the process of European integration were intergovernmen-tal in nature, why challenge the legitimacy of supranational institutions created by such processes? (Scharpf 2001: 355).

The argument based on the transmission belt theory offers a strong case for supporting an acceptable degree of democratic legitimacy and accountability to the ECB. As a by-product of the transmission belt theory two sorts of arguments claim how the ECB can be enough legitimate from the democratic viewpoint: arguments highlighting its constitutional dimension, and arguments relying on a technocratic dimension of legitimacy.

Starting with the constitutional dimension of ECB's legitimacy, some authors claim that the central bank's legitimacy comes from the treaty provisions that laid down the foundations for its creation and subsequent operation (Dyson 2000a: 17, and Issing 1999: 509). Since these treaty provisions received the consent of each and every member state through the vote delivered by each national leader, this is enough to award EMU as a whole, and the ECB in particular, with a mantle of democratic legitimacy. The mere constitutionalisation of EMU and its institutional settlement is the strong evidence of how democratic the central bank is. Furthermore, the fact that the process of ratification of the Maastricht treaty involved national parliaments (and in some cases even the citizens through referendum) is the clear-cut evidence of the democratic legitimacy owned by EMU (and the ECB). Accordingly, the ECB is accountable *vis-à-vis* the European peoples (Issing 1999: 509).

Others claim that EMU and the ECB have legitimacy backed on technocratic arguments. The general principle stands from the huge complexity of macroeconomic policy as the case for accepting ECB's current status of accountability. The justification comes from an extension of Dahl's reasoning that explains why international organisations remain closed to the public (Dahl 1999: 24): the outstanding example is foreign affairs, where issues are so complex and intricate that the general public necessarily has to remain outside of decision-making arenas and bargaining fora. The public is marginalised not for reasons of secrecy (as long as Dahl recognises that these are powerful enough to admit public's segregation, otherwise some results wouldn't be feasible) but for the lack of understanding about these issues. The same could easily be said of monetary policy. Thus the argument of accentuated expertise deemed necessary to interpret monetary policy is the main baseline to back up the concept of technocratic legitimacy associated to the ECB.

Within this conceptual framework, some scholars claim that technocratic legitimacy broadened the acceptance of the ECB as a legitimate institution, because the ECB had the positive input of opening monetary policy to the public. Prior to EMU monetary policy was more secret than now, and it was based on a complex and rather obscure complicity between national executives and central banks (Gowan 1997: 98, and Leino 2001: 27). An extension of this argument sees EMU as an enhanced site for democratic legitimacy because it was responsible for opening up financial markets that previously were closed to the general public's perception (Moran 2002:

275). For all these reasons, EMU (and the ECB) can be seen as being legitimised for the technocratic expertise associated to the issues they govern.

As complexity is so huge, more expertise is needed to deal with the challenges that arise. As more expertise is involved in monetary policy, the more citizens have difficult points of access to the overall framework that ends up in a monetary policy strategy (Dyson (2002a: 8). The expertise needed fuels the technocratic model of democratic legitimacy, going hand in hand with the contemporary tendency for delegating governance powers upon the shoulders of regulatory agencies (Verdun and Christiansen 2000: 167–8). Extending the line of reasoning to encompass a parallel between the ECB and traditional regulatory agencies, Majone (2001: 262) adds an interesting question: if member states were a paradigm in feeding regulatory agencies, thus empowering non-elected officials without being worried with their genuine democratic legitimacy and accountability, why is there so much concern with the ECB? The point is that it seems unfair (and intellectually dishonest) to accept a certain characterisation at the national level and then urging against that same model at the supranational level.

As a result of this line of reasoning, another helpful argument is put forward to demonstrate how the current status of accountability afforded to the ECB is satisfactory (Winkler 2000: 8): more important than calling for an open ECB is to battle for clarity in the information the central bank releases (Amtenbrink 2002: 151). The reasons are related with requests of information efficiency, a general principle the ECB should respect. As less clear and honest the information is, the less likely citizens are able to monitor monetary policy. The main goal associated to information efficiency by the ECB is to contribute for common understanding about monetary policy, adding the perception receivers have on how monetary policy is run by policy-makers, as well as the outcomes it provides.

As an application of the technocratic legitimacy argument, Cukierman (2001: 40–75) offers additional valuable arguments. The author makes a distinction between narrow accountability and broad accountability. The former refers to the objectives central bankers are committed to (in the ECB context, price stability), while the latter encompasses the scenario where elected officials are able to change central bank's objectives at any time. The concept of narrow accountability is crystallised in the ECB constitutional status. Furthermore, the author argues the ECB is transparent enough not to put in jeopardy its status of democratic legitimacy and accountability. He offers three powerful reasons: a high degree of independence, the ECB constitutional status can only be changed by treaty amendment requiring unanimity, and the Stability and Growth Pact preventing politicians' indirect interferences with monetary policy.

For Cukierman the concepts of transparency and accountability are intimately related, because he concludes there is as much transparency as the central bank is committed to a single objective. This is the case of the ECB, thus being possible to infer from the author's conceptualisation that the ECB is already enough transparent, accountable and democratic legitimate. Issing reaches a similar conclusion, asserting that the ECB is one of the most accountable and transparent central banks in the world, despite its infancy. The claims for more transparency are dismissed because elsewhere central banks don't rank on such high degree of transparency, and because in the specific context of central banking activity it is an absurd to envisage a system of absolute transparency (Issing 1999: 505–7).

4 THE SOLUTION PROPOSED

Let's get back to the crucial questions addressed in the chapter

i) Is the ECB accountable?

ii) Is the ECB lacking democratic legitimacy? Or, worse, it is just undemocratic?

iii) Did EMU deepen the democratic deficit that allegedly affects the European integration process?

iv) And finally, is EMU a mirror of pressures stemming from globalisation, thus opening the window for a differentiated concept of democratic legitimacy that comes in line with markets' requests and not so much with a traditional anchoring point upon the citizenry?

An attempt to provide answers leads to the previous knowledge of the specific context within which European integration moves on. Indeed it is not unsurprising to claim uniqueness is the crucial feature of the European integration process (Laffan 1998: 236, Wiener 2000: 319, and Stone Sweet, Fligstein and Sandholtz 2001: 3). Starting from this assumption, an important proposition is suggested: the nature of the EU as an emerging polity, a non-state type of polity (Eriksen and Fossum 2000: 6, and Shaw and Wiener 2000: 67). Thus when critics of ECB's record of democratic legitimacy and accountability present their arguments they fall on a conceptual trap: their mistake is to address European integration, and monetary union in special, as resulting on a state-like entity.

The conceptual mistake they run into is to look at EMU as a mere replication of existing monetary unions within nation-states, notably because they address the evolution of European integration in close connection with existing federal states (McKay 1999: 5–6, and Dyson 2000a: 155). In a short, the problem with the critical literature is their methodological shortcoming of assessing the most prominent events of European integration in the light of state-centric concepts. The danger in this methodological approach is to bear in mind that it is difficult to compare the incomparable. The EU is a specific, unique polity that cannot be easily compared with any other form of political organisation. A persuasive account of this line of reasoning stands on the perception that the EU is more than a regime and less than a nation-state (Wallace 1983).

The opposite argument that the process of monetary integration in Europe served to 'rescue the nation-state' (Milward 1992) can be reversed when its practical effects are carefully examined. Looking back to the ideas processed by this line of reasoning, their proponents claim EMU was the scapegoat to prevent the annihilation of the European nation-state(s) by the powerful, influential forces working in international markets. For those who advocate the 'rescue of the nation-state' argument, EMU is devised as an attempt to domesticate the so-far uncontrolled forces of globalisation that undermined national governments' ability to independently pursue their own macroeconomic policy objectives (Dyson 2000b: 651, and Rhodes 2002: 310).

But, ironically, this argument serves to reveal the fallacy of conventional criticisms directed to the ECB and to the political-economic model underneath EMU. For one side, because the recognition that EMU was created to tame international markets amounts to the awareness that EMU acts as an externality, as something that pictures a powerful influence from aboard undermining national governments' ability to autonomously run macroeconomic policy. Thus, EMU didn't rescue the nation-state at all. On the contrary, the transition towards monetary union had the straightforward significance of clearly showing how fragile and dependent upon external, uncontrolled events member states are. They were forced to proceed to EMU just because they recognised this was the best solution to match the demands of powerful international markets, as a means envisaged to react collectively to the challenges from accentuated economic interdependence (Peterson and Bomberg 2000: 20–1). Habermas (2000: 30) argues globalisation forces states to be thinner because they are compelled to enforce restrictive policies at home. Habermas (1997: 261) furthermore suggests that through European integration the outstanding evidence is that the nation-state is undergoing a process of erosion. According to this reasoning, nation-states are the dependent variable within the process that lead to monetary union in Europe, and not the independent variable as defended by the proponents of the 'rescuing the nation-state' argument.

Secondly, and as a consequence of the preceding reason, it is important to acknowledge the motivations that contributed to EMU's specific institutional architecture, notably the ECB-centric model (Dyson 2000a: 11). Even if one relies on state-centric accounts of monetary union in the EU it is instructive to conclude that the final institutional outcome member states influenced was pervasive for the specific purposes they allegedly run after—the rescuing of nation-states against the dictatorship of international finance markets, or the creation of monetary union as a mere reflection of the most powerful member states' interests.

In fact EMU rests on the prominence of the monetary authority, and invested the ECB with strong, independent powers. Therefore the supra-national central bank is immune from political pressures that eventually national governments exert. The single recognition of the ECB's independence status would be enough for finding the conceptual incoherence of those who see EMU as a mirror of member states' interests (acting as a mere instrument for praising member states' goals), or as an evidence of a life-belt to which member states anchor themselves. Moreover, the ECB was empowered with strong powers as the factual recognition that the central bank was well equipped to deal with powerful financial markets in the international arena (Pollack 2000: 267). More than national governments, with low skills to interpret the challenges coming from those markets, a general feeling emerged that central bankers possessed more qualifications to provide optimal policies that don't go against markets.

The aforementioned three arguments aim to provide an answer to the fourth question that constitutes a core aspect of this chapter. Indeed it is plausible that EMU was a reaction to globalisation and its challenges. It is wrong to suppose this reaction was akin to a rejection of the overall climate of intense economic interdependence that dominates world economics and politics. On the contrary, EMU must be correctly interpreted as the satisfactory answer found at the European level to the challenges of globalisation. In this context, the partial answer to the fourth question is that yes, EMU mirrored globalisation and matched its demands. The other point that remains to be answered—whether this amounts to a process of de-democratisation—will be addressed now.

The final (and third) reason that must be emphasised is linked with one important question: who decided to anchor EMU to this peculiar political-economic model of monetary integration? Who contributed for EMU with this particular ECB-centric institutional apparatus? The literature suggests a mixed perception: national politicians were decisive in giving their acquiescence to a monetary union that resembled the proposals made by the Delors Committee (Verdun 2000: 102), but on the backstage EMU was mainly influenced by the work done by central bankers within that Committee (Verdun 1999: 323). Without going deep into this discussion, it is important to show up how member states (be it national politicians or national central bankers) were the most enthusiastic supporters of monetary union approved in the Maastricht intergovernmental conference. The crucial aspect to be retained is the final approval by the highest national representatives in the European Council.

True, politicians ended up by giving their consent to the previous work undertaken by central bankers within the Delors Committee. Nonetheless this evidence, it is important to be acquainted that national representatives sanctioned EMU. They agreed with the institutional details, with the over-arching theoretical model behind EMU. They gave their consent, not only contributing for an indirect legitimisation of EMU and its institutional set-tlement, but also agreeing with the consequences underneath those specif-ic options.

Can we believe national politicians that accepted EMU ignored the specific content of monetary union? Can we admit they neglected the medi-um-to long-term implications EMU could impinge, not least upon their conventional patterns of autonomy related with macroeconomic policy? To anticipate this behaviour on national representatives is the same than recog-nising two important realities: they were in the forefront implicitly acknowl-edging that globalisation constrained their autonomy; and they provided an answer, through the peculiarities of EMU, that equates to the recognition that a different yardstick for assessing democratic legitimacy must come to the surface. A yardstick that directs its attention more to the demands made by markets, departing from the traditional conceptualisation of democracy as the mere reflection of popular claims (Campanella 2000: 112).

Summing up, where is the undemocratic nature of EMU after all? EMU cannot be accused being undemocratic just because directs its attention to market claims instead of addressing the requests made by citizens. The point that was missing to answer to the fourth question is thereby uncovered.

To further progress towards the remaining questions calls for renewing the assessment of the political-economic model that dominates EMU. A clear-cut political-economic orthodoxy exerts its domination, one of price stability. The main issue brought to discussion here is whether this anchor point for EMU has a democratic foundation—and if the answer is affirma-tive, where such an anchor point for domestic legitimacy lies.

Doubts could arise as to which extent the deliberate option for a certain model of macroeconomic orthodoxy, with all its economic and political implications, could be genuinely democratic in its essence. What is at stake is the deep commitment towards price stability, and the second-ary—if not absent—role attached to other goals, which resonates with too much rigidity. In this sense, EMU architects would have tied the hands of their successors in member states' governments and supranational insti-tutions alike, thus imprinting an exacerbated picture of doubtful demo-cratic legitimacy.

Here again some elements point to inconsistency. In the first place, because those who urge against this feature ignore the powerful intergov-ernmental democratic legitimacy basis underneath the decisions under-taken at the European Council. Moreover, there is a lot of rigidity in the reasoning of all those who accuse EMU of being rigid. Of course EMU constitutionalised an unambiguous roadmap for price stability; this poli-cy orthodoxy impinges several consequences for politics, both at the supranational and at the national level; furthermore, the option for low levels of inflation also carries noticeable economic consequences that cannot be underestimated. All of this is truth. But more important is to acknowledge that the constitutional roadmap is likely to be changed in the future. The only pre-requisite is a common understanding among EU institutions and national officials that another set of priorities should be associated to monetary union. If this comes to the surface, and if there is unanimous willingness among national governments to change the EMU constitution, who can predict that the current rigidity falls apart and pave the way for another political-economic paradigm[3]?

Aside these methodological aspects, others should be raised to understand where EMU's democratic legitimacy lies. It is interesting to open the doors for new conceptions of democracy outside state-centric commonplaces. Here is the question again: where is the democratic legitimacy when EMU architects picked up a political-economic model so heavily dependent on a culture of stability? The first source is the outstanding past record observed in Germany (McNamara 2001: 163–4). For decades Germany was a hallmark for economic policy biased towards price stability, with monetary policy driven by the Bundesbank which was immune to political interferences. Seeing Germany as the most outstanding example of macroeconomic success after the second world war, all member states accepted to gear their economic policies towards the German paradigm. This process of 'informally-geared' convergence occurred within the EMS, erasing the differences between Germany and the other member states.

As it was already asserted elsewhere in this chapter, during the years of the EMS all member states had formal competences to run their own monetary policies, but in practice this wasn't taking place: instead, all member states focused in mimicking the monetary policy implemented by the Bundesbank, giving Germany a de facto leadership role. What was the democratic legitimacy of monetary policy strategies defined in Germany and imitated by the remaining national governments in the EU? How could it be reasonably justified that all member states but Germany were deprived from running monetary policy autonomously? Here the main problem is the divorce between theory and practice—that is, while in theory all member states had the formal competences to define and implement their monetary policies, in practice such power of decision had vanished.

With the creation of the ECB, a material transformation took place. Where before national central bankers of all member states except Germany were deprived from having an autonomous voice for purposes

---

[3] McKay (2002: 84) emphasises this crucial feature in EMU: the citizenry is strong enough to drive change and force a retrenchment in current EMU orthodoxy. Thus fiscal policy tightness is not inevitable forever, according to the author.

of monetary policy discussions, now this no longer happens. National central bankers of the Euro-Zone member states have equal voting powers within the Governing Council. This amounts to a vigorous changing pattern due to EMU: all member states that were prevented from contributing for at least a coordinated monetary policy setting in the EMS, now have a say in shaping the single monetary policy.

The symbolic meaning of this constitutional landmark of EMU is the revelation of a crucial aspect for my arguments: EMU erased a source of inequality among the EU member states in what concerns monetary policy. The completion of monetary union in the EU amplifies the prominence of monetary policy. Thus it would be necessary to restore an organisational character conducive of equal voting powers for all member states included in EMU's final stage. Now, for a crucial policy arena as monetary policy, all member states have the same voting power. Of course this institutional innovation re-installs a more democratic legitimate system of decision-making, where all member states give their contribution to the common perception of priorities that should shape monetary policy.

This aspect contains a valuable element to validate an enhanced democratic legitimacy to EMU. Comparing the pre-EMU to the post-EMU scenario the observation is outstanding as to whether monetary union increased or decreased democratic legitimacy associated to the overall economic policy-making. Before the inception of EMU the picture was the factual domination by German authorities, without being legally established that such dominance was accepted by the remaining member states; after the creation of monetary union a more balanced institutional system was launched, since all member states are equipped with the same voting power. This comparison is favourable to EMU when examined through the lens of balanced inter-state powers.

Even though more elements were added to conclude for the democratic legitimacy of EMU, some reservations could be added regarding the consequences from the political-economic orthodoxy of price stability. The next issue for assessment is how democratic legitimate is the obligation imposed upon the ECB to be deeply committed to price stability? Here the answer must be found in a new concept of democratic legitimacy—output legitimacy[4] (Fossum 2000: 114), against a conventional conception of procedural legitimacy. Contrary to the traditional observation of yardsticks measuring how democratic a certain policy is, European integration brought to the surface an alternative dimension for measuring democratic legitimacy. The process of European integration appeals to a

---

[4] Scharpf (2001: 358) works out this conceptual dimension, making a distinction between input legitimacy and output legitimacy (respectively government *by* the people and government *for* the people). Using a different terminology to address the same reality, Arnull (2002: 4) speaks of social legitimacy.

different conceptualisation. Indeed the EU is a polity where uniqueness is the keyword, a polity that calls for a post-national, post Westphalian state-centric nature (Bellamy and Castiglione 2000: 68, and Shaw 2000: 291). Being different from member states, and not aspiring to be a nation-state in the medium term at least, the EU has to rely on a different conceptualisation of democratic legitimacy.

According to the theorisers of output legitimacy, the genuine essence of democracy should be observed in the light of results provided by policies. To the extent that such policies are able to provide results that improve citizens' welfare, such policies entail a powerful source of democratic legitimacy (Menon and Weatherill 2002: 115). The focus on output legitimacy presents a case for underestimating the means through which results are achieved (input legitimacy), and concentrates its attention on the ends itself. Instead of focusing on procedures, it is policies' performance that is at stake. Citizens are affected by the output, not so much by the input side of policies. Hence, a qualitative dimension of democracy pays attention to policies delivered, not to how they were delivered. (Issing 1999: 509, Leino 2001: 22, Cukierman 2001: 40–75, and Wessels and Linsenmann 2002: 67). Rather than focusing on procedures, it is the performance of policies that is important and which affects citizens. Hence, a qualitative dimension of democracy is the policies which are delivered rather than the manner in which they are delivered.

From the above mentioned elements (the democratic foundation of price stability and the shift towards output legitimacy) stand three important conclusions:

a) Sovereignty has changed with the ongoing process of European integration (Cameron 1998: 191, Dyson 2002a: 26, and Bellamy and Castiglione 2000: 69). EMU gave a boost on the conventional notion of sovereignty by absorbing or transforming some elements of national governments' core activity in economic policy. Some were transferred from the national to the supranational arena, thus splitting into pieces the ancient national economic sovereignty. Currently it makes sense to speak of shared sovereignty, where a supranational institution (the ECB) performs a prominent role in shaping economic policy.

b) Also democracy means a different thing in the specific context of European integration (Laffan 1998: 330–1, Bellamy and Castiglione 2000: 69, Dobner 2000: 17, and Mény 2003: 11). Democracy is an evolving concept. It is no longer reasonable to address democracy as something that can only be achieved through the nation-state, moreover because challenges come from abroad and not only from within the nation-states. Other modalities of political organisations are keen to respect the fundamental values of democracy, even though if they come out in a fresh conceptualisation. Bearing in mind the uniqueness of the European integration process, remembering the huge complexity of contemporary policy-making, taking into account the impact globalisation has on traditional forms of decision-making—all these elements together pave the way for an alternative democratic legitimacy based on output legitimacy.

c) From the interlacing of the previous two conclusions derives a third assertion: accountability has a new format under the auspices of the ECB. Therefore the supranational central bank is held accountable for its outcomes, assuming it provides the minimum of information for the public in order to make an alternative model of democracy operational—deliberative democracy (Eriksen and Fossum 2000: 2–17).

These conclusions are reinforced because powerful evidence suggests member states are unable to perform well enough when the assessment of state-centric conditions applies to them. Even those landmarks used to analyse nation-states come to poor results when member states in the EU are examined through this lens. Two dimensions matter. In the first place, member states are unable to deal efficiently with the challenges arising from contemporary macroeconomics. Pressures from intense economic interdependence worldwide diminish the extent to which national governments possess the efficient tools for redressing the problems inherent to globalisation. Since member states face this constraint and cannot provide valuable solutions, a dangerous desert could arise if they resisted transferring economic competences to transnational or supranational spheres. Acknowledging national governments' inability opens the doors for a black hole of competences that would be detrimental for citizens' welfare interests. In this context, a crisis of democratic legitimacy would happen: what would matter for assessing the impact of this situation is not the possibility elected officials being endowed with formal competences to run economic policy; more important is the recognition that elected officials in each country no longer hold the tools to tackle problems derived from globalisation.

To avoid the black hole scenario, the only solution is to displace economic competences towards the supranational level. Requests of efficiency call for this solution, and it is possible to infer that member states' politicians acknowledged this inevitability when they accepted to move towards monetary union. In the sense that democratic legitimacy has revolved towards output legitimacy, the obvious conclusion is that the concentration of crucial economic policy competences on the supranational level cannot be interpreted as undemocratic. On the contrary, for purposes of output legitimacy as a solid foundation for democratic legitimacy, the ensuing exercise of monetary policy by the ECB is genuinely democratic because it creates the (at least) theoretical conditions for providing excellent results for the sake of citizens' welfare.

The second dimension focus on the crisis of parliamentary democracy that affects EU member states (not in exclusivity). Considering the traditional and ancient solid foundations of democracy as being backed on structural competences associated to the parliamentary institution, the contemporary tendency runs against this. More and more there is a displacement of competences and tasks that once were reserved to the parliament and now are monopolised by the executive branch (Eriksen and Fossum 2000: 8). More recently another aspect deepened the dilution of parliamentary powers and the genuine essence of parliamentary democracy: the sub-delegation of powers governments made upon regulatory agencies.

The discussion is whether this transference of competences is democratically legitimate, notably when such re-allocation of competences occurred in default of constitutional change that could have been required for that purpose. If relying on the theoretical conception of the 'principal-agent' model, the delegation of powers from governments to regulatory agencies is acknowledged as being democratically legitimate. Indeed principals (the executive) decide whether or not to create regulatory agencies, and the extent to which they are empowered with certain functions and competences. The principal dominates the creation of the agent. But it can happen that agents can subvert their mandate. Of course the principal has the possibility to override the agent's boldness, reviewing the mandate or introducing rules that prevent the distortion of the mandate. Let's take here only the essence of the 'principal-agent model' and ask whether the ECB can be examined through this lens. Apart from all other justifications that consolidate supranational central bank's democratic legitimacy and accountability, the aspects imported from the 'principal-agent' model are useful for supporting democratic legitimacy. On the EU case, however, the 'agents' (supranational institutions) must be guaranteed against intrusions from the 'principals' (member states). Otherwise they will not be efficient and their output legitimacy can be put in jeopardy (Menon and Weatherill 2002: 119).

5 CONCLUSIONS

After reviewing the arguments offered by theoretical dimensions, after extracting some consequences from a mere deductive approach, the clock is ticking asking for the answers to the three questions that remain open for the moment.

i) Is the ECB accountable?

Section three focused on the main theoretical arguments presenting the case for a democratically legitimate and accountable ECB. Together with the uniqueness that characterises European integration, a strong case exists for concluding that the ECB is accountable sufficiently. A different conceptualisation, where more accountability would be required for the ECB, could entail detrimental effects. Not only because national or supra-national politicians (depending on the anchor point to which the ECB should be accountable) would have a meaningful say on monetary policy, eventually lacking the technical expertise to do so; but also because pre-venting effective independence as a core organisational aspect of the ECB, this would harmfully affect the central bank's credibility. Hence the achievement of price stability could be in danger, and the whole constitu-tional model of monetary union at risk of being threatened.

ii) Is the ECB lacking democratic legitimacy? Or, worse, is it undemocratic?

The answer depends on the previous one. In fact the conclusion that the ECB is sufficiently accountable drives to the subsequent assertion that there is no reason for fearing that the supranational central bank faces lower levels of democratic legitimacy, not to say an undemocratic pattern at all. Concerns about the scarce democratic assessment of the ECB are supported by the opinion that the central bank is timid in releasing infor-mation to the public. The ECB argues that only selected information should become available in order to make fundamental information about economic activity accessible. On the opinion of leading scholars on central banking it is redundant to release all information for a twin reason: such scenario entails the dispersal of information, making private agents unable to make an accurate selection among the relevant information; and the publication of economic forecasts can induce private agents to incor-porate such data in their expectations, thus creating the conditions for a prospective distortion because agents' expectations can deviate from the observed results (Winkler 2000: 16). Bearing in mind all these aspects, my inclination is to answer that the ECB is democratically legitimate.

iii) Did EMU deepen the democratic deficit that allegedly affects the European integration process?

The answer is also negative. The main reason is that the EU democratic deficit is questionable. Some authors insist the EU is plagued with sever-al sins affecting its democratic foundations. Such is the case of Weiler (1997: 273). Not so sceptical, Dahl (1999: 20) compares the EU with other international organisations. The latter are characterised by the existence of democratic deficit; hence it is no surprise European integration also pos-sesses some deficiencies in respect of with democratic standards. The author's idea is the following: how can international organisations (and the EU by extension) be criticised if nation-states themselves fail to meet the basic requirements of democratic legitimacy? Moravcsik (2001: 164) adds some more illuminating pieces to this discussion. For him the existing institutional architecture of the EU is democratically legitimate[5], because in the member states those functions assigned to the EU are not subject to citizens' participation and majority decision-making.

Against the democratic deficit argument, others highlight that the EU cannot be assessed by a conventional, state-centric approach to measure how democratic it is. Being so specific, European integration calls for an alternative conception of democratic legitimacy—one embracing output legitimacy, one that pays attention to deliberative democracy.

Moreover it cannot be ignored the fallacy underneath the methodology that uses state-centric concepts for examining the extent to which the EU is scarcely democratic. Firstly, because this methodology is not appropriate—it compares two political organisations that are difficult to be accurately compared (nation-state versus a supranational organisation); then, nation-states themselves are plagued with many deficiencies in what concerns the respect for many of the conventional yardsticks measuring how democratic they are (Mény 2003: 9). Thus, one important question discards these arguments: if member states show several drawbacks when assessed through the lens of conventional democratic legitimacy, how honest is the same qualification when the analysis shifts towards to the EU?

If EMU itself cannot be seen as a pillar for undemocratic legitimacy, of course it doesn't produce any harmful effect on the democratic legitimacy of the European integration process. On the contrary, for all the aspects that have been raised throughout this chapter, EMU is seen as a device that feeds a different conception of democratic legitimacy. If any lesson is to be drawn from the implications of the institutional architecture of monetary union in Europe, is that the monetary authority is shaped in such a way that it lays the foundations for a new conception of democratic legitimacy—focusing on output legitimacy, based ideally on price stability, drawing on the accountability towards the European peoples through the constitutional dimension EMU and the ECB possess.

REFERENCES

AMTENBRINK, FABIAN, 'On the legitimacy and Democratic Accountability of the European Central Bank: Legal Arrangements and Practical Experiences', in ARNULL, ANTHONY and DANIEL WINCOTT (eds), *Accountability and Legitimacy in the European Union*, (Oxford, Oxford University Press 2002.)

[5] Although subsequently Moravcsik (2002: 603–624) highlighted the ECB stands outside this line of reasoning, thus portraying the supranational central bank as clearly not democratically legitimate.

ANDERSON, PERRY: 'The Europe to Come', in GOWAN, PETER AND PERRY ANDERSON (eds), *The Question of Europe*, (London, Verso 1997.)

ARNULL, ANTHONY 'Introduction: The European Union's Accountability and Legitimacy Deficit', in ARNULL, ANTHONY and DANIEL WINCOTT (eds), *Accountability and Legitimacy in the European Union*, (Oxford, Oxford University Press 2002.)

BAIMBRIDGE, Mark, Brian Burkitt and Philip Whyman: *The Bank that Rules Europe?—The ECB and Central Bank Independence*, The Bruges Group Occasional Paper 1999 No 37.

BEGG, IAIN and GREEN, DAVID: *The Political Economy of the European Central Bank*, South Bank European Papers, 1998 No 1/98.

BEGG, IAIN and HODSON, DERMOT: *Is Keynes Alive, Dead, or in Need of Re-incarnation in the EU?*, www.sbu.ac.uk/euroinst/oneeurope/Keynes.pdf (in 09 07 01), also published as 'Está Keynes vivo, muerto o necesita rencarnaerse en la Unión Europea?' in 2000 Vol 155–156, *Sistema*, pp 15–30.

BELLAMY, RICHARD and DARIO CASTIGLIONE, 'The uses of democracy—Reflections on the European democratic deficit', in ERIKSEN, ERIK ODDVAR and JOHN ERIK FOSSUM (eds), *Democracy in the European Union—Integration Through Deliberation?* (London, Routledge 2000.)

BOBBITT, PHILIP: *The Shield of Achilles—War, Peace and the Course of History*, (London, Penguin Books 2002.)

BOYER, ROBERT: 'The Unanticipated Fall out of European Monetary Union: The Political and Institutional Deficits of the Euro', in CROUCH, COLIN (ed), *After the Euro—Shaping Institutions for Governance in the Wake of European Monetary Union*, (Oxford, Oxford University Press 2000.)

BUITER, WILLEM H: 'Alice in Euroland', (1999) Vol 37, No 2 (June) *Journal of Common Market Studies*, pp 181–209.

BUTT PHILLIP, ALAN: 'The Coordination of Budgetary Policy in the Context of the Stability and Growth Pact', in PITTA E CUNHA, PAULO and MANUEL PORTO (eds), *The Euro and the World*, (Coimbra, Almedina 2002.)

CAMERON, DAVID R: 'Creating Supranational Authority in Monetary and Exchange-Rate Policy: The sources and Effects of EMU', in SANDHOLTZ, WAYNE and ALEC STONE SWEET (eds), *European Integration and Supranational Governance*, (Oxford, Oxford University Press 1998.)

CAMPANELLA, MIRIAM L: 'The Battle between ECOFIN–11 and the European Central Bank: A Strategic Interaction Perspective', in GREEN COWLES, MARIA and MICHAEL SMITH (eds), *The State of the European Union: Risks, Reform, Resistance, and Revival*, (Oxford, Oxford University Press 2000.)

CROUCH, COLIN: 'The Euro and Labour Market and Wage Policies', in DYSON, KENNETH (ed), *European States and the Euro: Europeanization, Variation, and Convergence*, (Oxford, Oxford University Press 2002.)

CROWLEY, PATRICK M and ROWLEY, ROBIN: 'Configurations and prospects for European integration and monetary unification', in PARASKEVOPOULOS, CHRISTOS C (ed), *European Union at the Crossroads—A Critical Analysis of Monetary Union and Enlargement*, (Cheltenham, Edward Elgar 1998.)

CUKIERMAN, ALEX: 'Accountability, Credibility, Transparency and Stabilization Policy in the Eurosystem', in WYPLOSZ, CHARLES (ed), *The Impact of EMU on Europe and the Developing Countries*, (Oxford, Oxford University Press 2001.)

DAHL, ROBERT A: 'Can international organizations be democratic? A skeptic's view', in SHAPIRO, IAN and CASIANO HACKER-CÓRDON (eds), *Democracy's Edges*, (Cambridge, Cambridge University Press 1999.)

DE GRAUWE, PAUL: *The Economics of Monetary Union* 3rd edition, (Oxford, Oxford University Press 1997.)

DOBNER, PETRA: *Politics Beyond Constitutionalism: Constitutional Restraints in the Transformation of the State*, Paper given at the 12th International Conference of Europeanists, Chicago, 2000 March 30th–April 2nd.

DYSON, KENNETH: *Elusive Union: the process of Economic and Monetary Union in Europe*, (London, Longman 1994.)

DYSON, KENNETH: *The Politics of the Euro-Zone—Stability or Breakdown?* (Oxford, Oxford University Press 2000a.)

DYSON, KENNETH: 'EMU as Europeanization: Convergence, Diversity and Contingency', 2000b Vol 38, No 4 (November), *Journal of Common Market Studies*, pp 645–66.

DYSON, KENNETH: 'Introduction: EMU as Integration, Europeanization, and Convergence', in DYSON, KENNETH (ed), *European States and the Euro: Europeanization, Variation, and Convergence*, (Oxford, Oxford University Press 2002a.)

DYSON, KENNETH: 'Conclusion: European States and Euro Economic Governance', in DYSON, KENNETH (ed), *European States and the Euro: Europeanization, Variation, and Convergence*, (Oxford, Oxford University Press 2002b.)

EIJFFINGER, SYLVESTER CW and JAKOB DE HAAN: *European Monetary and Fiscal Policy*, (Oxford, Oxford University Press 2000.)

ERIKSEN, ERIK O ERIK and JOHN E FOSSUM: 'Post-national integration', in ERIKSEN, ERIK ODDVAR and JOHN ERIK FOSSUM (eds), *Democracy in the European Union— Integration Through Deliberation?*, (London, Routledge 2000.)

FOSSUM, JOHN E: 'Constitution-making in the European Union' in ERIKSEN, ERIK ODDVAR and JOHN ERIK FOSSUM (eds), *Democracy in the European Union— Integration Through Deliberation?*, (London, Routledge 2000.)

GOWAN, PETER: 'British Euro-solipsism', in GOWAN, PETER and PERRY ANDERSON (eds), *The Question of Europe*, (London, Verso 1997.)

HABERMAS, JÜRGEN: 'Reply to Grimm', in GOWAN, PETER and PERRY ANDERSON (eds), *The Question of Europe*, (London, Verso 1997.)

HABERMAS, JÜRGEN: 'Beyond the nation-state? On some consequences of economic globalization', in ERIKSEN, ERIK ODDVAR and JOHN ERIK FOSSUM (eds), *Democracy in the European Union—Integration Through Deliberation?*, (London, Routledge 2000.)

HARDEN, IAN: 'The European Central Bank and the role of National Central Banks in Economic and Monetary Union', in GRETSCHMANN, KLAUS (ed), *Economic and Monetary Union: Implications for National Policy-Makers*, (Doordrecht, Martinus Nijhoff Publishers 1993.)

HEISENBERG, DOROTHEE: 'Explaining the Dominance of German Preferences in Recent EMU Decisions', in LAURENT, PIERRE-HENRI and MARC MARESCEAU (eds), *The State of the European Union (vol 4)—Deepening and Widening*, (Boulder, Lynne Rienner 1998.)

ISSING, OTMAR: 'The Eurosystem: Transparent and Accountable or 'Willem in Euroland'', 1999 Vol 37, No 3 (September), *Journal of Common Market Studies*, pp 503–519.

KEOHANE, ROBERT O and JOSEPH S NYE Jr: *Between Centralization and Fragmentation: The Club Model of Multilateral Cooperation and Problems of Democratic Legitimacy,* John F Kennedy School of Government Working Paper (Harvard University), 2001 N° 04/01.

LAFFAN, BRIGID: 'The European Union: a distinctive model of internationalization', 1998 Vol 5, No 2 (June) *Journal of European Public Policy.*

LEINO, PÄIVI: *The European Central Bank and Legitimacy: Is the ECB a Modification of or an Exception to the Principle of Democracy?,* Harvard Jean Monnet Working Paper 2001 1/01.

MAJONE, GIANDOMENICO: 'Regulatory Legitimacy in the United States and the European Union', in NICOLAIDIS, KALYPSO and ROBERT HOWSE (eds), *The Federal Vision—Legitimacy and Levels of Governance in the United States and the European Union,* (Oxford, Oxford University Press 2001.)

MCKAY, DAVID: *Rush to Union—Understanding the European Federal Bargain,* (Oxford, Clarendon Press 1996.)

MCKAY, DAVID: *Federalism and European Union—A Political Economy Perspective,* (Oxford, Oxford University Press 1999.)

MCKAY, DAVID: 'The Political Economy of Fiscal Policy under Monetary Union', in DYSON, KENNETH (ed), *European States and the Euro: Europeanization, Variation, and Convergence,* (Oxford, Oxford University Press 2002.)

MCNAMARA, KATHLEEN R: 'Consensus and Constraint: Ideas and Capital Mobility in European Monetary Integration', 1999 Vol 37, No 3 (September), *Journal of Common Market Studies,* pp 455–76.

MCNAMARA, KATHLEEN R: 'Where do Rules Come From? The Creation of the European Central Bank', in STONE SWEET, ALEC, NEIL FLIGSTEIN and WAYNE SANDHOLTZ (eds), *The Institutionalization of Europe,* (Oxford, Oxford University Press 2001.)

MENON, ANAND and STEPHEN WEATHERILL: 'Legitimacy, Accountability, and Delegation in the European Union', in ARNULL, ANTHONY and DANIEL WINCOTT (eds), *Accountability and Legitimacy in the European Union,* (Oxford, Oxford University Press 2002.)

MÉNY, YVES: 'De la Démocratie en Europe: Old Concepts and New Challenges', 2003 Vol 41, No 1 (March), *Journal of Common Market Studies,* pp 1–13.

MILWARD, ALAN S: *The European Rescue of the Nation-State,* (Berkeley, University of California Press 1992.)

MORAN, MICHAEL: 'Politics, Banks, And Financial Market Governance in the Euro-Zone', in DYSON, KENNETH (ed), *European States and the Euro: Europeanization, Variation, and Convergence,* (Oxford, Oxford University Press 2002.)

MORAVCSIK, ANDREW: 'Federalism in the European Union: Rhetoric and Reality', in NICOLAIDIS, KALYPSO and ROBERT HOWSE (eds), *The Federal Vision—Legitimacy and Levels of Governance in the United States and the European Union,* (Oxford, Oxford University Press 2001.)

MORAVCSIK, ANDREW: 'In Defence of the 'Democratic Deficit': Reassessing Legitimacy in the European Union', (2002) Vol 40, No 4 (November), *Journal of Common Market Studies,* pp 603–24.

PETERSON, JOHN and ELIZABETH BOMBERG: 'The EU after the 1990s: Explaining Continuity and Change', in GREEN COWLES, MARIA and MICHAEL SMITH (eds), *The State of the European Union: Risks, Reform, Resistance, and Revival,* (Oxford, Oxford University Press 2000.)

PETERSON, JOHN and LAURENCE J O'TOOLE JR: 'Federal Governance in the United States and the European Union: A Policy Network Perspective', in NICOLAIDIS, KALYPSO and ROBERT HOWSE (eds), *The Federal Vision—Legitimacy and Levels of Governance in the United States and the European Union*, (Oxford, Oxford University Press 2001.)

POLLACK, MARK A: 'A Blairite Treaty: Neo-Liberalism and Regulated Capitalism in the Treaty of Amsterdam', in NEUNREITHER, KARLHEINZ and ANTJE WIENER (eds), *European Integration After Amsterdam—Institutional Dynamics and Prospects for Democracy*, (Oxford, Oxford University Press 2000.)

RHODES, MARTIN: 'Why EMU Is—or May Be—Good for European Welfare States', in DYSON, KENNETH (ed), *European States and the Euro: Europeanization, Variation, and Convergence*, (Oxford, Oxford University Press 2002.)

SCHARPF, FRITZ W: 'Democratic Legitimacy under Conditions of Regulatory Competition: Why Europe Differs from the United States', in NICOLAIDIS, KALYPSO and ROBERT HOWSE (eds), *The Federal Vision—Legitimacy and Levels of Governance in the United States and the European Union*, (Oxford, Oxford University Press 2001.)

SCHMIDT, VIVIEN: 'Federalism and State Governance in the European Union and the United States: An Institutional Perspective', in NICOLAIDIS, KALYPSO and ROBERT HOWSE (eds), *The Federal Vision—Legitimacy and Levels of Governance in the United States and the European Union*, (Oxford, Oxford University Press 2001.)

SHAPIRO, IAN and CASIANO HACKER-CÓRDON: 'Outer edges and inner edges', in SHAPIRO, IAN and CASIANO HACKER-CÓRDON (eds), *Democracy's Edges*, (Cambridge, Cambridge University Press 1999.)

SHAW, JO: 'Constitutional Settlements and the Citizen after the Treaty of Amsterdam', in NEUNREITHER, KARLHEINZ and ANTJE WIENER, *European Integration After Amsterdam—Institutional Dynamics and Prospects for Democracy*, (Oxford, Oxford University Press 2000.)

SHAW, JO and ANTJE WIENER, 'The Paradox of the 'European Polity', in GREEN COWLES, MARIA and MICHAEL SMITH (eds), *The State of the European Union: Risks, Reform, Resistance, and Revival*, (Oxford, Oxford University Press 2000.)

STASTNY, DAN: *Economic and Politics: Mutual Relationship*, Working Paper delivered at the Austrian Scholars Conference, Auburn, 2002 March 15–16.

STONE SWEET, ALEC, NEIL FLIGSTEIN and WAYNE SANDHOLTZ: 'The Institutionalization of European Space', in STONE SWEET, ALEC, NEIL FLIGSTEIN and WAYNE SANDHOLTZ, *The Institutionalization of Europe*, (Oxford, Oxford University Press 2001.)

TAYLOR, CHRISTOPHER: 'The Role and Status of the European Central Bank: Some Proposals for Accountability and Cooperation', in CROUCH, COLIN (ed), *After the Euro—Shaping Institutions for Governance in the Wake of European Monetary Union*, (Oxford, Oxford University Press 2000.)

UNDERHILL, GEOFFREY R D: 'Global Integration, EMU, and Monetary Governance in the European Union: The Political Economy of the 'Stability Culture", in DYSON, KENNETH (ed), *European States and the Euro: Europeanization, Variation, and Convergence*, (Oxford, Oxford University Press 2002.)

VERDUN, AMY: 'The Institutional Design of EMU: A Democratic Deficit?', 1998 Vol 18, Part 2 (May–August), *Journal of Public Policy*, pp 107–132.

VERDUN, AMY: 'The role of the Delors Committee in the creation of EMU: an epistemic community?', 1999 Vol 6, No 2 (June), *Journal of European Public Policy*, pp 308–328.

VERDUN, AMY: 'Monetary Integration in Europe: Ideas and Evolution', in GREEN COWLES, MARIA and MICHAEL SMITH (eds), *The State of the European Union: Risks, Reform, Resistance, and Revival*, (Oxford, Oxford University Press 2000.)

VERDUN, AMY and THOMAS CHRISTIANSEN: 'Policies, Institutions, and the Euro: Dilemmas of Legitimacy', in CROUCH, COLIN (ed), *After the Euro—Shaping Institutions for Governance in the Wake of European Monetary Union*, (Oxford, Oxford University Press 2000.)

WALLACE, WILLIAM: 'Less Than a Federation, More than a Regime: The Community as a Political System', in WALLACE, HELEN, WILLIAM, WALLACE and C WEBB (eds), *Policy-Making in the European Community*, (New York: John Wiley 1983.)

WESSELS, WOLFGANG and LINSENMANN, INGO: 'EMU's Impact on National Institutions: Fusion towards a '*Gouvernance Économique*' or Fragmentation?', in DYSON, KENNETH (ed), *European States and the Euro: Europeanization, Variation, and Convergence*, (Oxford, Oxford University Press 2002.)

WEILER, JOSEPH HH: 'Does Europe Need a Constitution? Reflections on Demos, Telos and Ethos in the German Maastricht Decision', in GOWAN, PETER and PERRY ANDERSON (eds), *The Question of Europe*, (London, Verso 1997.)

WEILER, JOSEPH HH: *The Constitution of Europe: 'Do the New Clothes Have an Emperor?' and Other Essays on European Integration*, (Cambridge, Cambridge University Press 1999.)

WELFENS, PAUL J: 'European Monetary Union: Post-Maastricht Perspectives on monetary and Real Integration in Europe', in WELFENS, PAUL J (ed), *European Monetary Integration—EMS Developments and International Post-Maastricht Perspectives* (3 edition), (Berlin, Springer 1996.)

WIENER, ANTJE: 'The Embedded *Acquis Communautaire*: Transmission Belt and Prism of New Governance', in NEUNREITHER, KARLHEINZ and ANTJE WIENER, *European Integration After Amsterdam—Institutional Dynamics and Prospects for Democracy*, (Oxford, Oxford University Press 2000.)

WINKLER, BERNHARD: *Which Kind of Transparency? On the Need for Clarity in Monetary Policy-Making*, European Central Bank 2000 Working Paper N° 26.

4

The Globalisation of International Justice

JG MERRILLS*

I INTRODUCTION

THE TITLE OF this paper is explained by its aims which are to show how international courts and tribunals of various kinds have proliferated in recent years, to suggest some of the reasons why this has occurred and to consider the implications of this development. This is, of course, a very large subject and many people, including a number of international judges, have written extensively about it already. Rather than attempting another general survey, this contribution to the debate therefore adopts a narrower focus and examines three cases, decided recently by different international courts, in order to see what they can tell us about the nature of international litigation today and any current trends.

Plainly, it is impossible for a study of just three cases to highlight every facet of current practice, or to be completely representative of what is an immensely varied scene. Nevertheless, by considering these decisions, not only handed down by different courts, but also involving quite different legal issues, some useful insights may emerge. The three cases selected for analysis are the *MOX Plant* case, where the proceedings with which we are concerned were held before the International Tribunal for the Law of the Sea in December 2001; the case of *Metalclad Corporation v Mexico*, decided in August 2000 by an arbitral tribunal convened under Chapter 11 of the North American Free Trade Agreement; and the *Ligitan and Sipadan* case, decided by the International Court of Justice in December 2002. The approach adopted in what follows will be to provide an overview of each case, to analyse what was decided more closely and then to consider the decision in a broader international context. A brief final section adds a general conclusion.

*Professor of International Law, University of Sheffield.

II THE MOX PLANT CASE

A An Overview of the Proceedings

This case involved a new international court, the International Tribunal for the Law of the Sea (ITLOS), which gave the decision with which we are concerned on 3 December 2001.[1] The proceedings here were brought by Ireland against the United Kingdom when it learned that the British Government intended to open a new facility at Sellafield in Cumbria to reprocess spent nuclear fuel into a new fuel, known as mixed oxide fuel (or MOX). The Irish Government claimed that as Sellafield is on the coast, operation of the new plant would contribute to the pollution of the Irish Sea and that transporting radioactive material to the plant by sea would involve further risks. In view of these dangers, Ireland claimed that the United Kingdom had breached its duties under the 1982 United Nations Convention on the Law of the Sea (LOSC), to which both States are parties, and which contains a number of provisions dealing with marine pollution.[2]

The 1982 Convention, as well as laying down rights and duties for States, also includes elaborate arrangements for resolving disputes about its interpretation and application.[3] These include arrangements for compulsory arbitration using what is called an Annex VII tribunal and Ireland's ultimate objective was (and is) to have the dispute over the MOX plant heard by such a tribunal. However, the LOSC also provides that while an Annex VII tribunal is being set up, a State may request ITLOS to order provisional measures of protection. Under Article 290(1) of the Convention these are available to protect the parties' rights or 'to prevent serious harm to the marine environment'. Provisional measures, as the name indicates, are only a temporary arrangement, but they can nevertheless be useful when the situation is one calling for immediate action. Ireland, accordingly, asked ITLOS for an order with the aim of delaying the opening of the MOX plant and suspending the movement of vessels associated with it, pending the establishment of the Annex VII tribunal.[4]

To deal with the Irish request ITLOS had to address two rather different issues. As a preliminary matter, it had to decide whether it was competent to deal with the case at all. This involved examining arguments

---

[1] *MOX Plant Case (Ireland v United Kingdom) Request for Provisional Measures*, Order of 3 December 2001, text in 41 *International Legal Materials* 405 (2002). For a summary of the Order see TL McDorman. Case-note, 12 *Yearbook of International Environmental Law*, 592 (2001).

[2] For the articles which Ireland relied on and the details of its claim see the Court's Order, para 26.

[3] See JG Merrills, *International Dispute Settlement*, 3rd edn (Cambridge, 1998), Ch. 8. Annex VII arbitration is discussed *ibid*, at pp 180–2.

[4] For the terms of Ireland's request see the Court's Order, para 29.

from the United Kingdom about the scope of the arrangements for the compulsory settlement of disputes in the Law of the Sea Convention and, more particularly, the relation between the Convention system and other treaties. These points, which will also be relevant to the jurisdiction of the Annex VII tribunal, were decided in favour of Ireland. Having resolved that matter, the Tribunal then had to address the main question and decide whether provisional measures were needed. Here it rejected Ireland's specific request, for reasons discussed below, but instead of simply dismissing the application, made an order requiring Ireland and the UK to enter into consultations and exchange information about the possible risks posed by the MOX plant. Thus in this case ITLOS made an order requiring certain provisional measures, but in terms different from those that had been requested.

In accordance with the terms of the Tribunal's order the two States undertook consultations and informed ITLOS of the results. In 2002 an Annex VII tribunal was appointed to hear the case, although the ITLOS order for provisional measures continued. At the time of writing the arbitration proceedings are under way.[5] Assuming the case goes forward and is not settled, the first task for the arbitrators will be to resolve the question of their jurisdiction, since the ITLOS ruling on Articles 282 and 283 concerned only the question of *prima facie* jurisdiction for the purposes of Article 290 and as such does not bind its successor. If the Annex VII tribunal decides that it has jurisdiction, it will then proceed to consider the merits.

Before we return to the ITLOS proceedings and consider the Tribunal's order in more detail, one further point should be mentioned. At the same time as Ireland initiated the Annex VII arbitration procedure under the Law of the Sea Convention, it requested arbitration in relation to the MOX plant under another international convention, the 1992 Paris Convention for the Protection of the Marine Environment of the North-East Atlantic (OSPAR Convention). Ireland's claim against the United Kingdom under this convention concerns an alleged breach of Article 9, which deals with access to information. Here also an arbitral tribunal has been established and proceedings have now begun.[6]

B   The Decision Analysed

The Irish request for provisional measures was made under Article 290(5) of the LOSC which provides that ITLOS may prescribe such measures when it is satisfied *prima facie* that the arbitral tribunal which is to be formed would have jurisdiction and that the urgency of the situation so

---

[5] This article was completed in April 2003.
[6] See EA Kirk, Note, 12 *Yearbook of International Environmental Law*, at p 227 (2001).

requires. As already noted, the United Kingdom denied that the jurisdictional requirement was satisfied and so this was the first issue that had to be considered. The British arguments here rested on Article 282 of the Convention, which deals with other agreed means of settlement, and Article 283 requiring a preliminary exchange of views.

As regards Article 282, the Tribunal agreed that this provision bars use of the Convention's procedures when the parties to a dispute over the Convention have agreed to resolve it through another binding procedure. It held, however, that the various conventions cited by the United Kingdom, including the OSPAR Convention, provide only for binding settlement of disputes arising under those conventions and hence are no obstacle when, as here, a dispute concerns the interpretation or application of the LOSC. Whilst it was true that the same issues might need to be decided under both procedures, this did not, according to the Tribunal, have any bearing on the jurisdiction of the Annex VII tribunal, because each of the treaties concerned creates separate rights and duties. The objection based on Article 282 was therefore rejected.[7]

The British argument based on Article 283 relied on the fact that under this provision the parties to a dispute are required 'to proceed expeditiously to an exchange of views' regarding its settlement by peaceful means. According to the United Kingdom no such exchange had taken place, with the result that the Annex VII tribunal was without jurisdiction. To decide this point the Tribunal reviewed the communications which had passed between the parties over the MOX plant, and, observing that a State 'is not obliged to continue with an exchange of views when it concludes that the possibilities of reaching agreement have been exhausted',[8] decided that what had been done was sufficient to satisfy the Convention. The objection based on Article 283 was therefore also rejected.

Having concluded that the Annex VII arbitral tribunal would *prima facie* have jurisdiction over the dispute, the Tribunal then turned to the substantive issue. Article 290(1) of LOSC, as noted earlier, provides that provisional measures may be prescribed 'to preserve the respective rights of the parties to the dispute or to prevent serious harm to the marine environment', and Article 290(5) makes urgency a further criterion in cases destined for arbitration. Although Ireland strongly argued that the provisional measures it sought were necessary, the Tribunal did not find that the urgency of the situation was such as to require them. Ireland, it will be recalled, was essentially asking for provisional measures to do two things: to delay the opening of the MOX plant; and to suspend the movement of shipping associated with it; both elements therefore had to be considered.

---

[7] See Order, paras 38–53.
[8] *Ibid.*, para 60.

In relation to the opening of the MOX plant the decisive factor appears to have been the Tribunal's awareness that the Annex VII tribunal would be set up very shortly, together with the lack of evidence that any serious environmental damage, or prejudice to Ireland's position, would occur in the meantime. A further factor which evidently influenced some of the judges[9] was the statement by the United Kingdom that neither the commissioning of the MOX plant, nor the introduction of plutonium into the system, was irreversible. As regards shipping movements, the Tribunal was quite explicit. The crucial factors here were a statement from the United Kingdom that there would be no additional marine transports of radioactive material as a result of the commissioning of the MOX plant[10] and a further assurance that there would be no import or export of nuclear fuel from the MOX plant until October 2002 at the earliest.[11] Here too, of course, expectations with regard to the setting up of the Annex VII tribunal were highly relevant.

Under Article 89(5) of its Rules ITLOS has the power to prescribe measures different in whole or in part from those requested. As mentioned earlier, it utilised this initiative in the present case, unanimously ordering Ireland and the United Kingdom to co-operate and to enter into consultations in order (a) to exchange further information with regard to possible consequences for the Irish Sea of the commissioning of the MOX plant (b) to monitor the risk or effects of the operation of the MOX plant for the Irish Sea, and (c) to devise, as appropriate, measures to prevent pollution of the marine environment which might result from operation of the plant. It also decided unanimously that Ireland and the United Kingdom were to report to the Tribunal on their efforts to co-operate which, as noted above, they subsequently did.

The justification which the Tribunal gave for placing the parties under the above obligations were that 'the duty to co-operate is a fundamental principle in the prevention of pollution of the marine environment'[12] and that 'prudence and caution require that Ireland and the United Kingdom co-operate in exchanging information concerning risks or effects of the operation of the MOX plant and in devising ways to deal with them, as appropriate'.[13] Two members of the Tribunal saw in this second justification a reference to the precautionary principle, now so prominent in environmental discourse, and which Ireland had urged should be taken into account by the Tribunal when assessing the urgency of the situation.[14]

---

[9] See the joint declaration of Judges Caminos, Yamamoto, Park, Akl, Marsit, Eiriksson and Jesus.

[10] See Order, para 78.

[11] See n 1 para 79.

[12] See n 1 para 82.

[13] See n 1 para 84.

[14] See the separate opinions of Judge Treves and Judge ad hoc Szekely, and McDorman, note 1 above at p 596. On the precautionary principle in general see P Birnie and A Boyle, *International Law and the Environment*, 2nd edn (Oxford, 2002), pp 115–21, with references to earlier literature.

This interpretation of the order may well be correct. If so, however, it is plainly a less forceful version of the precautionary principle than Ireland had advocated in its pleadings.

C   The Case in Context

Viewed in its wider context, as an illustration of the role and significance of international courts and tribunals today, the *MOX Plant* case merits attention in the first place on account of its subject matter, international environmental law, that is, the rules and principles of international law concerning protection of the environment. This aspect of international law has grown enormously over the last thirty years or so, since the celebrated Stockholm Declaration of 1972, as can be seen, for example, from the inclusion of provisions on conservation and pollution in the 1982 Law of the Sea Convention, the negotiation of specific agreements like the 1992 OSPAR Convention, the emergence of the precautionary principle in international practice and similar developments.[15]

With the growth of international environmental law has come an increase in litigation in which the scope of States' obligations in this field has needed to be determined. Prior to *MOX Plant* case ITLOS addressed environmental issues in the *Southern Bluefin Tuna* cases[16] (also a provisional measures request), and there have been several other ITLOS cases. The International Court of Justice has heard the *Gabcikovo-Nagymaros Project* case[17] and the *Nauru* case,[18] and there have been cases raising environmental issues in human rights tribunals and the World Trade Organisation. Not all of these cases have proceeded to a final decision on the merits, but the general lesson is clear. Extending the scope of international law to include environmental obligations has had a major impact on the work of international courts and tribunals.

The second point which may be made about the *MOX Plant* case is related to the first and concerns how this case was brought to ITLOS and, more generally, why it was possible for Ireland to begin proceedings against the United Kingdom. This is an important question as it is a fundamental principle of international law that the jurisdiction of international courts and tribunals rests on consent, with the result that unless the parties to a dispute have all accepted the adjudicators' authority, a case

---

[15] See Birnie and Boyle, above n 14.

[16] *Southern Bluefin Tuna Cases (New Zealand v Japan; Australia v Japan), Request for Provisional Measures*, Order of 27 August 1999, text in 38 *International Legal Materials* 1624 (1999). For an outline of the Order see RR Churchill, Case-note, 49 *International & Comparative Law Quarterly* 979 (2000).

[17] *Gabcikovo-Nagymaros Project (Hungary/Slovakia)*, Judgment, ICJ Rep. 1997, 7.

[18] *Certain Phosphate Lands in Nauru (Nauru v Australia), Preliminary Objections*, Judgment, ICJ Rep. 1992, 240.

cannot proceed. Such a requirement can obviously make it difficult for a State to vindicate its rights through litigation, if its opponent has no desire to go to court, as will often be the case. It is therefore worth noticing why Ireland was able to begin proceedings here.

The claim in the *MOX Plant* case, as we have seen, is based on the 1982 Law of the Sea Convention and Ireland was able to initiate the Annex VII arbitration, and engage ITLOS, by virtue of the arrangements for the compulsory settlement of disputes contained in the Convention. In this respect the LOSC is like the 1995 World Trade Organisation Agreement[19] and a number of similar treaties creating new international tribunals with compulsory jurisdiction. Admittedly, these networks of jurisdictional obligations are binding only on those States which have accepted the treaties concerned. They are therefore not an exception to the principle that international jurisdiction is consensual, but an illustration of it. However, because the treaties in question have been widely ratified, their significance can scarcely be overstated. The second point, then, which can be seen from the *MOX Plant* case is how new judicial institutions are functioning in novel systems of compulsory jurisdiction.

The third and final point to make about this case concerns its lessons as regards the relation between different dispute settlement procedures. The role of ITLOS, as we have seen, was to consider the parties' submissions on the question of provisional measures and, after dealing with the issue of *prima facie* jurisdiction, to decide what measures, if any, were needed, pending the establishment of the Annex VII tribunal. Here, then, is a dispute settlement system featuring separate tribunals engaged successively—first ITLOS, then the Annex VII tribunal. That in itself is interesting, but the value of a provisional measures stage, here and in other international litigation should also be noted. Adjudication, in other words, is not just about final rulings, but may also require preliminary decisions, usually from the same tribunal, but sometimes not, and in either case of considerable importance to the litigants.

To deal with the issue of *prima facie* jurisdiction, it will be recalled, ITLOS had to address the British arguments on Articles 282 and 283 of the LOSC. Although the questions here arose in the context of a particular convention, it is worth pointing out that they are of a type which now frequently has to be considered by international courts and tribunals. Thus the Article 283 argument over the requirement of a preliminary 'exchange of views' raised the question of the relation between recourse to arbitration and negotiation,[20] while Article 282, which was also in issue in the *Southern Bluefin Tuna* cases, required ITLOS to determine how arrangements for dispute settlement under different treaties may be

---

[19] Text in 33 *International Legal Materials* 1125 (1994). For discussion of the system for dispute settlement established by the Agreement see Merrills, above n 3 at pp 197–220.
[20] On this issue see Merrills n 3 pp 17–22.

reconciled.[21] As systems and forums for dispute settlement proliferate, making the same issue justiciable under different procedures, such problems of determining when and how each should be employed can be expected to multiply.

III   THE METALCLAD CORPORATION CASE

A   An Overview of the Proceedings

The case of *Metalclad Corporation v Mexico*[22] was decided on 30 August 2000, by an arbitral tribunal convened under Chapter 11 of the North American Free Trade Agreement (NAFTA). The claimant was a United States corporation which had constructed a landfill site for hazardous waste near the Mexican city of Guadalcazar, but had then been prevented from operating it, despite having earlier obtained the permission of the state government of San Luis Potosi and the Mexican federal authorities. The arbitration proceedings resulted in Metalclad being awarded a substantial sum of damages for Mexico's violation of its obligations under NAFTA. There were then further proceedings in the Supreme Court of British Columbia which resulted in the damages being varied slightly and soon afterwards an agreement to settle the case.

The 1992 North American Free Trade Agreement[23] is a treaty to which Canada, Mexico and the United States are currently parties. It came into force in 1994 with objectives which include eliminating barriers to trade in goods and services, promoting fair competition and investment and protecting intellectual property rights in the Member States. As well as a large number of provisions dealing with substantive obligations, it contains a number of distinct procedures for dispute settlement.[24] The latter include not only arrangements for dealing with inter-State disputes, but also arrangements for mixed arbitrations, that is proceedings between States and non-State entities (corporations or individuals) and it was those, contained in Chapter 11 of NAFTA, that were utilised in the *Metalclad* case.

---

[21] See Churchill, above n 16 at p 984. In the subsequent proceedings before the arbitral tribunal in 2000 the issue of jurisdiction was considered on the basis of Article 281, rather than Article 282 and the tribunal held by a majority that it lacked jurisdiction to adjudicate on the merits.

[22] *Metalclad Corporation v Mexico*, ICSID Case No. ARB(AF)/97/1, text in 40 *International Legal Materials* 36 (2001). For a summary of the case see WS Dodge, Case-note, 95 *American Journal of International Law* 910 (2001).

[23] Text in 32 *International Legal Materials* 289 and 605 (1993).

[24] For an outline of these see J Collier and V Lowe, *The Settlement of Disputes in International Law*, (Oxford, 1999), pp 111–116.

The provisions of Chapter 11 entitle investors of one State party to initiate proceedings in respect of disputes concerning the treatment of their investments by another State party under the Treaty. Disputes not resolved by negotiation may be submitted to arbitration, with the investor able to choose between several different forms, including arbitration under the International Centre for the Settlement of Investment Disputes (ICSID), the form which was selected here. The State's consent to arbitration is already provided for in Article 1122 of NAFTA and the investor's consent is given by initiating the Agreement's procedures. When, as in the *Metalclad* case, arbitration is invoked, use of other procedures is precluded. Metalclad brought its claim under Chapter 11 in January 1997.

The background to the claim was rather complicated. The project to build the landfill facility had originally been conceived by a Mexican company, COTERIN, which Metalclad purchased in September 1993, following the grant of permits by the federal and state authorities and assurances by the Mexican government that no further permissions were required. The landfill was constructed between May 1994 and March 1995, but demonstrations prevented it from opening and the municipality then obtained an injunction from the Mexican courts prohibiting operation of the site. Initially the problem was that Metalclad lacked a municipal construction permit which the city authorities claimed was needed. However, a further obstacle appeared when the governor of San Luis Potosi issued an Ecological Decree declaring the site a Natural Area for the protection of rare cactus. This decree was made in September 1997 after the arbitration had begun.

Deciding whether on these facts Mexico was liable to Metalclad required the Tribunal to interpret and apply the safeguards for investment in NAFTA States set out in Chapter 11 of the Agreement, and specifically those contained in Article 1105(1), guaranteeing 'fair and equitable treatment', and Article 1110, which provides a guarantee against expropriation. For reasons discussed below the Tribunal decided that Metalclad's inability to obtain a municipal construction permit had violated both provisions. It then added, by way of *obiter dictum*, that the implementation of the governor's Ecological Decree would by itself qualify as an act of expropriation. For the above violations Metalclad was awarded more than 16 million dollars compensation.

The case was then taken to the Supreme Court of British Columbia[25] because, as the site of the arbitration had been Vancouver, that court had jurisdiction to review the award. Interpreting his powers rather broadly, the Canadian judge decided that the Tribunal's ruling on the issue of fair and equitable treatment went beyond the scope of the submission to arbitration and that its ruling on expropriation was similarly vitiated. He then

---

[25] See *Mexico v Metalclad Corporation*, 2001 BCSC 664.

held, however, that the decision could be upheld on the basis that the Ecological Decree issued by the governor of San Luis Potosi amounted to an expropriation. These decisions too are further discussed below. As the Tribunal's award had been upheld, albeit on a narrower ground, the Court reduced the damages slightly to take account of the new findings as to when the breach occurred and this reduction was reflected in the eventual settlement.

B   The Decisions Analysed

Since the award of the arbitral tribunal and the ruling of the Canadian court each contain matter of wider interest, both decisions must now be examined in a little more detail. As regards the Tribunal's decision, a preliminary point which is worth noting is that the arbitrators prefaced their ruling on the substantive issue by holding that Mexico was responsible under NAFTA for the acts of both the regional and the municipal authorities. This decision was based on the express words of Article 105 of NAFTA which requires the parties to ensure implementation of the Agreement 'by state and provincial governments', and which, as the Tribunal observed, also reflects the position under customary international law. With Mexico's responsibility thus established, the Tribunal then turned to the content of its obligations.

The first provision to be applied, Article 1105(1), lays down an obligation to 'accord to investments of investors of another Party treatment in accordance with international law, including fair and equitable treatment and full protection and security'. Interpreting the reference to 'fair and equitable treatment' as importing a requirement of transparency, on the ground that this is an objective of NAFTA under Article 102(1), the Tribunal decided that transparency calls for both initial clarity on the legal requirements for investment and the prompt clarification by the host of any misunderstanding or confusion. Judged by these criteria the Tribunal found the handling of Metalclad's case to be seriously defective. To the uncertainty as to whether a municipal construction permit was required, had been added the problems Metalclad had then experienced in trying to obtain one. The lack of transparency at all stages had therefore resulted in a violation of Article 1105(1). The other relevant provision was Article 1110 which lays down that expropriation may only take place under certain carefully defined conditions. In applying this provision the Tribunal's starting point was that expropriation was not confined to deliberate taking of property, but was a concept broad enough to include covert or incidental interference which had the effect of depriving the owner of its economic benefit. Having regard to what had happened, the Tribunal was satisfied that by permitting the municipality's unfair and inequitable treatment Mexico had taken a measure 'tantamount to expropriation'.[26] Moreover, taken together with the federal government's assurances to Metalclad and the absence of a proper basis for the denial of a construction permit, the municipality's conduct amounted to an indirect expropriation. On this basis there had therefore also been a violation of Article 1110.

In view of the finding just mentioned, and in particular the Tribunal's approach to the concept of expropriation, it is not surprising that in the final part of its judgment it observed that implementation of the governor's Ecological Decree would by itself 'constitute an act tantamount to expropriation',[27] adding that this would be so regardless of the motivation for the decree. However, this finding was not necessary to the decision, the earlier rulings having fully vindicated Metalclad's claim for damages. As Metalclad had completely lost its investment, the Tribunal decided that damages under Articles 1105 and 1110 would be the same. Since the landfill had never functioned, and any award based on loss of profits would be speculative, the Tribunal awarded Metalclad damages based on its actual investment, plus interest from the date the municipality denied the construction permit, giving a total sum of $16,685,000.

When Mexico took the case to the Supreme Court of British Columbia, the question was whether the award should be set aside which depended in part on the scope of the Canadian court's power of review. After hearing the parties' arguments on the matter, the court decided, first, contrary to Mexico's submissions, that the relevant national law was British Columbia's International Commercial Arbitration Act, and then, contrary to the submissions of Mexico and Canada, that the Tribunal's award could only be reviewed on the grounds set out in section 34(2) of that Act. This meant that the crucial question was whether 'the Tribunal made decisions on matters beyond the scope of the submission to arbitration by deciding upon matters outside Chapter 11'.[28] The unusual way the Canadian court chose to answer this question was the most controversial part of its decision.

In ruling that the Tribunal's finding of unfair and inequitable treatment, contrary to Article 1105, went beyond the scope of the submission to arbitration, the Canadian court held that the crucial points were that there are no explicit transparency obligations in Chapter 11 and that the Tribunal had failed to show that transparency has become part of customary international law. As regards Article 1110, the court held that the Tribunal's decision that an indirect expropriation had occurred rested on its treatment of the transparency issue and was therefore also vitiated. On the other hand, the court decided that the award could be upheld on the

---

[26] See the Award, para 104.
[27] *Ibid.*, para 111.
[28] Supreme Court judgment, para 67.

basis of the Tribunal's concluding comment that the Ecological Decree could itself be regarded as an expropriation. Without necessarily endorsing the Tribunal's assessment, the court ruled that how an expropriation should be defined was a question of law which a national court, with a circumscribed power of review, was not entitled to interfere with.

As already indicated, having upheld the award in substance, the court reduced the amount of compensation to reflect its decision on when the breach occurred. The Canadian court gave its decision in May 2001 and later in the same month Mexico filed a notice of appeal. In June however, the parties reach a preliminary agreement to settle the case for $15,626,260.

C   The Case in Context

Although the circumstances of *Metalclad* were a long way from those of the *MOX Plant* case in every sense, here, as in the case considered earlier, the dispute and how it was handled have some important general implications. Taking first the subject matter, *Metalclad* is a case about trade and international economic relations and in this respect is certainly representative of much contemporary litigation. Since the World Trade Organisation (WTO) was set up in 1995 many cases have been dealt with through its dispute settlement system and this jurisprudence, which is constantly being added to, provides a growing body of case law on international trade. NAFTA, though perhaps less well known, is a regional trade agreement with similar effects and *Metalclad*, as an arbitration under Chapter 11, is not untypical of its jurisprudence.

It would, of course, be misleading to suggest that litigation over commercial matters began with NAFTA or the WTO. Between the conclusion of the General Agreement on Tariffs and Trade in 1947 and the creation of the WTO nearly fifty years later, a panel system for dealing with trade disputes evolved which provided the basis for the current WTO arrangements.[29] ICSID, which supplied the framework for the *Metalclad* arbitration was concluded in 1965 and, like the Arbitration Rules of the United Nations Commission on International Trade Law (UNCITRAL), adopted in 1976, has often been used.[30] Moreover, disputes involving issues of trade and investment were arbitrated, or sometimes referred to adjudication, even before the United Nations era. Thus cases in this field are by no means a novelty. The broad point, however, remains valid. With trade and economic relations, as with environmental issues, more law has meant more cases.

[29] See Merrills, above n 3 at p 199.
[30] See Collier and Lowe, above n 24 at pp 59–73.

Reflection on how and why the *Metalclad* dispute could be arbitrated suggests a further parallel with the *MOX Plant* case. For, as already explained, this was possible because NAFTA, like the Law of the Sea Convention, contains provisions for compulsory dispute settlement. In other words, instead of relying on the consent of the parties given *ad hoc* in each case, the treaty provides that such consent is given in advance through the State's acceptance of the treaty. Arrangements of this kind are now common in the field of trade and economic relations and their significance is reflected in the work of the courts and tribunals which exist to resolve disputes in this field. As already noted, the WTO system has proved particularly prolific, but several other international and regional arrangements are also influential.

In this connection it is also important to note the identity of the claimant in *Metalclad*. International litigation used to be thought of as the prerogative of States, but a glance at the range of claims falling within the jurisdiction of international courts and tribunals today reveals that this is plainly no longer so. The 1991 Mercosur Agreement,[31] for example, like NAFTA, now has a dispute settlement system providing for mixed arbitrations, as well as for the resolution of disputes between States; ICSID, as already mentioned, has provided facilities for mixed arbitrations since 1965; the Iran-United States Claims Tribunal[32] has handled about 4,000 such cases since its inception in 1981 and the 1982 Law of the Sea Convention provides for the Sea-Bed Disputes Chamber of the International Tribunal for the Law of the Sea, when it is established, to deal with disputes involving non-State entities.[33] In a different sphere international human rights law provides some particularly striking examples of courts and tribunals with the competence to hear claims brought by individuals.[34] Mixed arbitrations under Chapter 11 of NAFTA are therefore just one illustration of how the reach of international jurisdiction is broadening.

The third and final point to make about the *Metalclad* case concerns its aftermath. Mexico, as has been seen, was unhappy with the Tribunal's decision and therefore sought to have the decision set aside by taking proceedings in the Supreme Court of British Columbia. It was entitled to do this because the recognition and enforcement of arbitral awards in the commercial field, including mixed awards, rely on national legal systems. As a consequence, in cases like *Metalclad* a dispute may be considered successively by an international and a national court. As the proceedings in

---

[31] For an outline see Collier and Lowe n 24 at p 116.

[32] See Collier and Lowe at pp 73–84.

[33] See Merrills, above n 3 at pp 187–190.

[34] For example, the European Court of Human Rights, the Inter-American Court of Human Rights and the African Commission of Human and Peoples' Rights. For a description of the work of these and other bodies see AH Robertson and JG Merrills, *Human Rights in the World*, 4th edn, (Manchester, Manchester University Press, 1996).

the Canadian court demonstrated, the relationship between the two levels of jurisdiction in such cases is particularly delicate. Whilst the arbitral tribunal has the main responsibility to decide the case, the national court has the last word. Consequently, the scope of the national court's power of review, as *Metalclad* shows, may well be crucial.

Although national courts necessarily have a key role in commercial litigation of this kind it has been suggested that their position could be improved by the creation of an international appellate body for Chapter 11 cases.[35] Such a development would have at least two advantages. Firstly, it would enable any errors of law by the tribunal to be corrected, thereby avoiding the tendency for national review proceedings to turn into disguised appeals. Secondly, it would ensure a consistent interpretation of concepts such as 'fair and equitable treatment' and 'expropriation', something that has not been achieved under the current arrangements. In the WTO system an Appellate Body was created for precisely these purposes—to provide a full legal review of the initial decision and to ensure consistent interpretation of treaty obligations. The final lesson of *Metalclad* is therefore that international and national systems for dispute settlement can be complementary, but to achieve their purpose fully, arrangements currently providing for only one international hearing, may require development and supplementation.

IV   THE LIGITAN AND SIPADAN CASE

A   An Overview of the Proceedings

The third case to be considered involved the International Court of Justice. On 17 December 2002 the Court gave its judgment in a dispute over two small islands in the Celebes Sea claimed by both Indonesia and Malaysia.[36] The islands in question, Ligitan and Sipadan, are located off the northeast coast of Borneo and lie approximately 15.5 nautical miles apart. Both are very small and Ligitan is uninhabited; Sipadan, on the other hand, was developed by Malaysia into a tourist resort for scuba diving in the 1980s. In 1998 Indonesia and Malaysia referred the dispute to the Court by means of a Special Agreement, asking for a decision 'on the basis of the treaties, agreements and any other evidence furnished by the Parties' on whether sovereignty over the islands belonged to Indonesia or to Malaysia.

---

[35] See Dodge, above n 22 at p 918, referring to his earlier recommendation in 95 *American Journal of International Law* at pp 191–2 (2001).

[36] *Case concerning Sovereignty over Pulau Ligitan and Pulau Sipadan (Indonesia/Malaysia)*, Judgment of 17 December 2002, ICJ Rep. 2002. For a summary of the decision see JG Merrills, Case-note, 52 *International & Comparative Law Quarterly* 797 (2003).

By March 2001 the two States had completed the three rounds of written pleadings specified in their Special Agreement. However, at that point the Government of the Philippines applied to intervene in the case on the basis of Article 62 of the Court's Statute and Article 81 of its Rules. The former allows a State to submit a request for permission to intervene when it considers that it has 'an interest of a legal nature which may be affected by the decision in the case' and the latter sets out various requirements that an application must satisfy. The Philippines maintained that its application fulfilled the requirements of Article 62 and those of the Rules, but Indonesia and Malaysia denied this, claiming that the necessary 'interest of a legal nature' was absent and that the Rules had not been complied with.

In a judgment on 23 October 2001[37] the Court rejected the Philippines application to intervene as failing to satisfy the Statute, and in its decision, as well as addressing Article 62, also discussed the scope of the Rules. Here the main objection raised had been that the Philippines had made its intervention too late and that its application should be denied on account of its 'untimely nature'. The Court, however, decided this point in favour of the Philippines, along with a further point relating to documents. This left it with one final preliminary issue to consider which was whether, as Malaysia maintained, a jurisdictional link with the parties was required before the application could be considered. However, the Court, following its previous jurisprudence, held that this was unnecessary and so dismissed this objection also.

The main issue in the 2001 case was whether the Philippines had demonstrated the existence of an 'interest of a legal nature' as Article 62 requires. The Philippines had no territorial interest in Ligitan and Sipadan, but considered that its claim to sovereignty over the adjacent territory of North Borneo (Sabah), one of the federated states of Malaysia, might be affected by the reasoning contained in the Court's decision. An initial question was therefore whether a State may intervene under Article 62 when it has no interest in the subject matter of the dispute as such, but rather asserts an interest in possible reasoning of the Court with a bearing on a different dispute between the intervening State and one of the parties. Indonesia and Malaysia maintained that this was not a sufficient basis for intervention, but the Court, in an important ruling, disagreed and decided this point too in favour of the applicant.

As the Court also agreed that the application to intervene had a legitimate objective, the crucial question was whether the Philippines' claim to North Borneo might be affected by the Court's reasoning. Here the

---

[37] *Case concerning Sovereignty over Pulau Ligitan and Pulau Sipadan (Indonesia/Malaysia)*, Application by the Philippines for Permission to Intervene, Judgment of 23 October 2001, ICJ Rep. 2001. For a summary of this decision see JG Merrills, Case-note, 51 *International & Comparative Law Quarterly* 718 (2002).

applicant faced a practical difficulty, having previously submitted a request to be provided with copies of the parties' pleadings and documents which the Court had rejected. Although this was plainly a handicap, the Court stated that the Philippines was nevertheless in a position to explain its claim and the relevance of interpretations of specific instruments which might affect it. Finding that the Philippines' claim rested mainly on a grant by the Sultan of Sulu, dating from 1878, the Court found that neither Indonesia nor Malaysia relied on this grant as a source of title to Ligitan and Sipadan and on this ground concluded that the applicant had failed to show the necessary 'interest of a legal nature'. The request of the Philippines was therefore rejected.

With the complications of third State involvement thus disposed of in the 2001 proceedings, the case became once again a straightforward clash of arguments between the two protagonists about the acquisition of territorial sovereignty. Indonesia's claim to the islands rested primarily on a Convention concluded by Great Britain and the Netherlands in 1891, supported by various Dutch and Indonesian acts which were claimed to show sovereignty (so-called *effectivités*) and on an alternative basis of title as successor to the Sultan of Bulungan. Malaysia, for its part, denied that the 1891 Convention had the effect alleged by Indonesia, advanced its own claim based on succession from the Sultan of Sulu and, like Indonesia, also cited *effectivités* (here British and Malaysian) to confirm its title. In its judgment the Court, after carefully reviewing the parties' arguments, decided the case by 16 votes to 1 in favour of Malaysia.

B   The Decision Analysed

As indicated above, the arguments over sovereignty in this case were addressed to three main issues: the effect of the 1891 Convention, the parties' rival claims to succession; and the significance of their actions on the ground (*effectivités*). Whilst detailed discussion of these issues is unnecessary for present purposes, an outline of the Court's reasoning may be useful to place the decision in its wider context.

The 1891 Convention, which really provided the basis of Indonesia's case, was an agreement concluded by the then colonial powers, Great Britain and the Netherlands, to establish a boundary between their respective territories. The crucial provision of the Convention was Article IV which established a dividing line across Sebatik Island and, according to Indonesia, then extended it seawards to the east, designating islands to the north as British and those to the south as Dutch. If this interpretation was correct, Ligitan and Sipadan, as islands to the south of the parallel, had vested in the Netherlands and now belonged to Indonesia. Malaysia, as might be expected, took a different view. It acknowledged that Article IV divided Sebatik, but maintained that it had no further effect, with the result that everything to the east, including, of course, Ligitan and Sipadan, was completely unaffected.

As the question here was one of treaty interpretation, the Court turned for guidance to Articles 31 and 32 of the 1969 Vienna Convention on the Law of Treaties which it said in this respect could be said to reflect customary international law. Examining in turn the text of the 1891 Convention, the historical context and the object and purpose of the agreement, the Court found no support for Indonesia's position. Further confirmation of the limited effect of Article IV was, the Court found, to be found in the subsequent practice of Great Britain and the Netherlands with regard to the 1891 Convention. It therefore concluded that whilst the Convention established the boundary across Sebatik Island, it did not effect an allocation further east.

On the question whether Indonesia or Malaysia had obtained title to Ligitan and Sipadan by succession the Court first considered the claim put forward by Indonesia. This was that Indonesia had succeeded to the title held by the Netherlands, which in turn had originally acquired title through contracts with the Sultan of Bulungan. The flaw in this reasoning, according to Malaysia, was that the Sultan himself never actually possessed the islands. The Court agreed with Malaysia. Finding that both the original contract with the Sultan in 1878 and an amendment in 1893 described his possessions in terms which were too narrow to include Ligitan and Sipadan, the Court accordingly concluded that Indonesia's argument that it had inherited the islands must be rejected.

Malaysia's submissions on the succession question, which formed a major part of its case, were somewhat similar. Here, however, the chain of title began with the Sultan of Sulu, who, according to Malaysia, passed title over Ligitan and Sipadan to Spain in 1878 and thence to the United States in 1900, to Great Britain on behalf of the State of North Borneo in 1930, to the United Kingdom when North Borneo became a colony in 1946, and finally to Malaysia in 1963. The essential weakness in this argument was that Ligitan and Sipadan were not mentioned by name in any of the international instruments relied on by Malaysia to establish the alleged transfers of title. As a consequence, it was unclear whether the islands, which are a considerable distance from the island of Sulu, were ever part of the Sultanate's dependencies. In view of this uncertainty the Court concluded that Malaysia's contention that it had inherited a treaty-based title must also be rejected.

Having rejected Indonesia's interpretation of the 1891 Convention and both States' claim to a title based on succession, the Court turned finally to the significance of their activities on the ground. Both States, as mentioned earlier, relied primarily on such *effectivités* to confirm an alleged treaty title, but since those titles had not been substantiated, the Court had to examine their respective actions as an independent and separate issue.

Indonesia's *effectivités* rested on the patrols of the Dutch Royal Navy in the area, together with the activities of the Indonesian Navy and Indonesian fishermen. Malaysia, in contrast, cited control which had been exercised over the taking of turtles and turtles eggs, the creation of a bird sanctuary on Sipadan in 1933 and the construction by the British colonial authorities of lighthouses on both islands in the early 1960s.

Evaluating the parties' conduct in the light of the Permanent Court's observations in the *Eastern Greenland* case,[38] the Court noted that none of the acts which Indonesia relied on was of a legislative or regulatory character, while the various maritime activities which it cited were adjudged to carry little weight. For Malaysia, on the other hand, the measures relating to turtles and the bird reserve could be treated as relevant assertions of legal authority and in the light of the Court's judgment in the recent *Qatar/Bahrain* case,[39] its construction of lighthouses could also be taken into account. In view of the character and diversity of these acts, and bearing in mind that when they were carried out neither the Netherlands, nor Indonesia ever expressed any disagreement or protest, the Court concluded that Malaysia had obtained title to Ligitan and Sipadan on the basis of its *effectivités*.

C   The Case in Context

At first sight the *Ligitan and Sipadan* case may seem a somewhat surprising choice as part of a review of the expanding role of international courts. What, after all, can be learned from the resolution by the International Court of Justice of a territorial dispute, similar to so many which had been resolved either at The Hague or by arbitration in the past? That, however, is precisely the point. Although international law now has much to say about trade, the environment etc, and cases like *MOX Plant* and *Metalclad* show the expanding role of international judges, States still also have old fashioned disputes about sovereignty over territory and continue to need courts and tribunals to resolve them. Thus one way in which the *Ligitan and Sipadan* case is significant is as a reminder that the traditional functions of adjudication and international law are still highly relevant.

Confirmation of the point just made can be seen in the number of cases involving territorial issues of one kind or another which have been decided in the last ten years, or which are currently pending. Thus in the first category we find a boundary dispute between Libya and Chad,[40] a dispute between Botswana and Namibia over an island and a river

---

[38] *Legal Status of Eastern Greenland*, 1933, PCIJ Series A/B No. 53.

[39] *Case concerning Maritime Delimitation and Territorial Questions between Qatar and Bahrain (Qatar v Bahrain)*, Merits, ICJ Rep. 2001. The point relevant to the *Ligitan and Sipadan* case was made in para 197 of the earlier judgment.

[40] *Territorial Dispute (Libyan Arab Jamahiriya/Chad)*, Judgment, ICJ Rep. 1994, 6.

boundary[41] and two cases involving both marine boundaries and territorial issues, the first between Qatar and Bahrain in 2001[42] and the other between Cameroon and Nigeria, decided in October 2002,[43] just two months before the Indonesia/Malaysia case. Cases of this kind currently pending include a maritime delimitation case between Nicaragua and Honduras,[44] a case involving maritime and territorial issues between Nicaragua and Colombia[45] and most recently a boundary dispute between Benin and Niger,[46] submitted to the Court in May 2002. To these, of course, must be added the cases of this type dealt with by arbitration.[47] It is clear therefore that in this field, as in others, the traditional subject matter of international litigation continues to keep courts and tribunals busy.

A second way in which this recent case is instructive is as a reminder of the continuing relevance—indeed one might say the indispensability—of the International Court. Not very long ago it was common to ask whether the creation of new international courts and tribunals might undermine the ICJ by drawing away all or most of its business. The danger was perhaps seen as particularly acute in relation to the International Tribunal for the Law of the Sea, which, after all, was created for the express purpose of supplying an alternative judicial forum. But a threat was also apparent from arbitration, correctly perceived as offering several advantages over the International Court, and again an alternative which the Law of the Sea Convention can be said to have encouraged. In retrospect, however, it now seems that those fears were exaggerated.

Far from being displaced, the International Court is now busier than ever, not just with cases involving territorial and maritime boundaries, although these, as we have seen, continue to figure prominently, but also with cases on a variety of other issues. This has happened not because other procedures have failed to flourish—ITLOS, as has been seen, has certainly begun to establish itself and the recent Eritrea/Yemen case[48] shows the continuing value of arbitration. Rather there appears to have been an overall increase in the amount of litigation from which the International Court has maintained its share. Why it has done so is a

---

[41] *Kasikili/Sedudu Island (Botswana/Namibia)*, Judgment, ICJ Rep. 1999, 1045.

[42] See above n 39.

[43] *Land and Maritime Boundary between Cameroon and Nigeria (Cameroon v Nigeria)*, Judgment, ICJ Rep. 2002.

[44] *Maritime Delimitation between Nicaragua and Honduras in the Caribbean Sea (Nicaragua v Honduras)*. This case was referred to the Court by Nicaragua in December 1999.

[45] *Territorial and Maritime Dispute (Nicaragua v Colombia)*. This case was referred to the Court by Nicaragua in December 2001.

[46] *Frontier Dispute (Benin/Niger)*. The two States referred this case to the Court on the basis of a special agreement signed in June 2001 which came into force in April 2002.

[47] Eg the *Eritrea/Yemen* case, below see n 48 .

[48] *Eritrea/Yemen Arbitration* (1998/1999), text in 40 *International Legal Materials* 900 and 983 (2001).

complex question, but points which may be significant are the decision to encourage the use of *ad hoc* chambers,[49] so bringing the Court's work closer to arbitration and the steps taken more recently to modernise the Court's procedures,[50] thereby enabling it to deal with cases more expeditiously and reducing the comparative advantages of ITLOS. Whatever the explanation, the Indonesia/Malaysia case, which could have been referred to arbitration but wasn't, shows that the ICJ is alive and well.

The third and final lesson which can be learned from this decision of the International Court concerns the technical aspects of international litigation and specifically the question of jurisdiction. As already noted, Indonesia and Malaysia took this case to the Court by means of a special agreement, that is a treaty under which they accepted the Court's jurisdiction for this particular dispute. As a result, the proceedings in the *Ligitan and Sipadan* case had a quite different legal basis from those in either the *MOX Plant* case, or the *Metalclad* case, both of which, as we have seen, were referred on the basis of multilateral treaties containing provisions for compulsory dispute settlement (in the first the Law of the Sea Convention, and in the second the NAFTA Agreement). Why, then, is this point significant?

Arrangements under which the jurisdiction of courts or tribunals are accepted in advance are now quite common in international affairs, as we have noted, and their use is certainly to be encouraged. It is, however, important to appreciate that alongside the growing network of such compulsory arrangements, there remains the possibility of making *ad hoc* references to the International Court of Justice, or to arbitration. Moreover, this is more than a theoretical possibility. As the *Ligitan and Sipadan* case and numerous others indicate, it is regularly being used, sometimes to obtain a decision where the States concerned have not accepted procedures which would enable a unilateral reference to be made, but sometimes also where they have. Why States utilise some arrangements rather than others is a question beyond the scope of the present paper, but two benefits of the special agreement can readily be identified. Firstly, it provides a way in which States with little or no experience of international litigation can test its benefits by making a limited commitment. Secondly, because it involves taking a case to court on an agreed basis, it tends to avoid wrangles over jurisdiction and admissibility that are so common in cases of unilateral reference. Neither Indonesia nor Malaysia had previously used the International Court, and apart from the issue of the Philippines' intervention, no questions of jurisdiction were raised during the proceedings. Both benefits of utilising a special agreement mentioned above can therefore be seen from the *Ligitan and Sipadan* case.

---

[49] See Merrills, above n3 at pp 140–145. In this connection it is interesting to note that the Benin/Niger case (above n46) has been referred to a chamber of the Court.

[50] For an outline of these measures see JR Crook, 'The 2002 Judicial activity of the International Court of Justice', 97 *American Journal of International Law* 352, at p 361 (2003).

V   CONCLUSION

No purpose would be served by merely reiterating points already made, so this conclusion will be brief. It was noted at the outset that three cases can never be fully representative of the work of international courts and tribunals, or exemplify all facets of their activity and that is surely beyond dispute. In the cases considered above it has nevertheless been possible to see how in cases like *MOX Plant* and *Metalclad* the scope of adjudication is visibly broadening, as law is extended to encompass more and more areas of international life, as well as a wider clientele. At the same time, however, adjudication continues to be highly relevant for conventional international disputes, such as the dispute over territorial sovereignty at the heart of the *Ligitan and Sipadan* case.

If one reason for the burgeoning of international litigation has been the progressive extension of international law into areas such as trade and the environment, another has been the move away from the traditional voluntary basis of international litigation, illustrated here by the International Court's decision, to new compulsory procedures (meaning by this procedures where the acceptance is made in advance), which may be seen in the *MOX Plant* and *Metalclad* cases. The last is also a reminder that international litigation is now no longer the exclusive prerogative of States, but is increasingly available to individuals, corporations and other entities, a lateral extension of the competence of international courts and tribunals which naturally has also increased their business.

Finally, by looking at what happened when these cases came to court, the student of international litigation can appreciate how adjudication today may raise technical questions of jurisdiction and procedure, involving *inter alia* the relation between different international tribunals (as in the *MOX Plant* case), between international courts and national courts (as in the *Metalclad* case), and between the parties to a case and third States (as in the Philippines' attempt to intervene in the *Ligitan and Sipadan* case). It is hardly necessary to add that the proliferation of courts and tribunals and the increasing volume of international litigation, are likely to make technical issues of this kind increasingly common.

Our three recent cases do therefore hold some important general lessons. Naturally, there is much more that could be said both about these cases specifically and about international litigation generally. But they perhaps are matters for another occasion.

5

The Security Council and the Challenges of Collective Security in the Twenty-First Century: What Role for African Regional Organisations?

ADEMOLA ABASS*

1 INTRODUCTION

THERE IS NO easy way to describe the relationship between the United Nations and regional organisations in the field of collective security. What is certain though is that the unfolding of the relationship largely reflects the unpredictable fate of the collective security embodied by the UN Charter. A reckoning of the Charter rules on collective security reveals that the rather complex nature of UN–regional organisation relationship has its pedigree in the historical evolution of the UN itself.

The authors of the UN Charter lay down different normative rules to govern the UN and regional organisations in the dispensation of their responsibility for the maintenance of peace and security in 1945. One set of rules, contained in Chapter VII, is entrusted to the small but omnipotent Security Council to administer. These rules are defined with great specificity, and so is the procedural manner in which the Council must regulate them. In contrast, the provisions concerning regional arrangements or agencies (both terms nowhere defined in the Charter) are set down in Chapter VIII with considerable vagueness and ambiguity. In addition, whereas the Security Council has total control of and absolute responsibility for the powers contained in Chapter VII, regional organisations share Chapter VIII powers with the Security Council.

The hazy nature of the provisions contained in Chapter VIII, particularly the absence of details as to how the interaction between the UN and regional organisations should work out in practice, meant uncertain

* Reader in Law, University of Reading, UK.

relationship between the UN and regional organisations during the Cold War. During this period, Chapter VIII provisions were inoperative. The Security Council could not utilise regional arrangements to maintain international peace and security. Conversely, where regional organisations take actions on their own initiative, such as the Organisation of American States did in the Cuban Missile crisis,[1] such actions often lead to protracted and tensed debate amongst the permanent members of the Security Council.[2] Furthermore, attempts by the General Assembly to accord some kind of recognition, even if limited, to regional organisations often met with condemnations from the UN member states.[3]

Despite the rigidity of the Cold War and the lacklustre relationship between the UN and regional organisations, the post Cold War world order ushered in a different attitude in the way the UN and regional organisations perceive each other. In Liberia, the UN and ECOWAS (Economic Community of West African States) undertook a historic joint-operation in order to restore peace and security to Liberia. Since then, the UN and different regional organisations have re-enacted this camaraderie in several situations to differing degrees. Thus, in Sierra Leone,[4] Haiti,[5] Georgia,[6] and Akbhiza,[7] the relationship between the UN and regional organisations continues to unravel to a greater extent than anticipated by Chapter VIII.

---

[1] Leonard Meeker, 'Defensive Quarantine and the Law', (1963) 57 *American Journal of International Law* 515; Carl Christol, 'Maritime Quarantine: The Naval Interdiction of Offensive Weapons and Associated Matériel to Cuba, 1962' *Ibid.*, 525; Abraham Chayes, 'Law and the Quarantine of Cuba,' (1962/63) 41 *Foreign Affairs* 550; A Eide, 'Peace-keeping and Enforcement by Regional Organizations,' (1966) 3 *Journal of Peace Research* 125; Mallison, 'Limited Naval Blockade or Quarantine Interdiction: National and Collective Defense Claims Valid Under International Law', (1962) 31 *George Washington University Law Review* 339–43.

[2] (1962) 47 *State Department Bulletin* 598–600.

[3] For a review of the qualification of the OAU, OAS, and the Arab League, see Erkki Kourula, 'Peace-keeping and Regional Arrangements' in Anthony Cassese (ed), *United Nations Peace-keeping: Legal Essays* (Alphens aan den Rijn: Sijthoff & Noordhoff, 1978) 102–06; Gray at 204–06; Quincy Wright, 'The Middle East Problem', (1970) 64 *American Journal of International Law* 270.

[4] Karsten Nowrot and Emily Schabacker, 'The Use of Force to Restore Democracy: International Legal Implications of the ECOWAS Intervention in Sierra Leone', (1998) 14(2) *American University Journal of International Law Review* 321; A Conteh, 'Sierra Leone and the Norms of Non-Intervention: Evolution and Practice' (1995) 7 *African Journal of International and Comparative Law* 166; Ademola Abass, 'The Implementation of ECOWAS New Protocol and Security Council Resolution 1270 in Sierra Leone: New Development in Regional Intervention', (2002) 10(1) *University of Miami International and Comparative Law Review* 177.

[5] For a full account of this conflict, see David Malone, *Decision-Making in the UN Security Council: The Case of Haiti, 1990–1997* (Oxford, Oxford University Press, 1998).

[6] For an excellent documentation and review of this case, see Neil MacFarlane, 'The CIS and the OSCE in Georgia's Wars' in Thomas Weiss, Thomas Weiss (ed), *Beyond UN Subcontracting: Task-Sharing with Regional Security Organisations and Service-Providing NGOs* (London, Macmillan Press Ltd., 1998), 115–136 especially at 120.

[7] SM Chervonnaya, *Abkhazia–1992: Post-Konnunisticheskaya Vandeya* (Moscow, Mosgorpechat, 1993).

Chapter VIII of the UN Charter envisages two levels of interaction between the UN and regional organisations. The first is where the Security Council approves, regardless of the time of doing so, a regional enforcement action undertaken at the initiative of regional organisations. The ECOWAS actions in Liberia and Sierra Leone were not authorised, at least prior to these actions, by the Security Council. Subsequent endorsement by the Council in the form of adopting resolutions in praise, rather than in condemnation of these actions has been widely perceived as retroactive approval. Whatever may be the correct interpretation of such gestures by the Security Council, there is no doubt that these actions have been taken exclusively by regional organisations with some kind of acquiescence of the Council.

The second type of action envisaged under Chapter VIII is that whereby it is the Council, and not a regional organisation, that initiates a regional enforcement action by expressly calling on (or utilising, as it appears in Chapter VIII) a regional organisation to take an enforcement action. In practice, such utilisation rarely occurs. Save during the crisis in Yugoslavia (Bosnia–Hecergovina), the Security Council has not made use of this provision in Article 53(1) of the UN Charter.

Notwithstanding the remarkable improvement in the UN/regional organisation relationship, recent developments all around the globe suggest that the Security Council needs to co-operate to a greater extent with regional organisations in order to find a lasting solution to the threat to international peace and security. The confounding incidence of terrorism that took place in the United States in 11 September 2001, the launch of several terrorist attacks on US embassies in Kenya and Tanzania in 1998, the targeting of civilian aircraft by terrorists in Kenya in 2002, the introduction of the orgy of terrorism to relatively stable African countries like Morocco, the continuing assault by Israel on Palestinians and unrelentless waive of suicide bombing of the former by the latter indicate that new wars have overtaken the UN Charter scheme of collective security.

This chapter ponders the challenges confronting collective security in the twenty-first century and how the UN could enhance its relationship with regional organisations to address the situation. It argues that as it stands presently, the developing of UN/regional organisation relationship, especially in Africa, has so far been shaped by chances and opportunism rather than by a carefully considered *modus operandi* such that the dire problems of the current global security demand. The economical vulnerability of many African countries and their particular susceptibility to sectional conflicts, make the continent particularly attractive to terrorists as opposed to most other continents. Therefore, I argue that a formal allocation of responsibility, a greater co-operation and more structured co-ordination of activities, between the UN and African regional organisations, more than what currently obtains, has become imperative in order to arrest what seemed destined to become a desperate security situation in Africa.

Although the Secretary-General Boutros-Boutros Ghali cautioned in the *Agenda for Peace*[8] against the regimentalisation of the UN/regional organisations relationship, the formalisation advocated by this chapter in no way compromises the malleability of the Charter the UN Secretary-General sought to preserve. It is undeniable that challenges far greater, more complex and systemic than those existing or imagined in 1945, or even when the UN and ECOWAS launched a historic joint-venture in Liberia in 1993, compel a more drastic and concerted effort by regional organisations and the UN. I argue that between the dysfunctional (or, for lack of better word to use, erratic) multilateralism, which the Security Council presently symbolises,[9] and the enthronement of unilateralism in regional organisations serves as a good bridge in the quest to maintain international peace and security. By focusing on African regional organisations, I demonstrate how the inroad made by UN regional organisations in Liberia and consolidated in the former Yugoslavia and Haiti in the 1990s can be enhanced.

Since the relationship between the UN and regional organisations, in the context of collective security, forms a part of, and is complimentary to, the overall scheme of collective security in the UN Charter, it is pertinent to understand the general framework of collective security of the UN Charter. From this preliminary assessment, I consider the particular problems encountered by African regional organisations in implementing collective security, especially in the 1990s. Here, I briefly revisit initial episodes of UN/regional organisations actions in Africa, such as in Liberia and Sierra Leone, and set this against contemporary order. After identifying what these new challenges are, I discuss the window of opportunity opened by the AU towards creating an effective strategy for securing the continent against the scourges of terrorism in Africa.

2 SECURITY COUNCIL, COLLECTIVE SECURITY AND THE UN CHARTER: THE ORIGINAL PLAN

The whole system of collective security envisioned in 1945 by the founders of the UN was based on certain great expectations.[10] In the

---

[8] *An Agenda for Peace: Preventive diplomacy, peacemaking and peace-keeping. Report of the Secretary- General pursuant to the statement adopted by the Summit Meeting of the Security Council on 31 January 1992*, UN GAOR, 47th Sess., Agenda item 10, at 1, UN Doc. A/A47, UN Doc S/2411 (1992).

[9] Liberia (1989–1997), Sierra Leone (1997–2002), Kosovo (1999), and the second Gulf conflict (2003), are examples of how the collective will of the international community has continued to be steadily highjacked by unilateral actions on the basis, inter alia, of the inability of the Security Council to act multilaterally.

[10] For a complete history of the evolution of the UN, see Ruth B Russell and Jeanette E Muther, *A History of the United Nations Charter: The Role of the United States 1940–1945* (Washington, DC: The Brookings Institution, 1958).

audacious world order that emerged after the Second World War, states gave up their police powers, which they had exercised with little or no legal constraints many centuries before the birth of the UN.[11] The Security Council became the new policeman of the world[12]. With the enormous powers conferred on it under Chapter VII of the UN Charter, the Security Council could determine that circumstances (whatever these might be) exist, anywhere in the world, which threaten international peace and security (Article 39). Once it has so determined, the Council may then decide to order cease-fire or any other interim measures in order to secure a temporary truce in the crisis to enable it assess the situation (Article 40). After such a preliminary assessment, the Security Council may impose non-military measures on a recalcitrant and/or the innocent party (Article 41). The Council may then follow such measures by military actions consisting of air, sea, and land firepower (Article 42).

However, if, with the gift of foresight it was assumed in 1945 that the Security Council would possess, it decides that an imposition of economic sanctions would not achieve desired effects in a particular situation, it could leapfrog from interim measures under Article 40 onto Article 42 enforcement measures, thereby circumventing non-military measures of Article 41. To enable the Council to discharge its responsibility under Chapter VII, UN member states agree to conclude special agreements under Article 43 to provide the Council with necessary military personnel. Once the Council takes a decision, it is not up to states to choose how to respond: they agree to implement such a decision under Article 25 of the Charter. The great legislative architecture of Chapter VII was erected on a Military and Staff Committee (MSC) which had the responsibility for taking all military decisions on behalf of the Security Council.[13] Thus was born in 1945 an ideal world order encrypted in the most malleable and self-generative legal instrument of all times, the UN Charter.

3   THE DEPARTURE FROM THE IDEAL WORLD ORDER AND THE TRIBULATIONS OF THE CHARTER COLLECTIVE SECURITY SCHEME: THE SUBSTANTIVE AND PROCEDURAL PROBLEMS

The Cold War was the first to reveal that the grand assumptions that lay at the very foundation of the collective security scheme under Chapter VII

---

[11] See Julius Stone, *Legal Controls of International Conflicts: A Treatise on the Dynamics of Disputes—and War—Law* (London, Stevens & Sons Limited, 1954) 324; Jean-Pierre Cot and Alain Pellet, *La Charte des Nations Unies: Commentaire article par article sous la direction de* 2e édition, (Paris, Economica, 1991) (hereafter Cot and Pellet); M Virally, *L'Organisation mondiale* (Paris, Collection U, 1972); JES Fawcett, *The Law of Nations*, (London, Allen Lane, The Penguin Press, 1968) at chapter 8.
Sir Robert Jennings and Sir Arthur Watts Oppenheim (eds), Oppenheim's *International Law*, vol.1, Peace 9th ed, (London, Longman, 1992).
[12] Article 24(1) UN Charter.
[13] Article 43.

were far too idealistic for the *realpolitik* of the world outside Dumbarton Oaks and San Francisco where the UN was conceived and born. The divide between vision and reality would haunt the UN collective security system for most of the twentieth century. The collective security system envisioned for the Security Council could not be operated with the exactitude of the Charter texts. States reneged on (or simply refused to fulfil) the special arrangement they agreed to undertake under Article 43. They could not set aside members from their national contingents for the exclusive use of the Security Council. Nor could the Security Council itself agree on the composition and leadership of such forces, a pragmatic problem that would make the MSC, expected to organise and deploy such forces,[14] live most of its life on the pages of the UN Charter.[15] It is worth noting that certain delegates to the San Francisco conference anticipated the non-realisation of such an ambitious project as an international police force.[16]

The first Gulf conflict (1990–1991)[17] revealed the Security Council to be hind not fore sighted—another blow to the great expectations of 1945. Under the grand design of Chapter VII, the Security Council was envisioned to be omnipotent, omnipresent and omniscient. These three immutable qualities (as they were perceived at least in 1945) set the Security Council light-years above any international institutions ever known to mankind. Indeed, the Council has worked extremely hard to preserve these qualities by enshrouding most of its decision-making processes in deepening inscrutability[18] and ingenuously reinventing the Charter provisions whenever formality stands between it and its

[14] Article 47 of the UN Charter.

[15] See Ralph Goldman, *Is it Time to Revive the UN Military Staff Committee*, Occasional Papers Series, (Los Angeles, California State University, 1990).

[16] Britain's Mr Whitehall noted that 'this postulates a greater advance of international cooperation than States are yet prepared to make, as it implies the existence of a world State. Practical questions of size, composition, maintenance, location and command would give rise to controversies on which international agreement would almost certainly be unobtainable. We conclude that the time has not yet come for the creation of such an international police force'. See tentative Proposals by the United Kingdom for a general International Organisation, Memorandum A, July 22, 1944, 1 Foreign Relations of the United States, 1944, 670 at 686–87, cited by Thomas Franck, *Recourse to Force: State Action Against Threats and Armed Attacks* (Cambridge, Cambridge University Press, 2002) at 47. The Soviet Union thought that the project was 'Utopian and unnecessary'. See The Ambassador in the Soviet Union (Harriman) to the Secretary of State, Moscow, July 24, 1944, 1 Foreign relations of the United States, 1944, 696, 695, cited by Franck, *ibid.*, at 47.

[17] Nico Krisch, 'Unilateral Enforcement of the Collective Will: Kosovo, Iraq, and the Security Council', (1999) 3 *Max Planck Yearbook of United Nations Law* 59; J Lobel and M Ratner, 'Bypassing the Security Council: Ambiguous Authorizations to Use Force, Cease-Fires and the Iraqi Inspection Regime', (1999) 93 *American Journal of International Law* 124; C Gray, 'After the Cease-Fire: Iraq, the Security Council and the Use of Force', (1994) 65 *British Yearbook of International Law* 135.

[18] See Martii Koskenniemi, 'The Place of Law in Collective Security', (1996) 17 *Michigan Journal of International Law* 455 at 460; See Olivier Russbach, ONU Contre ONU: *Le Droit International Confisqué* (1994).

goals.[19] There is no doubt that in the Charter world, the Security Council is *primus inter pares*.

The Charter leaves no room for procedural tawdriness. Hence, the awesome powers entrusted to the Council under Chapter VII are attended by stringent in-built regulation. In the first Gulf conflict, the Security Council first imposed non-military measures on Iraq shortly after the invasion of Kuwait, and hoped that these would compel Sadam Hussein to abandon its aggression and withdraw his troops from Kuwait. Under Article 40, once the Council decides to *first* impose the non-military measures under Article 41, it must, without exceptions, await the outcome of such measures before unleashing the devastating actions under Article 42. Clearly on this occasion, when the Security Council imposed economic sanction on Iraq in 1990, it did not wait for the sanctions to achieve desired effect before adopting Resolution 678 authorising military action against Iraq.[20] Cuba and Yemen challenged Resolution 678 as ill timed and one taken in violation of Chapter VII because it was adopted in breach of the procedure enumerated under Chapter VII.[21]

Unravelling in tandem with the dissonance between the Charter texts and their implementation by the Council are incidents of civil wars, terrorism, small-arms proliferation, and a host of other situations that were not contemplated by the authors of the Charter in 1945, and for which the Charter contains no palliative prescriptions. The euphoria of the demise of the Cold War was soon doused by an instantaneous explosion of civil conflicts in erstwhile satellite conclaves of the US and the Soviet Union. From Somalia to Liberia, from Congo to Sierra Leone, Yemen to Yugoslavia, civil wars sacked and collapsed many member states of the UN.

4 REINVENTING AND LIFTING THE VEIL OF SOVEREIGNTY: THE SECURITY COUNCIL AS A THINKER

The Security Council, unable to deal decisively with the emergent situations on the basis of the UN Charter's formal provisions, evolved operational formulae that were nowhere mentioned in the Charter, as a pragmatic means of containing and dealing with the new menaces. Whereas, after determining that the invasion of Republic of Korea by North Korea constituted a breach of international peace and security,[22] it had called on

---

[19] For an account of how the Security Council was able to prevent collective security from total collapse in the stasis of the Cold War, see particularly Thomas Franck, *Fairness in International Law and International Institutions* (Oxford, Oxford University Press, 1995).

[20] UN Doc. S/RES/678 (1990) 29 Nov., 1990.

[21] Although China also abstained from voting, it did not however cast a veto vote and thus, its abstention did not prevent the adoption of Resolution 678.

[22] SC Resolution 82 (1950) 25 June 1950.

member states 'to render every assistance to the United Nations in the execution of this resolution.'[23] The Security Council would repeat this formulae in 1991 when, in the prelude to Operation Desert Storm, it called on states 'co-operating with Kuwait' to use all necessary means to repel Iraqi aggression and restore international peace and security.[24] Clearly, in both instances, the Security Council had to face up to the brutal realisation that the promise made by states to furnish it with ready troops under Article 43, in order for it to carry out the measures of Article 42, had not materialised. It then had to make an option: to view itself as incapable of implementing Article 42 measures in the absence of Article 43 forces, as was probably thought of in 1945, or to creatively untangle the implementation of the two provisions even if it acknowledged that they were legislative Siamese. In Korea and Kuwait, the Security Council adopted the second option and thus brought its ingenuity to rescue the UN collective security from a total collapse.[25]

The flagellation of the creative process, by which the Security Council authorises, rather than mandates UN members to take collective actions, is generically known as the 'coalitions of the willing.' This practice has now come to be known as a decentralised military option[26] or more broadly, an incident of the delegation of enforcement powers by the Security Council to states.[27] Such adaptation of the Charter rigid provisions on collective security to meet the constant reconfiguration on the world political landscape, although flourished in dealing with inter-state conflicts (since these are the primary targets of collective security and the ban on the use of force) they could not tackle civil wars without upsetting

---

[23] UN Doc. SCOR, 5th Sess., 473rd mtg, S/PV.473 (1950) 25 June 1950.

[24] UN Doc. S/RES/678 (1990) 29 Nov., 1990.

[25] There is continuous debate whether in the absence of special forces agreed on by states under Article 43 the Security Council can undertake the measures contained in Article 42. According to the *travaux preparatoires* of the UN, this was what was originally intended. In the words of US Secretary of State, '[t]he whole scheme of the Charter is based on this conception of collective force made available to the Organization for the maintenance of international peace and security'. See Report of the President on the Results of the San Francisco Conference, June 26 1945, US Congress, Senate Committee Hearings, 79th Cong., vol 767, 34 at 55. However, as some writers have argued, even if the authors of the Charter did not 'envisage such Council-mandated use of force in the absence of an Article 43-based military capability [there] is no reason, however, why the Council's responses to aggression cannot be understood as a creative use of Article 42, severed from, and unencumbered by, the failed Article 43'. See Thomas Franck, *Recourse to Force: State Action Against Threats and Armed Attacks* (Cambridge, Cambridge University Press, 2002), 26.

[26] Nigel White and Özlem Ülgen, 'The Security Council and the Decentralised Military Option: Constitutionality and Function', (1997) XLIV *Netherlands International Law Review* 378 at 380 *et seq*. This is system by which the Security Council delegates to UN member states the powers to intervene in a crisis in accordance with its resolution rather than the UN Charter.

[27] See Danesh Sarooshi, *The United Nations and The Development of Collective Security: The Delegation by the UN Security Council of its Chapter VII Powers* (Oxford, Clarendon Press, 1999).

one of the Charter's golden rule: the preservation of sovereignty of member states.[28] Civil wars, by their very nature, are incidents that Article 2(7) refrains the UN from intervening in since they are deemed to be matters essentially within the domestic jurisdiction of member states.

Despite Article 2(7) of the Charter, as early as 1960s, the UN, or some of its powerful members, had begun to perceive certain 'domestic matters' as capable of constituting threat to international peace and security. Thus, the United States viewed the crisis in the Congo republic not as internal conflict but one that constituted a 'clear threat to international peace and security *because* of the actual involvement or potential involvement of outside powers.'[29] Although the US had cautiously precipitated the UN to remove the protection afforded states by Article 2(7), partly on the ground of invitation from the government of Congo and partly because of actual involvement of outside powers, the UN had all but discarded such qualifications in 1966 when both the Security Council and General Assembly mandated member states to impose Chapter VII sanctions against the minority racist government of Ian Smith in South Rhodesia.[30]

Curiously however, this early 'victory' of principle over the formality of the Charter provisions would be conveniently side-tracked decades later in the crises in Liberia and Chechnya.[31] On these occasions, the Secretaries General of the UN had pronounced that the situations in the two countries were not such that the UN could intervene. Changes to this attitude would not begin until around the middle 1990s when civil wars, *coup de tats*, armed conflicts in Somalia, Democratic Republic of Congo, Rwanda, Yemen, Socialist Federal Republic of Yugoslavia, Former Republic of Yugoslavia (Serbia and Montenegro), Haiti, became too dire and too destructive for the UN to ignore. Alongside these armed hostilities of different forms were the explosion of HIV/Aids all over the world, especially in Africa, hunger and poverty, and gross violations of human rights. The net effect of all these on the UN was to compel a rethink of how it should interpret the provision of Article 2(7) of its Charter. Indeed, the UN Secretary-General,[32] the Security Council and the General Assembly

---

[28] The UN Secretary General Janvier Pere de Cuellar had insisted in 1990 that the conflict in Liberia was not such that the UN could intervene. See *Report of the Secretary-General on the Work of the Organisation*, UN GAOR, 46th Session., Supp. No. 1, at 3, UN Doc. A/461/1 (1991). The same opinion was expressed by the UN in the conflict between Russia and Chechnya. See Larry King Live: Interview with Boutros-Boutros Ghali (Cable Network News Broadcast, December 22 1994) Transcript no 1312, available in Lexis, New Library, CNN File.

[29] Department of State Press Release No 99, Feb., 22 1963.

[30] S/Res. 232 (1966) 16 Dec., 1966. See also S.Res. 418 4 Nov., 1977 with respect to South Africa.

[31] Peter Daniel DiPaola, 'A Noble Sacrifice? Jus Ad Bellum and the International Community's Gamble in Chechnya', (1997) 4 *Indiana Journal of Global Legal Studies* 435.

[32] See the Report of the Secretary General on the Work of the Ogranization, GAOR, 54th Sess., 4th Plen. Mtg., A/54/1, 20 September 1999.

united in relying on these modern day challenges to collective security to lift the veil of sovereignty under Article 2(7). This pragmatic approach also received judicial blessing when the International Criminal Tribunal for the Former Yugoslavia noted that the practice of the Security Council 'is rich with cases of civil war or internal strife which it classified as a 'threat to the peace' and dealt with under Chapter VII, and concluded that the 'threat to peace' of Article 39 may include, as one of its species, internal armed conflicts'.[33]

Thus, in response to civil wars and other activities previously regarded as falling essentially within the domestic jurisdiction of member states, the Security Council began to encourage UN member states to take necessary measures to facilitate the delivery of humanitarian assistance to needy populace, as in Somalia. In other situations, it would simply complement an effective intervention by a regional organisation such as the Organisation of the American States in Haiti, and ECOWAS in Sierra Leone to restore overthrown democratic governments.

5   THE UNSECURED FRINGES: BETWEEN THE ADAPTATION OF CHAPTER VII AND THE BAN ON THE USE OF FORCE

It could be said that with the broad-minded approach adopted by the Security Council concerning the substantive shortfalls between the provisions of the Charter and their implementation, it has saved the Charter scheme of collective security from two most daunting challenges it confronted in its earlier years. The first is the non-materialisation of the special arrangements that would facilitate the implementation of collective security under Chapter VII. The second is the removal of the veil of territorial sovereignty under which states have hidden for decades to decimate their own populations and wreak havoc on the very ideals the UN stands for.

The close of 1990s and the opening of 2000 would yet bring another shocking realisation to the Security Council: that there are still unsecured fringes of collective security that are by far more devastating. The most prominent of these is terrorism which, since 1990s has become more or less a growth industry, and one that probably presents collective security with its most daunting challenge yet. Although it is not the intention here to go into any details about terrorism, much less to pontificate about its definition, I briefly highlight what particularly makes the problem of terrorism one that cannot be easily dealt with within the paradigmatic framework of the Charter or the existing creative reinterpretation of its provisions by the UN organs.

---

[33] See *Prosecutor v Tadic*, IT–94–1–AR 72 (October 1995) para 30.

5.1   Terrorism and the UN Charter

The UN's ban on the use of force and its mechanism for collective security, constitute a statecentric system. The charter does not address non-state uses of force. Terrorism is often operated by non-state entities, acting on their own or with active support of mostly anonymous state entities. Terrorist groups often adopt means of operation that frequently defy easy classification under the Charter norms, such that could instigate the Charter defence mechanisms against its occurrence. The ban contained in Article 2(4) of the Charter restrain states in their international relations from the threat or use of force. Hence, when terrorists mounted their most daring campaign yet against the United States on 11 September 2001, the Charter had simply and (probably innocently too) gone to sleep. Terrorist organisations are mostly amorphous and amphibious. They sometimes have operational cells in several countries some or most of which may not genuinely have the knowledge of their presence within the polity.

Except for the generic phrase 'maintenance of peace and security' found all over the UN Charter, there is no single legislative prescription in the Charter that could come to the aid of a deeply frustrated United States, a constant victim of an untraditional enemy, unknown to the UN Charter. Although the US had vindicated its self-defence right under Article 51 of the Charter, and had been assisted by NATO states in doing this, that was possible because of a host of factors that may not be present in every situation of terrorism. The Al-Qaeda network allegedly responsible for the September 11 acts were all linked with a particular state—Afghanistan—the government of which was known to protect those terrorists either by commission or omission, and had such had thus opened itself up for imputability of the act. Hypothetically, had the terrorists not been linked so compellingly to Afghanistan, it remains to be seen how the issue would have been dealt with. Even then, the question must be raised how may the Security Council deal with terrorism within the framework of collective security when the UN Charter contains no provision that deal with non-state uses of force?

With regard to the attacks on the United States, the Security Council had proved tremendously unresourceful in dealing with this issue at the crucial moment. It seems appropriate to conclude that as the UN Charter presently stands, the global role of the Security Council in dealing with terrorism may not go beyond encouraging states which have become victim to deal with the issue as best as they wish. Thus, unlike its ingenuous reaction to the problems of civil wars created by and common to small and weak states, the Security Council has not been able to address, in like manners, the problems besieging its most powerful members. As to be expected, the Security Council adopted resolutions declaring terrorist attacks as acts that constitute threats to international peace and security, it had, however, left the victims to help themselves to whatever measures they deemed fit in self-defence to counter the menace. This, as we know, was not what was envisaged under Article 51 of the UN Charter which negotiating history suggests that once the Security Council has taken measures necessary to maintain international peace and security, this terminates the right of self-defence of the victim.

6   REGIONAL ORGANISATION AND THE CHALLENGES OF COLLECTIVE SECURITY: THE AFRICAN DILEMMA

In the overall design of the Charter collective security, little regard was paid by the founders of the UN to the role to be played by regional organisations. The only instance it appears that the authors of the UN Charter were inclined to leave some powers out of the Security Council's control was the inclusion of the very marginal framework of Chapter VIII in the Charter. This chapter contains provisions that allow regional organisations to take pacific measures in respect of their members' disputes (Article 52). They also allow the Security Council to utilise any such organisations, as it may deem fit, in order to maintain international peace and security in areas not explicitly stipulated in (Article 53(1). However, this article forbids regional arrangements or agencies to take enforcement actions without the authorisation of the Security Council. In the assumption of the authors of the Charter, the Security Council would always be in the position to authorise regional enforcement actions.

Even then, the inclusion of regional arrangements in the UN Charter cannot be credited to the foresight of the Founding States. Chapter VIII came into the Charter as an afterthought in San Francisco. Regional arrangements for collective security were never part of the original negotiation at Dumbarton Oaks. It was the insistence of the Latin American states, which feared that the Security Council might be given too much power and wanted their organisation to be named as an exclusion to the Council's powers that led to the compromise that became Chapter VIII. American states also feared that a non-American permanent member of the Security Council (in particular they had Soviet Union in mind) could use the veto power, a power that is nowhere found in the Charter in the sense that it is today known, to prevent their regional organisation from acting within the Western Hemisphere. Far from it being a stroke of genius, it was a combination of the fear of the unknown and the selfishness of a few states in the Americas that led to the singular instance of devolution of collective security powers in the Charter.

Nonetheless, the Cold War effectively prevented regional organisations from acting in their regions, except with respect to peacekeeping operations, such as the OAU undertook in Chad and the League of Arab States in Lebanon. The Security Council could not utilise regional organisations as Article 53(1) anticipates and attempts by regional organisations to impose measures sometimes perceived as fringing too closely on enforcement action resulted in tensed debates in the Security Council as seen in the Cuban Missile crisis in 1962. Decisions even by the General Assembly to accord observer status in its proceedings to regional organisations were hotly contested by UN member states. However, the end of the Cold War signified a rejuvenation of the relationship between the UN and regional organisations and indeed, a reinvention of Chapter VIII by regional organisations themselves.

7   REINVENTING CHAPTER VIII AND THE ARTICULATION OF NEW COLLECTIVE SECURITY SYSTEM IN AFRICA

7.1   ECOWAS and UN in Liberia and Sierra Leone

There had been sufficient coverage of the Liberia crisis by legal writers to justify dispensing with recounting that episode in great details here. Furthermore, considerable attention has been focused on how this crisis has helped foster a greater complementarity between the UN and regional organisations to a greater extent than possible during the Cold War.[34] Also, much has already been said about how this situation has engendered a regime of cooperation between the UN and regional organisations, a development that was virtually unthinkable during the Cold War. The intention here is to set these two conflicts as a background to new collective security challenges facing African states and their interaction with the UN.

The intervention of ECOWAS, a hitherto sub-regional economic grouping, in the Liberian crisis is standard setting for, at least, African regional organisations. The crisis in Liberia, which broke out in 1989, was due to well-known facts. Briefly recounted, this conflict came into existence because of the insurrection led by Charles Taylor, a former Minister under Samuel Doe's regime, against the latter's government. The magnitude of the massacre committed by both sides to the conflicts, the potential destabilisation it would cause to West Africa's peace and security, the decline of the Security Council to intervene in a civil conflict all led to the decision by ECOWAS to intervene in Liberia in 1990. At the time ECOWAS intervened,

---

[34] Georg Nolte, Restoring Peace by Regional Action: International Legal Aspects of the Liberian Conflict, 23 *ZaöR V* 53/3, 603; Kofi Oteng Kufor, 'The Legality of the Intervention in the Liberian Civil War By the Economic Community of West African States', (1993) (5) *African Journal of International and Comparative Law* 525; Funmi Olonisakin, *Reinventing Peacekeeping in Africa: Conceptual and Legal Issues in ECOMOG Operations* (The Hague, Kluwer Law International, 2000); Ademola Abass, 'The New Collective Security Mechanism of ECOWAS: Innovations and Problems' (2000) 5(2) *Journal of Conflict and Security Law*, 211.

it only could do so by relying on then a decade old protocol[35] without the institutional facilities that would make such an intervention legal.[36] Although there are contained, in PMAD, legal bases for ECOWAS to intervene in Liberia, the required bodies that could take such decisions were non-existent. This vacuum led certain commentators to conclude that the action in its entirety was illegal.[37]

The conclusion by legal commentators that ECOWAS' enforcement action in Liberia violated the Charter was based on the assumption that the action, at inception, was a peacekeeping operation. This assumption is not without serious problems. In fact, the Gambian President, who was involved in the Committee that established ECOMOG, and in whose country this force was born, rebutted such an assumption.[38]

Importantly, the Security Council had not only kept silent when ECOWAS began to use force against rebel groups, it adopted resolutions commending ECOWAS 'peaceful' efforts although these efforts had glaringly been anything but peaceful. Thus, ECOWAS had stepped out of the Chapter VIII of the UN Charter, the first time any regional organisation had unequivocally done so, and had not only got away with it, but also won tacit approval of the Security Council.

The legal furore generated by ECOWAS' seemingly illegal act—according to legal commentators but not necessarily in the understanding of the Security Council—did not convincingly clear the legal quandary created by the action. For sure, if the Security Council accepted the action as legitimate, serious problems arise as to how it can otherwise be perceived. This is especially so if the generality or the majority of states in the international community do not share the view of the writers that ECOWAS action is illegal simply because it was taken without conformity to Article 53(1) of the Charter. Afterall, when it comes to interpreting treaties, such as the UN Charter, international law attach a great importance to how states interpret treaty provisions in practice.[39]

Importantly, no single state, either of ECOWAS, or the UN itself, has come out to challenge ECOWAS' intervention in Liberia as illegal. Nor has any member of the Security Council or General Assembly done so. In fact, when Belgium argued its case in the suit brought against it and nine

---

[35] *Protocol relating to Mutual Assistance* (PMAD) adopted 29 May 1981. See ECOWAS Doc. A/SP3/5/81. Printed also in the *Official Journal of ECOWAS*, Vol 3, June 1981 pp 9–13.

[36] Kofi Oteng Kufor, 'The Legality of the Intervention in the Liberian Civil War By the Economic Community of West African States', (1993) (5) *African Journal of International and Comparative Law* 525 argued that the 'decision making process was subverted', at 538.

[37] Christine Gray, *International Law and the Use of Force* (Oxford, Oxford University Press, 2000), 213, but see Georg Nolte, 'Restoring Peace by Regional Action: International Legal Aspects of the Liberian Conflict', 23 ZaöR V 53/3, 603 at 615.

[38] A/Dec.1/8/90 of *First Session of the Community [ECOWAS] Standing Mediation Committee*, Banjul, The Gambia 6–7 August 1990.

[39] Article 31 Vienna Convention on the Law of Treaties 1969.

other NATO states by FRY for violation of Article 2(4), it had cited the ECOWAS' action in Liberia as a precedent for humanitarian intervention.[40] In the light of the silence of the Security Council, the General Assembly and the entire international community of states, it is difficult not to conclude that ECOWAS action in Liberia set a standard for regional collective security, extended the interpretation of Chapter VIII provisions, and erected a signpost for the future.

8 UN AND AFRICAN REGIONAL ORGANISATIONS: THE PROBLEM OF ASSOCIATION AND CO-OPERATION

Although there was some kind of relationship between the UN and ECOWAS during the Liberia crisis, it is submitted that the significance of such on collective security development seemed a bit over-exaggerated by legal commentators. It appears that the cacophonous reception of the UN/ECOWAS interaction in Liberia owes more to the symbolic importance of that unprecedented camaraderie, especially just as the Cold War collapsed, rather than its practical implications on the future of collective security in Africa. The Security Council itself would appear to pander to this view when it specifically mentioned the episode in its resolution as the first time that the UN had co-operated with another organisation.[41]

Certainly, the relationship was brought about by fortuitous circumstances rather than any planned or premeditated delegation of authority by the UN to regional organisations under Chapter VIII as some writers have apparently assumed.[42] The Security Council had declined a request by Liberia to intervene in the crisis, a situation that compelled Nigeria, the subregional power, to intervene under ECOWAS auspices for reasons certain writers believe were not totally altruistic. On the field, UNOMIL had come under rebel fire, forcing the lightly armed Blue Helmets to seek protection from ECOMOG forces. Nevertheless, the interaction between UN and ECOWAS in Liberia was a remarkable departure from Cold War era of disconnection between the UN and regional organisations and an encouraging signpost into the future.

The deployment of ECOMOG to Sierra Leone is even more telling on the implication of ECOWAS' action in Liberia in particular, and its cooperation with the UN in developing capacities to meet challenges to collective

---

[40] *Legality of Use of Force* (*Yugoslavia* v *Belgium*) CR99/15 10 May 1999; (1999) ICJ Pleadings http://www.icj cij.org/icjwww/idocket/iybe/iybeframe.htm

[41] UN Doc. S/RES/866 (1993) adopted on 22 September.

[42] Sarooshi, for instance, wrote that 'In its response to the *coup* ... the Security Council delegate (sic) to ECOWAS by resolution 1132 the power to carry out a naval interdiction against the country (Sierra Leone)' See D Sarooshi, '*The Development of Collective Security: The Delegation by the UN Security Council of its Chapter VII Power*' (Oxford, Clarendon Press, 1999) at 249, n 4.

security problems in the region. In reality, this mission is by far more significant for its impact on the relationship between the UN and regional organisations in Africa than the one in Liberia. It contains the varied features of joint venture—mutual distrust and subsequent understanding, tension and ease, divergent and unified visions, unity in diversity, trials, errors and triumph. These were the direct consequences of the mission in which both international actors, UN and ECOWAS, had squared up in tackling serious issues of collective security and not just supervising the reconstruction of local markets in Monrovia.

The ECOWAS action in Sierra Leone was in response to the overthrow of a legitimate government by certain elements of the Sierra Leone National Army.[43] In this case, ECOMOG went into Sierra Leone to do one and only one thing: to restore the democratic government of Tejan Kabah by forceful means. As with Liberia, the UN had not been particularly keen on intervening. For ECOWAS, there was no problem with intervening since, while the Liberian crisis lasted, it had already stationed, pursuant to a Status of Force Agreement,[44] its troops in Freetown, Sierra Leone capital, in order to prevent spill-over as the two countries share borders. Decisively, ECOWAS altered its troops' mandate and handed them a new one: to take enforcement actions to remove the rebels and restore the exiled president.

ECOWAS's action in Sierra Leone not only affirmed my position that the Liberian action constituted a standard setting in regional collective security, it also, for the first time, established a regime of decentralised collective security whereby ECOWAS asserted its right (perhaps forever more) to undertake enforcement action without the authorisation of the Security Council.[45] In all probability, ECOWAS was fully aware of the implications of its actions in Sierra Leone, and unlike Liberia, it did not grope for legal justification for its action. Based on its experience with the Security Council in Liberia, in which the Security Council had authorised UNOMIL to go into Liberia, only after ECOWAS had done most of the ground work and, at least, stamped out rebels from Monrovia, ECOWAS concluded that it would no longer await the authorisation of the Security Council before acting.[46]

---

[43] See above.

[44] For a renewal or negotiation of a new SOFA with Sierra Leone, see *Final Communiqué Meeting of Chiefs of Defence Staff of Contributing States to ECOMOG* in Sierra Leone Abuja, 15 April 1999.

[45] See Ademola Abass, 'The Implementation of ECOWAS New Protocol and Security Council Resolution 1270 in Sierra Leone: New Development in Regional Intervention', (2002) 10(1) *University of Miami International and Comparative Law Review* 177.

[46] The present writer confirmed this view in an interview he conducted with the Legal Director of ECOWAS in 2000. See Ademola Abass, n 45.

In Sierra Leone, ECOWAS drew inspiration from its new protocol.[47] The protocol does not only allow ECOWAS's Mediation and Security Council (MSC) to decide on 'all forms of intervention',[48] it also empowers it to dispense with consent of member states as it would have been necessary had its actions been peacekeeping. ECOWAS member states have dispensed with their customary right to specifically invite, or consent to, any other member or members wishing to intervene in their conflict. They agree, under the new legal regime, that the organisation has the competence to take such decisions. They even go thus far to agree, under the procedural rules, that a withdrawal of such member, in respect of which ECOWAS may be taking collective action, will not frustrate the action. Such a withdrawal notice can only take effect one year after it is served, time enough for ECOWAS to have brought the conflict under control (which could then encourage the member to revoke its withdrawal notice) or to withdraw its troops from the state.

The important lesson here is that, in adopting a new protocol, ECOWAS shows acute awareness of circumstances in which member states can frustrate its activities in respect of their disputes. President Abdel Nasser of Egypt withdrew the consent he gave UNEF to serve as a buffer zone between Egypt and Israel during the Suez Canal crisis in the 50s. Likewise, the Chadian President Goukouni implicitly withdrew his support for OAU in 1981 when the organisation refused to be used by the President to fasten his hold on powers.[49] When such withdrawal come *in media res*, the effect can have wider implications. Hence, in the Chadian crisis, the tacit withdrawal of Chad's consent effectively ended the fledgling relationship between the UN and the OAU in which the former had assisted the latter to raise funds towards the mission in Chad.

Undoubtedly, there were moments of tension, bitter quarrel and mutual distrust between the UNAMSIL and ECOWAS such that led to the withdrawal of Indian contingents and their general, Vijay Kumah as UNAMSIL commander.[50] Yet, such were the necessary learning processes which the UN and regional organisations must undergo before achieving a clear-cut *modus operandi* in joint-operations. An eventual triumph came in the form of the UN's ability to persuade Nigeria, the largest and most significant player in ECOWAS collective security, to rejoin the mission in Sierra Leone. This time, Nigeria joined as part of UNAMSIL, although minor differences still existed in the approaches adopted by ECOWAS

---

[47] *Protocol Relating to the Mechanism for Conflict Prevention, Management, Resolution, Peacekeeping and Security*, adopted in 1999. Text in Abass, 'The New Collective Security Mechanism of ECOWAS: Innovations and Problems', (2000) 5(2) *Journal of Conflict and Security* 211.

[48] Article 10.

[49] *Keesing's Contemporary Archives* (1982) 31677–31680.

[50] See Abass, *above* n 4.

and UNAMSIL in implementing their mandates. The most important achievement of this mission was that the two organisations truly functioned initially side-by-side, then together, and brought about a restoration of the democratic government to Sierra Leone.

Problematic, however, in the joint action between UN and ECOWAS in Sierra Leone especially are issues such as command and control, unification of mandate, mission control, composition, funding, and such other practical problems that also made the realisation of the special agreement on international police force under Article 43 impossible. Apart from these, bigger challenges to peace and security in the region manifest in the forms of arms proliferation, incessant border-crossing by rebels, inadequate capacity by ECOWAS to deal with the situation and the over-dependency of ECOWAS on Nigeria for its financial and material healthiness. In the next section, I demonstrate how some of these problems have been addressed by African organisations. Particular attention is focused here on the effort of the Security Council and African organisations to address the problems of terrorism and allied issues such as the proliferation of small arms.

9   AFRICAN REGIONAL ORGANISATIONS AND THE CHALLENGE OF TERRORISM

Aside from the problems bedevilling collective security identified above, and the particular problems of association and cooperation between UN and African regional organisations, one significant problem that has also emerged is with regard to terrorism. At its Second Ordinary Session between 10–12 July 2003, the African Union considered a *Code of Conduct for Combating Terrorism* (hereafter Maputo Code) as proposed by Tunisia.[51] This followed the conference of African Union in Algiers, Algeria, in September 2002. At this meeting, a planned of action was agreed on towards implementing the 1999 OAU Convention on Preventing and Combating Terrorism.[52] It is not the intention here to engage in analysis of these codes and treaties, but to highlight certain areas in which the UN and regional organisations can cooperate towards the implementation of these instruments.

The background to the *Maputo Code*, as enumerated by African states, was the 'lack of progress in formulating an international convention on Terrorism in the Committee VI of the United Nations General Assembly'.[53] Such blistering indictment of the admittedly slow progress

---

[51] Assembly/AU/8(II)Add.11 Assembly of the African Union, Second Ordinary Session 10–12 July 2003, Maputo, Mozambique.

[52] http://www.iss.co.za/AF/RegOrg/unity_to_union/oautr.html

[53] See above n 52 at 1.

of the General Assembly is not unjustified in the face of enormous challenge posed by terrorism. Significantly, the Maputo Code is not designed to replace a universal obligation on terrorism as may emerge from the General Assembly or the Security Council's stable in the future. Hence, the Code 'would serve as an intermediary stage mobilizing all the states around a consensus on the issue'.[54]

The AU hopes to establish a code of 'ethnics (sic) among States to avert tensions, disagreement and confrontations and establish stable and fruitful relations among them, based on the principle of collective security in conformity with the United Nations Charter'.[55] The Code alludes to UN's efforts towards fighting terrorism such as contained in Security Council's Resolutions 1373 and 1456, adopted on 28 September 2001 and 20 January 2003 respectively. Accession to the Maputo Code shall be on a voluntary basis—apparently to encourage wide participation by member states—and its nature shall be similar to the Code of Conduct against the Proliferation of Ballistic Missiles, and the Code of Conduct on Terrorism, adopted by the Organisation of Islamic Conference (OIC) and the OAU.[56]

Several issues arise concerning the nature of the Code and the obligation it seeks to impose on member states. Since accession is on a voluntary basis, it is clear that the Code established a soft law obligation as against any hard rules on member states. Given the significance of terrorism, it is doubtful whether soft obligations will suffice to tackle the problem of terrorism in Africa.

Considering the plethora of treaties, protocols and treaties existing within African organisations, and the rather tepid manner in which several African states take their international obligations under these legal regimes, the Maputo Code can only make a real difference if its obligations were hard. Here is where the cooperation of the UN and African states becomes more crucial. Granted that the UN is expected to, at some point in the future, come out with a decisive instrument on terrorism, it seems that the way forward for now is to adopt a holistic and complementary approach in combating terrorism[57] rather than a disjunctive approach.

It is interesting that the AU linked the principles and ethics of its code with the principle of collective security. As noted above, some level of cooperation already exists between the UN and African regional organisations in the areas of collective security. Therefore, the extension of such relationship to cover areas such as terrorism—which is not explicitly catered for in the UN Charter—appears a useful means of enlarging the syllabus of regional arrangements ingrained in the Chapter VIII of the UN

---

[54] *Ibid.*
[55] See above n 52.
[56] See above n 52 at 2.
[57] See above n 52 at 1.

Charter. There is no prospectus for regulating the developing of the inter-action between the UN and regional organisations. Thus, it entirely depends on the creativity of the organs of the UN, especially the Security Council and the General Assembly, and regional organisations to contin-ue to fathom ways in which the legislative gulf in the Chapter VIII of the UN Charter can pragmatically be filled.

Perhaps the UN should emulate the approach adopted by the US in co-ordinating its campaign against terrorism in Africa. The US has engaged African countries in several ways to enhance their counterterrorism capa-bilities.[58] One important method adopted by the US is through the *Pan Sahel Initiative* (PSI).[59] This is an initiative of the US State Department to enhance the capacity of specific African states such as Mali, Chad, Niger, and Mauritania, in protecting their borders, tracking movement of peo-ple, combating terrorism, and enhancing regional stability.[60] Given the extremely porous nature of most African borders, as well as the relative free flow of small arms across African frontiers, the PSI is a practical and pragmatic step which, if effectively implemented, is capable of thwarting efforts of unscrupulous elements from slipping through borders to perpe-trate havoc without the national governments even being aware of their presence. In addition, intelligence sharing among states is extremely cru-cial, and indeed *desideratum* to the global effort at combating terrorism. By focusing on a small group of states, it is possible that the PSI is able to achieve its objectives more quickly and pointedly than if it were to con-centrate of all African states at once.

In this connection, it is suggested that the Security Council could, through appropriate resolutions, give support to the *Maputo Code* and put logistical support in place towards enhancing the AU's capability to imple-ment the Code. Such support does not have to be continent-wide based. The Security Council could target sub-regional groupings, such as the ECOWAS, IGAD, SADC, and Mahgreb Union, within the AU. Focusing on subregion-al organisations within the framework of the AU at one and the same time commit African states within their respective regions and on a continent-wide basis. Such an approach, it is submitted, could make it much easier for a more universal instrument on terrorism to be readily applied in Africa since similar frameworks would already have been in place.

10 CONCLUDING REMARKS

The challenges to collective security in the twenty-first century are enormous and have been made more complex by the aggravation in the

---

[58] See *US Department of State*, Pattern of Global Terrorism, 2002—Africa. Also in http://usinfo.state.gov/topical/pol/terror/2002patterns/africa.htm
[59] *Ibid.*, 1.
[60] *Ibid.*, 1.

incident of terrorism in recent times. The nature of these challenges, whether concerning the implementation of collective security provisions contained in the UN Charter or the more subtle issues such as proliferation of light arms, or more egregious ones like terrorism, is such that cannot be tackled alone either by the UN or regional organisations.

There is a desperate need for the UN to extend a much stronger hand of fellowship to regional organisations in addressing the problems facing collective security especially terrorism. The General Assembly could continue to search for a universally accepted definition and concept of terrorism while at the same time co-operating with member states which have come up with functional definitions and conceptions of terrorism to enable them deal with the matter in their locality. Broad and concerted approach rather than narrow and disjointed ones are required to effectively address the many problems of collective security. Addressing the problems may also mean that the UN, through its political organs, would confront certain issues such that make some of its member states support, either overtly or covertly, terrorism as a mean of airing their view on global issues or registering their disapproval on such matters.

Where there is a sufficient or evident political will to combat problems facing collective security, the lack of logistical means of achieving desired objectives can compromise the whole mission and retard progress. This is particularly true of many African states. The UN must do a lot more to empower regional organisations, especially those with very limited means, to enhance their capabilities. A proactive rather than reactive method is required when dealing with issues like terrorism.

> Particular attention also must be paid to cultural and social diversity when defining and conceptualising collective security issues, such as terrorism. African countries, for instance, have taken steps to reaffirm the 'legitimate right of peoples for self-determination and independence pursuant to the principles of international law and the provisions of the Charters of the Organization of African United Nations (sic) as well as the African Charter on Human and Peoples' Rights'.[61]

This does mean that recourse to often forceful means towards dismantling colonialism (which itself in most cases is installed by some violence and repression) by colonised peoples cannot constitute an act of terrorism. This position by African states calls for a clear demarcation of the province of terrorism by the UN and an unequivocal articulation of what and what does not constitute terrorism.

The future of collective security remains precarious especially in the light of development in the Gulf region in 2003. The Security Council

---

[61] See *OAU Convention on the Prevention and Combating of Terrorism*, Algiers, Algeria, 14 July 1999, available at http://www.africa-union.org/home/welcome. htm. accessed on 4 feb 2005.

continues to encounter difficulty in discharging its collective security responsibility under the UN Charter. Given the antecedents of the Security Council development, it is uncertain whether the peculiar problem of the threat or actual use of the veto power constantly hindering its work would abate in any near future. Such bleak prospects can only (and had indeed been inviting) unilateral actions by states. Kosovo (1999) and Iraq (2003) are blatant reminders that all is not at present well with collective security. There is a need to devise a bridge between the dysfunctional collective security system (under the Security Council) and the rabid recourse to unilateral actions (by powerful members of the UN) so that anarchy would not overtake the Charter legal regime. Such a bridge can convincingly be built through the institution of regional organisations. Some of these organisations, such as NATO, the OAS, and ECOWAS, have proved that given the necessary legal and material support by the universal body, the UN, they are willing and able to secure their regions from the scourges of terrorism, civil disturbances and other challenges that continue to breathe noxious fume into the lungs of collective security.

6

WTO Law and Environmental Standards: Lessons from the TRIPS Agreement?

PROF DR PETER ROTT*

WHETHER ONE WELCOMES or dislikes this development, the World Trade Organization (WTO) has, as a matter of fact, extended its scope of regulation beyond the traditional regulation of free trade, and the WTO Members have decided to proceed on this line. In particular, the Uruguay Round brought not only the foundation of the WTO, in 1994, but also an expansion of subject-matter covered by this intergovernmental organisation. The one area that has been included most clearly was the protection of health, a classic area of human rights law as well as of social policy. The relation between free trade and health-related measures has found its regulation in the TBT Agreement and, more specifically, in the SPS Agreement, and the TRIPS Agreement has created new rules for balancing intellectual property rights and the protection of public health and nutrition. The relationship between free trade and environmental law has been debated for a long time and was, in Doha in November 2001, put on the agenda for the next round of negotiations.[1]

This development does not only create problems on the institutional level, where several specialised intergovernmental organisations have been active for decades in the fields that we now absorbed, some of them with competing dispute settlement regimes.[2] Even more worrying, from the views of many, is the danger of international economic law dominating social policy, and even human rights law, through this

---

* Junior Professor for Private Law with a focus on European Private Law, University of Bremen.
[1] See the Ministerial Declaration, WTO–Document WT/MIN(01)/DEC/1. See also below, at II. 4.

[2] In favour of a specialised environment organisation, eg, CF Runge, 'A Global Environment Organization (GEO) and the World Trading System', (2001) 35 *Journal of World Trade* 399 ff. In favour of the WTO, eg S Shaw & R Schwartz, 'Trade and Environment in the WTO' (2002) 36 *Journal of World Trade* 129, at 154.

absorption.[3] This paper argues that the inclusion of social policy issues into WTO law has, until now, proved not to be a one-way road but that it has influenced, and maybe even changed international trade law to some degree. In a very pragmatic perspective, WTO law may increase legal certainty about the relationship of trade and non-trade issues, and it may offer economically weaker countries some protection from undue pressure since it prohibits WTO Members from using any unilateral measures in the field regulated by WTO law.[4]

A   SOCIAL POLICY AND THE TRIPS AGREEMENT

I   Historical overview

Patent law has been subject to controversies between developed countries and developing countries since the 1960s. On the international level, the World Intellectual Property Organization (WIPO) co-ordinated the efforts to create an international patent law system.[5] However, these efforts proved unsuccessful after 1967 when developed countries pressed for (higher) national minimum standards for the protection of intellectual property whilst developing countries voted for preferential treatment in this field.[6] No common ground could be found, and in the following, developing countries came under bilateral pressure from developed countries, such as the US[7] but also the EC,[8] to adopt certain patent law standards.[9] For example, the US made the protection of intellectual property a precondition for participation in their preferential trade system.[10]

[3] See eg, S Dillon, 'Trade and the Environment: A Challenge to the GATT/WTO Principle of "Ever-freer Trade"' (1996) 11 *St John's Journal of Legal Commentary* 351 ff.; A Orford, 'Contesting Globalization: A Feminist Perspective on the Future of Human Rights', (1998) 8 *Transnational Law and Contemporary Problems* 172 ff.

[4] See the Panel report in *United States—Sections 301–310 of the Trade Act of 1974*, WT/DS152/R. See also D Jakob, 'Die Zukunft US-amerikanischer unilateraler Section 301–Maßnahmen', (2000) *Gewerblicher Rechtsschutz und Urheberrecht—Internationaler Teil* 715 ff.

[5] See eg, K-F Beier, 'Hundert Jahre Pariser Verbandsübereinkunft—Ihre Rolle in Vergangenheit, Gegenwart und Zukunft', (1983) *Gewerblicher Rechtsschutz und Urheberrecht—Internationaler Teil* 339–40.

[6] See H Forkel, 'Das Erfinder- und Urheberrecht in der Entwicklung—vom nationalen zum internationalen Schutz des "geistigen Eigentums"', (1997) *Neue Juristische Wochenschrift* 1672 ff.

[7] See eg, FM Abbott, 'Protecting First World Assets in the Third World: Intellectual Property Negotiations in the GATT Multilateral Framework', (1989) 22 *Vanderbilt Journal of Transnational Law* 689, at 709 ff.

[8] For pressure on Korea, see S-H Song & S-K Kim, 'The Impact of Multilateral Trade Negotiations on Intellectual Property Laws in Korea', (1994) 13 *UCLA Pacific Basin Law Journal* 118, at 125–6.

[9] For an overview, see E Simon, 'GATT and NAFTA Provisions on Intellectual Property', (1993) 4 *Fordham Intellectual Property, Media & Entertainment Law Journal* 267, at 270 ff.

[10] See RE Hudec, *Developing Countries in the GATT Legal System* (Aldershot, Gower, 1987), at 112 ff.

Finally, the WTO took over. Despite strong objections by a number of developing countries, the issue of intellectual property protection had been included in the negotiations on the Uruguay Round of GATT, the result being the TRIPS Agreement.[11] The TRIPS Agreement has been condemned by some as a neo-colonialist intervention into the economic development of developing countries.[12] Indeed, the TRIPS Agreement forces developing countries to grant patents in most fields of technology for a duration of 20 years. It also established rules on exceptions from patentability and from the rights of the patent owner. On the other hand, it is obvious that the developed countries have not achieved all their goals concerning the international protection of intellectual property.[13] The question is whether at last, the TRIPS Agreement (as one part of WTO law) was detrimental or beneficial to developing countries.

II Appraisal

1 A good bargain and a safe harbour

Developing countries accepted the adoption of the TRIPS Agreement for two reasons. The first one was a bargain. In return, they negotiated significant tariff reductions and largely improved market access in the fields of textiles[14] and tropical agricultural products[15] that are crucial for their economies. The other incentive for developing countries to finally accept the TRIPS Agreement was to avoid further bilateral trade measures by bringing intellectual property law under the multilateral dispute settlement system of the WTO,[16] and in fact a number of disputes between

---

[11] For a historical overview, see JC Ross & JE Waterman, 'Trade-Related Aspects of Intellectual Property Rights' in TP Stewart (ed), *The GATT Uruguay Round: a negotiating history (1986–1992)*, Vol 2 (Deventer, Kluwer, 1999) 2241, at 2264 ff.; J Croome, *Reshaping the World Trading System—A History of the Uruguay Round*, 2nd edn (The Hague, Kluwer, 1999), at 109 ff., 215 ff., 244 ff.; C Raghavan, *Recolonization* (London et al, Zed Books, 1990), at 265 ff.

[12] See eg, M McGrath, 'The Patent Provisions in TRIPs: Protecting Reasonable Remuneration for Services Rendered—or the Latest Development in Western Colonialism?', (1996) *European Intellectual Property Review* 398 ff.

[13] For a detailed analysis, see P Rott, *Patentrecht und Sozialpolitik unter dem TRIPS-Abkommen* (Baden-Baden, Nomos, 2002), ch 4. See also JJ Schott & JW Buurmann, *The Uruguay Round—An Assessment* (Washington, Institute for International Economics, 1994), at 115; ML Doane, 'TRIPS and International Intellectual Property Protection in an Age of Advancing Technology', (1994) 9 *American University Journal of International Law and Policy* 465, at 468.

[14] See X Tang, 'Textiles and the Uruguay Round of Multilateral Trade Negotiations', (1989) 23 (3) *Journal of World Trade* 51 ff.

[15] See A Koekkoek, 'Tropical Products, Developing Countries and the Uruguay Round', (1989) 23 (6) *Journal of World Trade* 127 ff.

[16] See eg, the message of the President of Brazil to the Brazilian people, see PB Casella, 'The Results of the Uruguay Round in Brazil: Legal and Constitutional Aspects of Implementation' in JH Jackson & AO Sykes (eds), *Implementing the Uruguay Round* (Oxford, Clarendon Press, 1997), 441, at 452. See also the comments by a number of developing countries in *United States—Sections 301–310 of the Trade Act of 1974*, WT/DS152/R.

developed countries and developing countries have been carried out under this system.[17] Compliance with the TRIPS requirements establishes a safe harbour in the sense that other WTO Members cannot retaliate within the scope of WTO law.[18] Since this scope has expanded immensely with the foundation of the WTO, in 1994, this safe harbour effect cannot be underestimated. Admittedly, the safe harbour established by the TRIPS Agreement is only relatively safe, and WTO Members continue to put pressure on, in particular, developing countries to go beyond the minimum standards required by the TRIPS Agreement.[19] Relevant fields are pharmaceutical[20] and biotechnological inventions.[21] However, their arsenal has become less deterrent. For example, pressure on developing countries through the potential withdrawal of voluntary preferences under the preferential trade systems of developed countries has decreased since tariffs have been drastically reduced as a result of the Uruguay Round anyway, thereby diminishing the importance of the preferential trade systems.[22] With the envisaged further reduction of tariffs in the sectors of agriculture and textiles, independency from preferential trade systems will further increase. Thus, WTO Members must offer more, nowadays, in order to bring unwilling developing countries in line with their ideas of the appropriate level of protection of intellectual property.

2   Balanced obligations and flexibility

Of course, this safe harbour can only be beneficial for developing countries if the requirements for reaching it are reasonable. In the opinion of

[17] However, only *India—Patent Protection for Pharmaceutical and Agricultural Chemical Products*, WT/DS79/R was decided upon by a panel. Others have been settled, see *Pakistan—Patent Protection for Pharmaceutical and Agricultural Chemical Products*, WT/DS36; *Brazil—Measures Affecting the Patent Protection*, WT/DS199/1 and/4; and partly *Argentina— Patent Protection for Pharmaceuticals and Test Data Protection for Agricultural Chemicals*, WT/DS171, and *Argentina—Certain Measures on the Protection of Patents and Test Data*, WT/DS196.

[18] See also CM Correa, *Intellectual Property Rights, the WTO and Developing Countries* (London et al, Zed Books, 2000), at 8. Nevertheless, the US have amended their trade laws in such a way that they can impose trade sanctions even on those countries that comply with TRIPS but still grant a low level of intellectual property protection, see FM Abbott, 'Commentary: The International Intellectual Property Order Enters the 21st Century', (1996) 29 *Vanderbilt Journal of Transnational Law* 471, at 477.

[19] For an overview, see P Rott, n 13, at 83–5.

[20] For an analysis of the conflict between the US and the Republic of South Africa, see SM Ford, 'Compulsory Licensing Provisions under the TRIPS Agreement: Balancing Pills and Patents', (2000) 15 *American University International Law Review* 941 ff.; D Nash, 'South Africa's Medicines and Related Substances Control Amendment Act of 1997', (2000) 15 *Berkeley Technology Law Journal* 485 ff.; F Woolridge, 'Analysis: Affordable Medicines—TRIPs and United States Policies', (2000) *Intellectual Property Quarterly* 103 ff.

[21] For the latter, see Genetic Resources Action International (GRAIN), *TRIPS-plus through the back door*, http://www.grain.org/publications/trips-plus-en.cfm.

[22] See R Blackhurst, A Enders & JF Francois, 'The Uruguay Round and market access: opportunities and challenges for developing countries' in W Martin & LA Winters (eds), *The Uruguay Round and the developing countries* (Cambridge, CUP–Cambridge University Press, 1996), 125 ff.

this author, the example of intellectual property law is encouraging. The TRIPS Agreement has established an entirely new balance between inventors and society, and between developed and developing countries which deviates largely from the Western determination of previous international patent law.[23] The principles of Article 7 TRIPS and the aims and objectives expressed in Article 8.1 TRIPS explicitly allow developing countries to pursue politics in favour of the protection of public health and nutrition as well as in favour of the public interest in sectors of vital importance to their socio-economic and technological development, and Article 27 et seq. TRIPS offer a number of mechanisms to render these principles and aims and objectives practicable. Article 27.2 TRIPS and the exceptions from the patent owner's rights show a high degree of flexibility. All these provisions have to be interpreted in the light of the aims and objectives of the TRIPS Agreement which are laid down in Article 8.1 TRIPS,[24] enabling WTO Members to integrate social policy considerations into their patent laws.[25] All the patent law mechanisms that developing countries were keen to keep available are still permitted even though conditions have been put on some of them. WTO Members can still reject patent applications under certain circumstances, under Article 27.2 TRIPS, although not in order to facilitate access to new inventions. They can issue compulsory licenses and allow the public use of patents, under Article 31 TRIPS. Article 30 TRIPS permits further exceptions from the patent owner's rights. Even the long contested domestic working requirements can arguably be brought in line with Article 27 TRIPS.[26] At the same time, the reduction of possibilities to totally reject patent applications have brought upon a better fine-tuning of patent law mechanisms. And the new rules force WTO Members to justify the rejection of patent applications and exceptions from the patent owner's usual rights, in particular with a view to their social needs. This may reduce the WTO Members' regulatory freedom but it makes patent law policy more rational.

In addition to this, the financial burden of having to establish a patent law system where none has existed before is somewhat eased by Article 41.5 TRIPS,[27] and, at least in theory, by technical assistance given by developed countries, under Article 67 TRIPS.[28]

---

[23] See P Rott, n 13, at 335-7.
[24] See especially the Panel in *Canada—Patent Protection for Pharmaceutical Products,* WT/DS114/R, at 7.26., with regard to Art. 30 TRIPS.
[25] For an in-depth analysis see P Rott, n 13, at 113–9.
[26] See P Rott, n 13, at 193–8.
[27] See C Heath, 'Bedeutet TRIPS wirklich eine Schlechterstellung von Entwicklungsländern?', (1996) *Gewerblicher Rechtsschutz und Urheberrecht—Internationaler Teil* 1169 ff.
[28] See I Elangi Botoy, 'Potential and Substantial Benefits of the Trips Agreement to the Member Countries of the African Intellectual Property Organization in the Patent Field', (2001) 4 *Journal of World Intellectual Property* 91 ff.

3   *Legal certainty through dispute settlement procedures*

One major problem for developing countries had been, in the aftermath of the foundation of the WTO, that they (as much as many developed countries) had difficulties to understand the full meaning of the new body of law.[29] Developed countries have tried to use the uncertainty for their purposes, alleging TRIPS violations by developing countries where they manifestly complied with the Agreement. The most notorious example was probably US American pressure on the Republic of South Africa to abandon the international exhaustion of patent rights in the field of pharmaceutical in the midst of a massive AIDS HIV crisis.[30] Public pressure in favour of developing countries was great, and it forced the US to give up their challenge to South Africa.[31]

Whilst the WTO itself has done remarkably little to shed light on the TRIPS Agreement,[32] other organisations, in particular UNCTAD but also non-governmental organisations, have been most active in preparing concise commentaries on the new law.[33] Legal certainty, however, was primarily fostered by the dispute settlement bodies. Their reports were highly consistent and of good legal quality. In particular, the inherent flexibility of the TRIPS Agreement has been recognised in the practice of the dispute settlement bodies. The Panel in *Canada—Pharmaceutical Products* has interpreted Article 30 TRIPS in the light of Article 8.1 TRIPS, and it has stressed the importance of exceptions from the patent owners' rights for the pursuance of public health goals.[34] In *Canada—Patent Terms*, the Appellate Body even mentioned the possibility of shortening the duration of patents for crucial pharmaceuticals,[35] a possibility that is far from obvious after a first glance at the patent law provisions of the TRIPS Agreement.[36] Overall, the dispute settlement body appears to be sympathetic to well-reasoned limitations to the inventors respectively the patent owner's rights, and they appear to be willing to take the particular circumstances of

---

[29] See JH Reichman, 'Universal Minimum Standards of Intellectual Property Protection under the TRIPS Component of the WTO Agreement', (1995) 29 *The International Lawyer* 345, at 388.

[30] See the references in n 20.

[31] See CM Correa, 'Implementing National Public Health Policies in the Framework of WTO Agreements', (2000) 34 *Journal of World Trade* 105, at 108; JA Harrelson, 'TRIPS, Pharmaceutical Patents, and the HIV/AIDS Crisis: Finding the Proper Balance Between Intellectual Property Rights and Compassion', (2001) *Widener Law Symposium Journal* 175, at 186.

[32] See the WTO website http://www.wto.org/english/tratop_e/trips_e/trips_e.htm.

[33] See the Capacity Building Project on Intellectual Property Rights (IPRs) and Sustainable Development by UNCTAD and the International Centre for Trade and Sustainable Development (ICTSD), http://www.iprsonline.org/resources/trips.htm.

[34] *Canada—Patent Protection for Pharmaceutical Products*, WT/DS114/R, at 7.26.

[35] *Canada—Term of Patent Protection*, WT/DS170/AB/R, at 101.

[36] See P Rott, n 13, at 273–4.

the WTO Member in question, including its state of development, into account.[37]

It was presumably this experience that has led developed countries to believe that it is wiser not to challenge patent laws of developing countries that cater for the social needs of their people in a reasonable and responsible way. A number of disputes, even between countries with some tradition of animosities, namely disputes initiated by the US against Brazil and Argentina, have been settled. Some of the controversial issues had gone to the core of the balance between the interests of inventors or patent owners and society, such as the international exhaustion of patent rights, in *Argentina—Certain Measures on the Protection of Patents and Test Data*,[38] and the domestic working requirement, in *Brazil—Measures Affecting the Patent Protection.*[39]

4   Confirmation of the new balance at Doha

In the Declaration on the TRIPS Agreement and Public Health,[40] adopted at the Doha Ministerial Conference on 14 November 2001, the developed countries finally formally accepted this new balance between the interests of the inventor or patent owner and society. Even though the Declaration brought, strictly speaking, nothing new,[41] it was nevertheless celebrated as a breakthrough in recognising the relevance of the health needs of developing countries for the interpretation of patent law.[42] Again, the new self-confidence of developing countries vis-à-vis their own position in international patent law and the developed countries' giving in at the Doha Ministerial affirm the importance of legal clarity and legal certainty.

5   Conclusion

Overall, one may conclude that the situation of developing countries has probably improved with respect to intellectual property law. Their obligations under the TRIPS Agreement are not small. However, interpreted correctly, they are not unreasonable either. Through intense academic discussion, their situation has been analysed with much more depth, and

---

[37] The Appellate Body has also shown sympathy for measures for the protection of public health under GATT. See especially the report in *European Communities—Measures Affecting Asbestos and Asbestos-Containing Products*, WT/DS135/AB/R.

[38] WT/DS196.

[39] WT/DS199. Most authors opine that domestic working requirements violate the TRIPS Agreement. For a different view, see P Rott, n 13, at 193–8.

[40] WTO document WT/MIN(01)/DEC/W/2.

[41] See P Rott, 'The Doha Declaration on TRIPS—Good News for Public Health?', (2003) *Intellectual Property Quarterly* 284, at 285–92.

[42] See eg, R Kampf, 'Patents versus Patients?', (2000) 40 *Archiv des Völkerrechts* 90.

with less prejudice, and their views have found much more sympathy even in developed countries. Much is yet to be done, and recent developments in the search for patent law mechanisms for developing countries with no or insufficient capacities for producing medicines for the treatment of AIDS HIV, malaria, tuberculosis etc. have been rather discouraging.[43] Still, and most importantly, it would be difficult for individual developed countries to blame developing countries for too low a level of protection of intellectual property so long as they comply with their obligations under the TRIPS Agreement.

B   ENVIRONMENTAL POLICY UNDER THE UMBRELLA OF WTO LAW?

Based upon the analysis of the sovereignty of WTO Members in pursuing their social policy goals under the framework of the TRIPS Agreement, one may try to draw conclusions as to whether it would be advisable to bring environmental standards into the framework of WTO law.

I   'Trade and environment' issues

The relationship of trade regulation and environmental policy is extremely complex and complicated, and it is certainly more complicated than the intellectual property law issue. Nevertheless, some parallels exist. Like low intellectual property protection standards, low environmental standards have come under attack by developed countries, even though no concrete attempt has been made yet to establish minimum environmental standards at WTO level.[44] A variety of interests is at stake, such as the destruction of global commons, including the ozone layer and climate. Environmental groups simply claim minimum environmental standards in all WTO Members for altruistic reasons.[45]

However, there is also the purely trade-related issue of so-called 'environmental dumping'. In the developed countries' eyes, low environmental standards offer the opportunity to produce goods cheaply, thereby increasing competitiveness with goods that have been produced in other countries under higher environmental standards, and more

---

[43] See P Rott, n 41, at 292–9.
[44] See E Neumayer, 'Greening the WTO Agreements', (2001) 35 *Journal of World Trade* 145 at 156.
[45] See T Oppermann & M Beise, 'Freier Welthandel und Umweltschutz nach der WTO-Doha-Konferenz 2001', (2002) *Recht der Internationalen Wirtschaft* 269 at 270.

costly.[46] Environmental concerns are frequently (mis)used in order to maintain competitiveness.[47] In a number of fields, standards have already been formulated in multilateral environmental agreements (MEAs), and trade restrictions are explicitly permitted in these MEAs with the aim of enforcing the respective standards. The most prominent examples are the Montreal Protocol on Substances that deplete the Ozone Layer, the Convention on International Trade in Endangered Species of Wild Fauna and Flora (CITES), and the Basel Convention on the Control of Transboundary Movements of Hazardous Wastes and their Disposal. A more recent agreement of high importance is the Cartagena Protocol on Biosafety, a proper trade and environment agreement that allows for import restrictions on living genetically modified organisms. In cases, where the conflicting parties are WTO Members as well as members to the relevant MEA, problems arise both on the institutional level and on the level of the applicable rules. However, not all WTO Members are member to these agreements, and their relationship with WTO law has remained unclear until now.[48]

The overlapping rules of WTO law and MEAs are by no means an issue for developing countries only.[49] In fact, the only dispute between two parties that are WTO Members and members to the relevant MEA, was brought by the EC. In *Chile—Swordfish*,[50] Chile has taken measures under the United Nations Convention on the Law of the Sea (UNCLOS), which the EC has regarded as GATT-inconsistent.[51] And amongst those potential disputes in which WTO Members are not both members to the relevant MEA, a dispute on the Cartagena Protocol appears to be the most likely

[46] The same argument goes, of course, with 'social dumping', related to the protection of workers. See eg, K Anderson, 'The intrusion of environmental and labor standards into trade policy' in W Martin & LA Winters (eds), *The Uruguay Round and the developing countries* (Cambridge, Cambridge University Press, 1996), 435, at 448 ff.; H-M Wolffgang & W Feuerhake, 'Core Labour Standards in World Trade Law', (2002) 36 *Journal of World Trade* 883, at 887. In fact, a study by K Maskus, 'Regulatory Standards in the WTO', (2002), spot.colorado.edu/~maskus/papers/wtostandardsrev.doc, has revealed that trade distortions through environmental dumping are low, and that trade distortions through social dumping are marginal at best.

[47] See eg, K Anderson, n 46, at 436 ff.

[48] For a comprehensive analysis of trade measures in MEAs, see the WTO document 'Matrix on Trade Measures Pursuant to Selected Multilateral Environmental Agreements, WT/CTE/W/160/Rev. 2 of 25/4/2003. See also H Ginzky, *Saubere Produkte, schmutzige Produktion* (Düsseldorf, Werner, 1997); D Abdel Motaal, 'Multilateral Environmental Agreements (MEAs) and WTO Rules', (2001) 35 *Journal of World Trade* 1215 ff.

[49] See also S Shaw & R Schwartz, n 2, at 131.

[50] *Chile—Measures affecting the transport and importation of swordfish*, WT/DS193. See G Marceau, 'Conflicts of Norms and Conflicts of Jurisdictions', (2001) 35 *Journal of World Trade* 1081, at 1123.

[51] Due to a provisional agreement, the establishment of a panel has been suspended, see WTO document WT/DS193/3.

since massive economic interests of exporters of seeds, in particular the US, are at stake.[52]

From a developing country's perspective, environmental protection is a matter of national sovereignty, and it must be balanced with other policy goals, such as industrial and economic development, food security etc. The developed countries' desire of urging developing countries to adopt high environmental standards is regarded as protectionist since such standards may close the door for exports into developed countries.[53] Indeed, the few disputes under GATT '47 and the WTO that turned on trade restrictions in the name of the protection of the environment, have demonstrated that the developing countries' suspicion is by no means groundless.[54] To date, no developing country WTO Member has formally objected under the WTO dispute settlement system to trade restrictions under the Montreal Protocol, CITES, or the Basel Convention. This might change, however, should developed countries introduce, for example, by a ban on tropical lumber aiming at the protection of the rain forest.[55]

II 'Trade and environment' in current international trade law

The preamble to the WTO Agreement already mentions the link between trade and environmental protection. The WTO Members recognise

---

[52] See JS Fredland, 'Unlabel Their Frankenstein Foods!: Evaluating a US Challenge to the European Commission's Labeling Requirements for Food Products Containing Genetically-Modified Organisms', (2000) 33 *Vanderbilt Journal of Transnational Law* 183 ff.; PWB Phillips & WA Kerr, 'Alternative Paradigms', (2000) 34 (4) *Journal of World Trade* 63 ff.; M Hilf, 'Freiheit des Welthandels contra Umweltschutz?', (2000) *Neue Zeitschrift für Verwaltungsrecht* 481, at 487. For an analysis of inconsistencies between the Cartagena Protocol and WTO rules see C Hutchison, 'International Environmental Law Attempts to be "Mutually Supportive" with International Trade: A Compatibility Analysis of the Cartagena Protocol to the Convention on Biological Diversity with the World Trade Organisation Agreement on the Application of Sanitary and Phytosanitary Measures', (2001) *Journal of International Wildlife Law and Policy* 1 ff.
The relationship between the Cartagena Protocol and WTO rules has already been subject to debate during the negotiation of the Cartagena Protocol, see eg, M Buck, 'Das Cartagena Protokoll über Biologische Sicherheit in seiner Bedeutung für das Verhältnis zwischen Umweltvölkerrecht und Welthandelsrecht', (2000) *Zeitschrift für Umweltrecht* 319, at 321; JH Adler, 'More Sorry than Safe: Assessing the Precautionary Principle and the Proposed International Biosafety Protocol', (2000) 35 *Texas International Law Journal* 173, at 189 ff.
[53] See eg, K Anderson, n 46, at 443; M Jacobs & J Wiers, 'The E in ICE: Is the Climate for Negotiations on Trade and Environment Heating Up?', (2002) 29 *Legal Issues of Economic Integration* 83 at 84; T Oppermann & M Beise, n 45, at 270. It was, however, argued that in some cases, developing countries have taken contradictory positions towards WTO law and towards international environmental law, due to a lack of co-ordination between the responsible government officials. See D Abdel Motaal, n 48, at 1220.
[54] See especially the Appellate Body report in *United States—Import Prohibition on Certain Shrimp and Shrimp Products*, WT/DS58/AB/R, at 161 ff. See also K Anderson, n 46, at 439.
[55] See K Anderson, n 46, at 446–7.

'that their relations in the field of trade and economic endeavour should be conducted with a view to raising standards of living, ensuring full employment and a large and steadily growing volume of real income and effective demand, and expanding the production of and trade in goods and services, while allowing for the optimal use of the world's resources *in accordance with the objective of sustainable development, seeking both to protect and preserve the environment and to enhance the means for doing so in a manner consistent with their respective needs and concerns at different levels of economic development'.*[56]

These general aims have been concretised in a number of the special agreements.[57]

In contrast, the GATT is lacking proper rules dealing with the relationship between trade and environment. Generally speaking, WTO law, and in particular Article XX b) GATT and the SPS Agreement, cater for the needs of countries that wish to protect their domestic environment from the importation of harmful products.[58] However, the situation is different with a view to the destruction of the environment during the production process in a foreign exporting country (the so-called non-product-related process and production methods, or PPMs).

1 The old dogma: No protection of the foreign environment

According to the established practice of the panel under the GATT 1947, Article XX b) GATT did not allow WTO Members to impose trade restrictions on other Members on the grounds of their domestic environmental behaviour. The crucial cases were the two *US—Tuna* cases[59] in which the US prohibited the importation of tuna from Mexico because Mexican fishing boats applied catching methods that led to the killing of a greater number of dolphins than those methods that US American fishing boats were forced to apply by domestic environmental law. In these cases, and also in the more recent *US—Shrimps* case,[60] the WTO dispute settlement body expressed its clear preference for multilateral

---

[56] Emphasis added.

[57] See Annex 2 of the Agreement on Agriculture, eg at 12; Art. 6 of the Agreement on the Application of Sanitary and Phytosanitary Measures; Art. 2 of the Agreement on Technical Barriers to Trade; or Art. 8.2 c) of the Agreement on Subsidies and Countervailing Measures.

[58] Specific problems relate to dangers to the environment that are not scientifically proven, such as genetically modified crops. See eg, R Howse & PC Mavroidis, 'Europe's Evolving Regulatory Strategy for GMOs—The Issue of Consistency with WTO Law: Of Kine and Brine', (2001) 24 *Fordham International Law Journal* 317 ff.; J Bohanes, 'Risk Regulation in WTO Law: A Procedure-Based Approach to the Precautionary Principle', (2002) 40 *Columbia Journal of Transnational Law* 323 ff.

[59] *United States—Restrictions on Imports of Tuna*, DS21/R (Tuna-Dolphin I), and *United States—Restrictions on Imports of Tuna*, DS29/R (Tuna-Dolphin II). See eg, PC Mavroidis, 'Trade and Environment after the *Shrimps-Turtles* Litigation', (2000) 34 *Journal of World Trade* 73, at 75 f.

[60] *United States—Import Prohibition on Certain Shrimp and Shrimp Products*, WT/DS58.

agreements over unilateral action.[61] This is, by the way, in line with
Principle 12 of the Rio Declaration on Environment and Development,
which states that unilateral actions to deal with environmental challenges outside the jurisdiction of the importing country should be
avoided, and the same approach has been taken by the European Court
of Justice when the Netherlands prohibited the importation of a wild
bird that was neither migratory nor endangered and which could law-
fully be hunted in the exporting Member State, the UK.[62]

2 New challenges: Global commons, subjects of global concern, and MEAs

The old dogma is not valid anymore. Today, there is considerable uncertainty as to whether WTO Members are permitted, under Article XX
GATT, to take unilateral measures for the protection of so-called global
commons or subjects of global concern,[63] and whether they may apply
trade restrictions under MEAs.

The case that brought new impetus to the debate was the famous *US—
Shrimps* case. Again, it was the US that prohibited the importation of
shrimps that were caught in a way that harmed the endangered sea turtles, whereas US legislation provided for more restrictive rules for domestic shrimp trawlers. The trade measures were imposed on India, Pakistan,
Thailand and Malaysia that had become important suppliers to the US
shrimps market. In this case, the Appellate Body held that sea turtles were
'exhaustible natural resources' in the terms of Article XX g) GATT,[64] and
that the US were entitled to prohibit the importation of shrimps that had
been caught in a way that harmed sea turtles because said sea turtles
migrated, amongst others, into US American waters. In addition, the
Appellate Body relaxed the link elements between measures and their
sought results, namely the 'necessity test' of Article XX b) GATT and the
'related-to test' of Article XX g) GATT.[65] However, the Appellate Body

---

[61] See especially T Cottier, E Tuerk & M Panizzon, 'Handel und Umweltschutz im Recht
der WTO: Auf dem Weg zur praktischen Konkordanz', (2003) *Zeitschrift für Umweltrecht* 155,
at 161–2.

[62] See ECJ, judgment of 23/5/1990, Case C–169/89 *Criminal proceedings against
Gourmetterie Van den Burg* [1990] ECR I–2143. See also E Neumayer, n 44, at 161.

[63] Global commons are usually said to comprise of the deep-sea bed, the Antarctic, and the
atmosphere, whereas the biodiversity was named, in the preamble to the Convention on
Biodiversity, a global concern of humankind.

[64] *United States—Import Prohibition on Certain Shrimp and Shrimp Products*, WT/DS58/
AB/R, at 132. See also PC Mavroidis, n 59, at 83 ff.

[65] See especially *European Communities—Measures Affecting Asbestos and Asbestos-
Containing Products*, WT/DS135/AB/R, at 170–5, and *United States—Standards for
Reformulated and Conventional Gasoline*, WT/DS52/AB/R, at 16–22. See also G Marceau & JP
Trachtman, The Technical Barriers to Trade Agreement, the Sanitary and Phytosanitary
Measures Agreement, and the General Agreement on Tariffs and Trade, (2002) 36 *Journal of
World Trade* 811, at 824 ff.; T Cottier, E Türk & M Panizzon, n 61, at 160–1.; J Neumann & E
Türk, 'Necessity Revisited: Proportionality in World Trade Organization Law After *Korea-
Beef*, *EC-Asbestos* and *EC-Sardines*', (2003) 37 *Journal of World Trade* 199 ff.

also stressed that measures for the protection of the environment had to be applied in a non-discriminatory manner, ie against all WTO Members that applied such fishing methods.[66]

Whilst this report was hailed by environmentalists as a breakthrough,[67] it has worried developing countries considerably.[68] Indeed, the reasoning of the Appellate Body scarcely veiled its attempts to allow for the protection of endangered species that is sought by CITES.[69] This may be laudable in the instant case but it has also created legal uncertainty. To what extent are WTO Members allowed to protect global commons, such as the atmosphere, in their trade policy?[70] Notably, there is not even consensus over what exactly such global commons are. Or does the mere existence of an MEA allow for unilateral trade restrictions once negotiations with a non-member to the MEA have failed?[71] And if so, what is the number of parties that makes an MEA relevant for the purposes of Article XX GATT?[72] Unsurprisingly, the US have concluded from their final victory in the shrimps case that they are now allowed to take unilateral measures, at least initially, to protect what they perceive as shared environmental resources.[73]

In contrast, it is rather certain that many such trade restrictions with a view to the protection of global commons would pick on production methods that are applied in developing countries and deteriorate their access to the developed countries' markets.

3 Influencing consumer behaviour through information

One increasingly important mechanism available to WTO Members aiming at environmental protection at a global scale is consumer information through labelling requirements, voluntary labelling schemes or reporting duties. For example, the EC intends to increase the consumers' awareness of detrimental production methods thereby creating incentives for those

---

[66] See eg, PC Mavroidis, n 59, at 79 ff.

[67] See T Oppermann & M Beise, n 45, at 273. The case also gave hope to the supporters of trade restrictions directed to labour standards, see R Wai, 'Countering, Branding, Dealing: Using Economic and Social Rights in and around the International Trade Regime', (2003) *European Journal of International Law* 35, at 61–2.

[68] See also F Biermann, 'The Rising Tide of Green Unilateralism in World Trade Law', (2001) 35 *Journal of World Trade* 421, at 432 ff.; D Abdel Motaal, n 48, at 1221; T Cottier, E Tuerk & M Panizzon, n 61, at 163; S Shaw & R Schwartz, n 2, at 152.

[69] *United States—Import Prohibition on Certain Shrimp and Shrimp Products*, WT/DS58/AB/R, at 132 ff.

[70] See also T Cottier, E Tuerk & M Panizzon, n 61, at 163.

[71] The Appellate Body report in *United States—Import Prohibition on Certain Shrimp and Shrimp Products*, WT/DS58/AB/R, at 122–3, is somewhat vague in this respect. The implementation panel has interpreted this as the possibility to adopt a 'provisional measure allowed for emergency reasons', see *United States—Import Prohibition on Certain Shrimp and Shrimp Products*, WT/DS58/WR, at 5.88.

[72] See also M Jacobs & J Wiers, n 53, at 90.

[73] See D Abdel Motaal, n 48, at 1219.

who produce in an environmentally sound manner, and this shall include, in particular, production in developing countries.[74] Such information schemes may impede on the marketing of certain products from developing countries. In principle, nothing in WTO law should prevent Members to apply such schemes as long as they are non-discriminatory and based on reasonable grounds, ie as long as they are not disguised restrictions to trade.[75] However, due to its potential negative consequences on market access, the issue of environmental labelling is subject to highly controversial discussion.[76]

4   *'Incentives' outside the WTO legal system*

Finally, measures to protect the foreign environment, or to protect domestic industry from environmental dumping, are carried out outside the framework of WTO law. For example, developed countries use their preferential trade regimes to give 'incentives' to developing countries to comply with minimum environmental standards, thereby raising the competitiveness of those that comply over those that do not comply.[77] Another mechanism is the adoption of bilateral agreements that incorporate environmental (and labour) provisions, such as a free trade agreement between US and Jordan.[78]

III   Future WTO 'trade and environment' rules as a safe harbour?

Until now, most developing countries have been unwilling to change WTO rules on trade and environment.[79] However, experience from intellectual property law might tell that they might be better off with an agreement on certain minimum environmental standards, provided certain conditions are fulfilled.

1   *Environmental standards as a safe harbour?*

As in the field of intellectual property law, the introduction of certain environmental standards could end unilateral trade measures in the field

---

[74] Decision No 1600/2002/EC laying down the Sixth Community Environment Action Programme, OJ 2002 L 242/1 (2, 5, 13, 14), and Green Paper on Integrated Product Policy, COM(2001) 68 final, 20. See also C Glinski & P Rott, 'Umweltfreundliches und ethisches Konsumverhalten im harmonisierten Kaufrecht', (2003) *Europäische Zeitschrift für Wirtschaftsrecht* 649 ff.

[75] See P Rott, 'Genetically modified products and consumer concerns under WTO law', (2003) 6 *Journal of World Intellectual Property* 571 ff.

[76] See eg, T Cottier, E Tuerk & M Panizzon, n 61, at 165–6; M Jacobs & J Wiers, n 53, at 92 ff.

[77] See eg, the EC preferential trade regime, Regulation (EC) No 980/2005, OJ 2005 L 169/1.

[78] See CF Runge, n 2, at 416.

[79] See D Abdel Motaal, n 48, at 1218.

of environmental protection through trade measures, an aim that is certainly desirable for developing countries.[80] Recently, India has successfully challenged the EC generalised tariff preferences scheme that accords tariff preferences for the protection of labour rights and the environment and also for combating drug production and trafficking.[81] This dispute provides evidence that there is a perceived need for a safe harbour.

2   Getting a good bargain

It should be possible for developing countries to strike a deal with developed countries that are interested in introducing environmental standards.[82] Evidence for this can be found in the negotiations of the Uruguay round as well as in the negotiations between developing countries and the EC in Doha. The EC 'paid' for the inclusion of a very limited mandate for negotiations on environmental matters[83] with concessions in the field of export subsidies on agricultural products.[84]

In fact, the Uruguay round, with all its improvements in the fields of tariff reduction for developing countries' products and with its re-inclusion of agricultural products and textiles into the GATT system, has left developing countries with much to desire.[85] In particular, the removal of tariff escalations and tariff peaks for forest and leather products, and of export subsidies paid by developed countries to their farmers, are high on the wish-list.[86] These issues could be addressed in return for concessions in the field of environmental protection.

3   Balanced obligations and flexibility

It has been proposed that any future WTO rules on trade and environment should embrace the achievement of a high standard of environmental protection as an aim, as EC law does.[87] As far as MEAs are already in place, they appear to have established reasonable standards that should simply

[80] See D Abdel Motaal, n 48, at 1221. See also the proposal by ASEAN 'The relationship between the Provisions of the Multilateral Trading System and Trade Measures for Environmental Purposes, Including Those Pursuant to Multilateral Environmental Agreements', WTO document WT/CTE/W/39 of 24/7/1996, in which the ASEAN states propose the opening of an 'environmental window' as a quid pro quo for a refrain from unilateral extra-jurisdictional trade measures for the protection of the environment.

[81] *European Communities—Conditions for the Granting of Tariff Preferences to Developing Countries*, WT/DS246/R.

[82] This was the experience with Mexico negotiating a side-agreement to the NAFTA with the US and Canada, see CF Runge, n 2, at 402 f.

[83] See below, at III. 15.

[84] See T Oppermann & M Beise, n 45, at 273.

[85] See J Whalley, 'Developing countries and system strengthening in the Uruguay Round' in W Martin & LA Winters (eds), *The Uruguay Round and the developing countries* (Cambridge, CUP–Cambridge University Press, 1996), 409, at 417 f.

[86] See S Shaw & R Schwartz, n 2, at 137.

[87] See E Neumayer, n 44, at 156.

be adopted by WTO law. This is demonstrated by the number of WTO members in general, and the number of developing countries in particular, that are part to most of these agreements.[88] Also, new standards should be elaborated in the specialised international environmental organisations and conferences. Generally speaking, it would seem to make sense to leave the legislative role to those who are experts in the field of environmental regulation, and to limit the WTO to its judiciary function.[89]

. Of course, the differentiation between developed countries, developing countries, and the least developed amongst them,[90] that is well-known to WTO law[91] as much as to MEAs,[92] would have to be applied to environmental regulation. Where environmental protection is a matter of technology, this would, in the first place, require reasonable phasing-out periods for currently applied technology, and phasing-in periods for new technologies, an issue that was also addressed by the Appellate Body in *US— Shrimps*.[93] The introduction of environmental standards would also have to be accompanied by financial support for and technology transfer to developing countries.[94] Again, the necessity to offer environmentally sound technology to potential addressees of trade restrictions has already been emphasised by the Appellate Body in *US—Shrimps*,[95] and it has also been claimed by developing countries in the CTE.[96]

---

[88] For an overview, see WTO document WT/CTE/W/160/Rev. 2 of 25/4/2003. See also F Biermann, n 68, at 424 f.

[89] See also PC Mavroidis, n 59, at 87. Also, the WTO dispute settlement body should use and would probably use the expertise of the officials of international environmental organisations if it came to interpreting an MEA in a dispute. See also G Marceau, n 50, at 1126–7. This is what the Panel in *United States—Section 211 Omnibus Appropriations Act of 1998*, WT/DS176/R, 6.1 ff., did with a view to provisions of the Paris Convention for the Protection of Industrial Property that were incorporated into the TRIPS Agreement.

[90] The categories of 'developed Members', 'developing countries' and 'least developed countries' have still not been defined under WTO law in general or the TRIPS Agreement. Therefore, some legal uncertainty remains in border-line cases. Whereas the UN list of 49 countries that are designated to be least developed provides some guidance for WTO law (although it should not be regarded as a binding classification), there is no such list available for the category of developing countries. For details and for possible classification criteria, see P Rott, n 13, at 143–61

[91] For an overview, see WTO document WT/COMTD/W/66. On the legal status of the principle of special and differentiated treatment in WTO law, see P Rott, n 13, at 132–3.

[92] For an overview, see N Michels, *Umweltschutz und Entwicklungspolitik: Mechanismen zur Berücksichtigung von Entwicklungsländern in internationalen Umweltschutzübereinkommen* (Frankfurt, Verlag Peter Lang, 1999).

[93] *United States—Import Prohibition on Certain Shrimp and Shrimp Products*, WT/DS58/AB/R, at 174.

[94] For the example of the Montreal Protocol, see F Biermann, 'Financing Environmental Policies in the South: Experiences from the Multilateral Ozone Fund', (1997) 9 (3) *International Environmental Affairs* 179–218.

[95] *United States—Import Prohibition on Certain Shrimp and Shrimp Products*, WT/DS58/AB/R, at 175. The expenses for using the so-called Turtle Excluder Devices were estimated to be $ 30,000 per boat and year, an amount that is unaffordable to shrimp fishers in India or Pakistan. See M Hilf, n 52, at 484.

[96] See D Abdel Motaal, n 48, at 1218.

Apart from this, any kind of regulation under WTO law can only be acceptable for developing countries if their obligations are sufficiently flexible for taking into consideration their respective needs in a long-term perspective. The current preamble to the WTO Agreement appears to be a good starting point since it aims at sustainable development, which is a holistic concept that integrates economic, social and environmental development.[97] For developing countries, it would be crucial to have provisions on principles and objectives in the line of Articles 7 and 8 TRIPS included. These provisions would have to allow WTO Members to take into account competing goals such as food security, or societal and industrial development.[98] This would again be in line with the Rio Declaration that regards environmental protection as an integral part of the development process that cannot be considered in isolation from it. Such a general clause would not render the whole agreement arbitrary and meaningless. Members that rely on specific grounds for deviating from otherwise reasonable standards would be obliged to justify their action.[99] The dispute settlement body has demonstrated in its reports on TRIPS that it is well equipped to deal with such an escape clause.

4 *Legal certainty*

From the developing countries' perspective, it may be beneficial to solve the issue of the protection of global commons or subjects of global concern by negotiations rather than through the WTO dispute settlement system. Not only is the WTO dispute settlement procedure costly and therefore almost unaffordable for some developing countries, but the current trend to allow the protection of global commons may prove to go beyond what developing countries have expected.[100] Indeed, some authors argue that the jurisprudence established by the Appellate Body in *US—Shrimps* could not have been reached by negotiation.[101] Surely, legal development through the Dispute Settlement Body creates uncertainty as to the legal status of different measures in different circumstances.[102] It would therefore be preferable to clarify by negotiation which multilateral environmental agreements may be enforced by trade restrictions, even against WTO Members that are not party to the respective environmental agreement,[103] instead of trying to reconcile WTO

---

[97] See M Jacobs & J Wiers, n 53, at 84.
[98] See also T Cottier, E Tuerk & M Panizzon, n 61, at 163.
[99] See P Rott, n 13, at 336.
[100] See also T Cottier, E Tuerk & M Panizzon, n 61, at 163.
[101] See M Jacobs & J Wiers, n 53, at 96.
[102] See also M Jacobs & J Wiers, n 53, at 96.
[103] See also F Biermann, n 68, at 426; S Shaw & R Schwartz, n 2, at 153.

rules and the rules of the various MEAs by interpretation only.[104] With a view to the developing countries' concerns, it was proposed to introduce a rule according to which new trade restrictions aiming at environmental protection have to be accepted by a qualified majority of the WTO Members. This would offer developing countries a way to block protectionist trade restrictions.[105]

5   *The Doha mandate*

In Doha, the relationship between trade and environment was addressed in paragraphs 31 to 33 of the Ministerial Declaration of 14 November 2001.[106] The WTO Members agreed, amongst others, to negotiations on the relationship between existing WTO rules and specific trade obligations set out in MEAs. These negotiations shall, however, be limited in scope to the applicability of such existing WTO rules as among parties to the MEA in question, and they shall not prejudice the WTO rights of any Member that is not a party to the MEA in question. The WTO Members also instructed the CTE to give particular attention to the effect of environmental measures on market access, especially in relation to developing countries, in particular the least-developed among them, and those situations in which the elimination or reduction of trade restrictions and distortions would benefit trade, the environment and development. Finally, they recognised the importance of technical assistance and capacity building in the field of trade and environment to developing countries, in particular the least-developed among them. This mandate is rather narrow in its scope, in particular since it does not encompass the problem of incongruent membership to the WTO and to MEAs.[107] Currently, the negotiations appear to be stalled. In Cancún, no progress was made on the issue.

C   CONCLUSION AND PERSPECTIVES

Environmental law and labour law have always been under the umbrella of WTO law. However, whilst developing countries seemed to be safe from trade restrictions aiming at the protection of their domestic environment, the Appellate Body report in *US—Shrimps* has blurred the picture. It has created room for interpretation of Article XX GATT that allows

---

[104] For such attempts see eg, G Marceau, 'A Call for Coherence in International Law: Praise for the Prohibition Against Clinical Isolation in WTO Dispute Settlement', (1999) 33 *Journal of World* Trade 5 ff.; G Marceau, n 50, at 1081 ff.

[105] See T Oppermann & M Beise, n 45, at 273. For other proposals, see F Biermann, n 68, at 437–42.

[106] WTO Doc. WT/MIN(01)/DEC/1.

[107] See also M Jacobs & J Wiers, n 53, at 86. For a more optimistic evaluation, see T Oppermann & M Beise, n 45, at 274.

WTO Members to resort to unilateral measures once attempts to co-operate have failed. Experience tells that some WTO Members will use the new potential and introduce new trade restrictions under the label of environmental protection.

It may therefore be wiser for developing countries to change their strategy towards explicit integration of environmental standards into WTO law. From their perspective, more intense regulation could serve two goals: (1) reducing legal uncertainty, thereby avoiding litigation costs for challenging trade measures adopted by developed countries, and (2) getting a good bargain for accepting certain minimum standards, for example, further tariff reductions in sensitive fields, and technology transfer. They should, however, take greatest care to have their flexibility in balancing environmental protection with other (legitimate) policy goals guaranteed. An agreement with the EC should be feasible on this basis. And once they are sufficiently isolated, even the US, the other important player that opposes a number of environmental standards, might agree if they achieve, for example, better access to the EC market in return.[108]

---

[108] See also D Abdel Motaal, n 48, at 1218 ff., and the scepticism expressed by CF Runge, n 2, at 416.

7

Legal Fetishism and the Contradictions of the GATS

JANE KELSEY*

THIS PAPER LOCATES the General Agreement on Trade in Services (GATS) within the broader ideological transformation of 'services' from fundamentally social relations that are embedded within communities to commercialised commodities traded within an international market place. It is written from the standpoint of someone actively engaged in the current campaign against the GATS as a social activist, trade unionist, media commentator, NGO lobbyist, adviser to indigenous Maori and international campaigner and as an academic who teaches and writes on international economic law and New Zealand's neoliberal revolution.[1] It seeks to explain the ways in which the normative dimension of the Agreement works to silence those whose conceptualisation of services falls outside the marketised paradigm. The aim is to delegitimate the strategy of those who avoid meaningful dialogue by retreating inside the text and to identify more clearly the barriers and opportunities that the Agreement itself presents to effective critical engagement.

THE CONTEXT

This analysis is premised on the view of law, described by Colin Sumner, as a 'politico-ideological phenomenon produced in a form of political practice, that practice geared to the creation, definition and maintenance of power relations'.[2] That approach raises crucial questions about the identity of the power bloc, the nature of the problem

* Professor Jane Kelsey, School of Law, University of Auckland, New Zealand.
[1] See Kelsey, J *Economic Fundamentalism. The New Zealand Experiment: A World Model for Structural Adjustment?* (London, Pluto 1996) and Kelsey J *Reclaiming the Future. New Zealand and the Global Economy* (Toronto, University of Toronto Press 2000).
[2] Sumner, C *Reading Ideologies in Law. An investigation into the Marxist Theory of Ideology and Law* (London, Academic 1979) p 268.

they want to solve, the ideologies in which they perceive and understand the problem, and the political opposition that confronts them. Seeing the GATS as ideology, and not simply as a technical legal text, is therefore pivotal to understanding how the interests of international capital are effectively privileged and how competing understandings that insist that GATS embodies and perpetuates the inequality of social relations are excluded.

My approach assumes that services are premised on the notion 'to serve'. They involve personal relationships that extend beyond the immediate parties to the transaction into families, communities and societies. Banks, railways, radio, post, sports, schools, hospitals, sewage schemes, lawyers, ports, electricity, telephones, old people's homes, kindergartens, libraries, movie theatres, research bodies, universities serve purposes that are intrinsically social, as well as environmental, cultural and economic. Moreover these social relations have traditionally been embedded in localised communities. Their form and content has been designed to deliver a range of functions: individual wellbeing, employment, training, infrastructure, communications, community development, regional development, economic development, and cultural transfer. For these reasons services have traditionally been provided by or at least mediated through the state and subject to extensive regulation. The result has often been expensive, stagnant, monocultural and dominated by bureaucrats, interest groups and professions. Services have therefore also been an important site for contest involving indigenous nations, women, trade unions, churches, rural communities and many more.

Since the 1970s the growth of transnational services firms has introduced a new and powerful party to this contest. Organised through lobbies like the United States Coalition of Services Industries and the European Services Forum, and smaller national equivalents, they have promoted the deregulation, liberalisation and privatisation of services in their home countries and the negotiation of binding international rules that guarantee long term, enforceable and infinitely expandable access to other countries' services markets. Their key goals have been

— weaker or no restrictions on foreign direct investment (FDI);
— guarantees that central and local government will not discriminate in favour of local services firms and employees;
— guaranteed access to countries' services markets, with no requirements to operate through joint ventures and no numerical limits on the size to which any services market could grow;
— no favouritism of one country's services firms over another;
— dismantling of public monopolies that lock up potential services markets;
— light handed regulation;
— free movement of capital;

— immigration rules that allow short term entry for key personnel for services firms; and
— enforcement of these rules with sanctions that bite.

The GATS, and related regional and bilateral free trade agreements, offer a framework for achieving this.

READING GATS IDEOLOGY

Alan Hunt helpfully distinguishes between the ideological content of the 'form of law', the ideological content of fundamental legal 'principles' and the ideological content of concrete legal norms.[3]

The Legal Form

The form in this case is that of an international economic treaty. The Uruguay Round agreements, including the GATS, are the product of social practices and relations, in which the political, economic and social interests of the major powers and related capital largely held sway over those represented by the governments of poorer and smaller countries. Once the requisite processes of international law were completed, their origins as a construct of a particular historical, economic and political conjuncture were obliterated.

The GATS was magically transformed into an expression of objective rationality and an abstract normative instrument based on general principles, rules and technical terms. Those who accepted its legitimacy represented the assumptions, values and interests that underpin the Agreement as unquestionable and timeless. Despite the constraints it imposes on the state's notional sovereignty, the GATS is also purported to be the product of that sovereignty. This confers legitimacy on its ideology and moves to enforce its rules, and a distance between these rules and the interests of capital that they benefit.

Because the GATS is binding, principles of non-discrimination, rules that limit permissible domestic regulation or preference for local firms, and technical terms like market access or disguised restrictions on trade are now treated as the absolute determinants of discussions about the international regulation of services and about the regulation of services that are provided by or to a foreigner. There is no option to see the artificial construction of services markets as a misrepresentation of social life. The rules define not only rights and obligations but exclusively determine

---

[3] Hunt, A *Towards a Constitutive Theory of Law* (New York, Routledge, 1993), p 127.
[4] Engels, F quoted in Hunt, A *Towards a Constitutive Theory of Law* (New York, Routledge 1993), p 19.

the legal personalities that are recognised, being WTO Members and 'services suppliers', in forms that are disembodied and decontextualised. In the words of Engels: 'the juristic form is, in consequence, made everything and the economic content nothing.'[4] The rules are then used to try to reconstitute the reality of services in the image of the ideal.

This is not to suggest that these norms go uncontested. But the critique is forced to occur outside the 'legitimate' discourse established by the Agreement. The advocates and the critics, by definition, talk past each other. Breaking this impasse requires either the collapse of the Agreement, the capitulation of the critics to accept adjustments within the market paradigm, or tactical manoeuvres to secure advances or retreats (however each side views them) within the scope provided by its structure, substance and terminology.

Fundamental Principles

The GATS defines the market driven model as the international norm for regulation and delivery of services. This was already part of the neo-liberal policy agenda that many countries had begun to implement since the late 1970s. But it was highly sensitive. The most common form of foreign provision of services was through foreign direct investment. There was strong opposition to international rules that provided guaranteed access by foreign firms to newly created services markets. A different organising idea was required.

'Trade' in services

The solution was to adapt the idea of 'trade in goods' to services as the basis for a binding international agreement. The accepted notion of international trade and the existence of the GATT gave the artificial construct of 'trade in services' some intrinsic legitimacy. Services 'exports' would be defined in terms of the national origin of the service provider and services 'imports' as the national origin of the consumer. These identities, and issues that arise from their relations, could be submerged in the technical jargon of trade.

In their account of the formative work in the OECD during the 1970s and early 1980s, Drake and Nicolaidis claim that an ideologically-driven group of intellectuals and trade officials set out to achieve a sea change in thinking about services, from a social, cultural and public good to a tradeable commodity.[5] They acknowledged the threat to erode democracy, cultural identity and social wellbeing, but saw this as acceptable and inevitable. The description of this fluid group as an 'epistemic community' of like-minded technocrats driven by rationality is itself an

[5] Drake, W and K Nicolaidis, 'Ideas, Interests and Institutionalization: 'Trade in Services' and the Uruguay Round', 1992 *International Organizations*, 46 (1), p 37.

important illustration of the ideology. Viewed from a Gramscian perspective, they were the organic intellectuals of capital constructing a new hegemony; critics of the GATS have since been engaged in a counter-hegemonic strategy to displace that organising idea by one where services are regulated to promote progressive social relations.

'Rules based' trade in services

Within this trade paradigm, the core principle of 'rules based' trade sets the parameters for the scope, function and content of the Agreement. This draws on the pre-existing notion of 'rules based' trade in goods under the GATT, and implies an equivalence between services and industrial and agricultural goods that forecloses a debate about their relative social roles. A generic set of rules that potentially covers all services also denies the substantive difference in the nature, function and social relations of particular services, such as education, health, transport, postal delivery, ports and construction.

Drawing on the GATT automatically justifies the choice of rules that are premised on liberalisation. Potential objections are pre-empted by pre-ambular objectives that appear to balance a diversity interests. The Preamble begins by promoting 'principles and rules . . . with a view to the expansion of such trade' and 'early achievement of progressively higher levels of liberalization'. It then provides two pieces of defensive rhetoric. The first is aims to disarm and reassure defenders of state sovereignty:

> *Recognizing* the right of Members to regulate, and to introduce new regulations, on the supply of services within their territories in order to meet national policy objectives and, given asymmetries existing with respect to the degree of development of services regulations in different countries, the particular need of developing countries to exercise this right;

The second deflects concerns about an imbalance of power between North and South in the global marketplace:

> *Desiring to* facilitate the increasing participation of developing countries in trade in services and the expansion of their service exports including, inter alia, through the strengthening of their domestic services capacity and its efficiency and competitiveness;

> *Taking* particular account of the serious difficulty of the least developed countries in view of their special economic situation and their development, trade and financial needs;

These objectives are essentially hortatory, unless they are reiterated in the GATS text itself. That rarely occurs. Article IV Increasing Participation of Developing Countries repeats the commitment to enhance the capacity, effectiveness and competitiveness of 'developing countries' and 'least developed countries' services exports, but it creates no enforceable rights, merely expectations on 'developed' countries to schedule their commitments with beneficent intentions.

Progressive Liberalisation

By contrast Part IV is headed 'Progressive Liberalisation'. Within that, Article XIX requires regular negotiations

> with a view to achieving a progressively higher level of liberalisation. Such negotiations shall be directed to the reduction or elimination of the adverse effects on trade in services of measures as a means of providing effective market access.

Article XIX also repeats the preambular language of 'promoting the interests of all participants on a mutually advantageous basis and to securing an overall balance of rights and obligations' and that 'the process of liberalisation shall take place with due respect for national policy objectives and the level of development of individual Members, both overall and in individual sectors.' But national policy objectives have already been framed by the context of progressive liberalisation. Articles XX and XXI reinforce this. New negotiations to extend country specific schedules were required to begin by 2000 and periodically thereafter. Amendments to existing commitments are deterred by the obligation, where an objection is raised, to provide compensatory liberalisation of services to an equivalent value of the loss such an amendment causes.

Non-discrimination

The GATS also imports the primary GATT rule of non-discrimination through the Most Favoured Nation Article II and National Treatment Article XVII. The concept is implicitly imbued with the virtuous human rights discourse of equality and equity. In the GATS context it formally guarantees equally liberal access for services suppliers to compete within the services 'markets' of the WTO's member countries. According to the theory of comparative advantage those suppliers who are more efficient will succeed, which in turn encourages the rationalisation of scarce resources into activities that produce the best returns.

Contextualised, MFN and national treatment intrinsically advantage transnational enterprises whose scale, technology, research and development capacity, access to capital, marketing and brand recognition, and patronage of major powers enables them to dominate less endowed competitors from poorer countries and small local services firms. It was precisely these concerns that underpinned the initial opposition from

Southern countries to the idea of the GATS. The need to protect their interests is partly reflected in the reservations to MFN, provided in Annex II. However there was only one opportunity to lodge these, back in 1994, and they were a matter for the 'importing' country to decide, not the beneficiary. Lack of foresight can have unintended consequences, as emerged from the European Union's failure to enter an MFN exemption for distribution of bananas from the Afro-Caribbean and Pacific countries. These exemptions are 'in principle' due to expire in 2005, but in practice are likely to remain.

Governments can defend their domestic service capacity by not listing them in country-specific schedules or making their commitments conditional. But that only applies to rules in Part III of the agreement relating to market access, national treatment and additional commitments; it provides no protection from rules on MFN, domestic regulation, monopolies and restrictive business practices. Moreover, the difficulties of exit make it extremely difficult to restore those defences once they are signed away in a country's schedule.

In summary, the fundamental principles of the GATS concede no possibility of market failure and offer limited opportunities to avoid the core principles of non-discrimination where their application may be politically or ethically unacceptable. They leave no space for the possibility of any alternative paradigm. Commenting on similar processes in the context of rights, Valerie Kerruish observes: 'This quality, in the legal norm, gives it a capacity to replace fact with fiction, to close the door on further inquiry and so to be that which we cannot go beyond in our legal understanding.'[6]

CONCRETE LEGAL NORMS

The operational layer of the Agreement, where the technicalities are found, reveals the ideology of the GATS at its most potent. This is the target of much of the current critique and has forced defenders of the GATS into highly contested debates about the meaning and implications of specific provisions.

Modes of Supply

The definition of 'trade in services' under Article 1.2 sets the technical boundaries of the Agreement and the operative elements of trade in services. It effectively shifts the focus from previous discourses where services were largely perceived as being experienced by people and

---

[6] Kerruish, V *Jurisprudence as Ideology* (London, Routledge 1991), p 124.

communities to the production of services by the transnational firm, its management and skilled workers. 'Trade' in services is fragmented into four modes of delivery, taking the discourse into an abstract realm that is stripped of any social or political dimension.

While the first two of these modes ('cross-border supply' and 'consumption abroad') refer to the service itself, the remaining two ('establishing a commercial presence' and 'temporary presence of services personnel') refer to the 'supplier'. This confers a privileged status on producers that has no parallel for industrial or agricultural producers in the GATT. The disembodied and neutral term disguises the overwhelming dominance of major transnational enterprises in these transactions.

Defining these activities as 'trade' excludes other ways of perceiving them that may raise more objections. The clearest example is Mode 3, which is essentially the right of foreign direct investment. This remains the predominant way in which foreign services firms operate. Its impact on services, from retail and railways to education and water, is highly controversial. Continued resistance to binding international rules that liberalise FDI and guarantee rights to foreign investors saw the failure of moves in the OECD to secure a Multilateral Agreement on Investment and of attempts to revive such a measure through the WTO. By defining FDI as a mode of trading, some such rules have been achieved in relation to the services sector through the GATS Mode 3.

Mode 4 is about preferential treatment under immigration laws. While the Annex on Movement of Natural Persons asserts that countries retain their right to make their own immigration laws, these cannot nullify or impair their scheduled commitments. As a concession to Southern governments, the Annex also affirms that commitments can apply to all natural persons supplying services.

Notionally, all governments can choose whether to schedule services in either of these modes. Most Northern governments want commitments in Mode 3 to benefit their transnational enterprises and want to limit the influx of lower skilled workers in hotels, catering, cleaning or call centres under Mode 4. Many Southern governments are dependent on FDI but are reluctant to make binding commitments under Mode 3; but they want access for their workers to secure remittances and develop skills under Mode 4. In practice, however, these negotiations do not take place on a level playing field. Pressures on Southern countries to open Mode 3 seem much more likely to be effective than their corresponding demands that richer countries liberalise even temporary lower skilled immigration under Mode 4.

Modes 1 'cross border supply' and 2 'consumption abroad' disguise further controversies, such as the provision of tele-medicine and internet education, and medical tourism for purposes of cosmetic surgery or unconventional treatment in foreign clinics.

Legitimate exceptions

The scope of the definition of 'trade inservices' is limited through four provisions that appear to offer more protection than they do. The first is the temporary exclusion of government procurement under Article XIII. This appears to protect the highly sensitive role of central and local government support for local firms and workers, local economies and communities. However this exclusion is only partial. In the opaque commercial terminology that pervades the Agreement, services must be 'purchased for governmental purposes' and 'not with a view to commercial resale or with a view to use in the supply of services for commercial sale'. Whether user charges for education or rubbish dumps are a commercial resale is very unclear. The exclusion also applies only to the MFN, market access and national treatment rules, and not to those on domestic regulation or monopolies. Further, mandatory negotiations to bring procurement under the GATS were to begin by 1997, although they are moving quite slowly.

The second provision appears to exclude 'public services' from the Agreement, and is frequently cited as such by defenders of the GATS. But the term 'public services' is never used; such an idea has no conceptual place in the Agreement. Its meaning is also fuzzy. Many services that were previously provided to communities by centralised and publicly owned agencies have been commercialised, contracted out or privatised. If public services are narrowly defined to exclude such activities, the scope of the protection is very limited. If public services are seen as services that have a public good dimension they are much more extensive, and would include services such as banking, transport and ports. This ambiguity has been a feature of exchanges between critics and advocates of the GATS, and suggests that 'public services' is not a useful term. Recently, for example, the ICFTU has preferred the phrase 'Public services and other services of general interest'.[7]

Article 1.3 (b) talks instead of 'services supplied in the exercise of governmental authority'. This is defined in 1.3(c) as 'any service which is supplied neither on a commercial basis, nor in competition with one or more service suppliers'. Again, the criteria are the purchasing agent and the market nature of the activity, not its social function. And again, it is limited to exclusively non-commercial activities where there is no private competitor. In the present highly liberalised and deregulated environment, very few 'public services' as traditionally defined come within that narrow window.

The only remaining generic exclusion that might accommodate social purposes is Article XIV on General Exceptions. The chapeau ensures there

---

[7] Trade Union Statement on the Agenda for the 5th Ministerial Conference of the World Trade Organisation (Cancun, 10–14 September 2003).

is no escape from the primacy of the liberalisation objective by requiring that such 'measures are not applied in a manner which would constitute a means of arbitrary or unjustifiable discrimination between countries where like conditions prevail, or a disguised restriction on trade in services'. This mirrors language of the GATT, again dispensing with any need for justification. Likewise specific grounds for exemption are required to meet a 'necessity' test, judged by a panel of trade experts at the WTO.

Significantly, however, the substance of the Article diverges from the comparable provision in the GATT in ways that limit its scope to protect societal interests. It retains the exceptions 'to protect public morals or to maintain public order;' and 'to protect human, animal or plant life or health'. But it omits the right to adopt measures that are '(e) products of prison labour', '(f) imposed for the protection of national treasures of artistic, historic or archaeological value' and '(g) relating to the conservation of exhaustible natural resources if such measures are made effective in conjunction with restrictions on domestic production or consumption'. One explanation might be that the 'bottom up' nature of commitments provides adequate protection, but that would logically mean no exceptions.

The potential for emergency safeguards in Article X to protect the supply of services is again framed within the norm of global services markets. It is not clear whether the trigger would be a crisis in the availability of services or the survival of local services firms, some of whom would be foreign investors under Mode 3. The focus on the product and producer means that neither would address crises in the social function of services. Whatever, the three-year mandatory deadline for concluding negotiations on safeguard provisions has passed, with major powers rejecting the need for any such provisions at all.

Product Classifications of Services

The most symbolic ideological device is the categorisation of services under the United Nations Central Product Classifications (CPCs). The term 'product' classification, identified by numbers, is emblematic in itself. Division of all services into eleven categories, with over a hundred and fifty subsectors and further sub-classifications with detailed descriptions of the activities they cover, reflect the perspective of the producer and deny any social context. Midwifery is a business services, broadcasting and postal delivery are communications services, rubbish dumps and sanitation are environmental services.

Services are not only abstracted, they are also fragmented. A unitary and integrated service as experienced by a family or community spans a number of sub-sectors. The core activities of a university, for example, fall under 92310 Post-secondary technical and vocational education services, 92390 Other higher education services, 92400 Adult education services, 9641 Sporting services, 8510 Research and experimental development services on natural sciences and engineering, 8520 Research and experimental services on social sciences and humanities, 8530 Interdisciplinary research and experimental development services, Libraries and Archives.

A social phenomenon such as culture is reconstituted under the categories of: Business: publishing and printing, translating; Audio-visual: projecting, production, broadcasting; Cultural services: entertainment, libraries, archives, museums.

Even when a government has split a previously integrated service into numerous activities, each of those activities may not coincide with a corresponding CPC sub-category. This is taken one step further in the case of Public Private Partnerships (PPPs) and Private Finance Initiatives (PFIs), where services are disaggregated in accordance with the operational imperatives of the contracted firms and reaggregated under a principal contractor. Those activities will span a wide range of CPCs.

A foundation hospital, for example, could involve contractors whose activities are split between: *Business services*: medicine, midwifery, dentistry, nurses, physiotherapists, paramedicals, placement and supply of personnel, data processing, data bases, management consulting, placement and supply of personnel, security services, research and development on natural sciences, technical testing and analysis, scientific and technical consulting, rental services related to machinery and equipment, building cleaning, translation; *Communications*: paging services; *Construction related services*: new and refurbished building; *Environmental services*: sanitation, refuse collection and disposal; *Tourism related services*: catering; *Health-related and social services*: inpatient-services that comprise medical and paramedical services, nursing services, laboratory and technical services including radiological and anaesthesiological services, ambulance services, social workers, outpatients services; *Financial services*: health insurance, lending, asset management. The existence of overlaps reflects the changing nature of previously integrated descriptors such as 'hospital services'. A charter school would cover many of the same CPCs, plus libraries, and possibly translating, printing and publishing.

A further variation arises where services firms develop transnational operations in one aspect of their activity, which then takes on a generic form. For example, the activities of a postal services firm that develops a consultancy arm that specialises in restructuring and privatisation of postal services internationally, and moves from there to secure contracts to privatise utilities such as ports or electricity systems, will be covered by Business services: consulting rather than Communications services: postal.

This categorical fragmentation has important practical consequences. Commitments made at one time can have unforeseen consequences when the nature of the service being provided or the identity of the provider is changed. Such commitments confer long term rights on a foreign contractor involved in one socially disengaged aspect of a service. Even if this occurs in relatively few aspects, protection of those suppliers' rights could make it extremely difficult to reintegrate services when the disaggregated approach fails or it is seen as desirable to adopt a more socially centred approach to basic services.

This analysis also illustrates how, under the GATS, services have become fetishised, a process that distorts reality by assimilating many diverse features of social life within a unified ideological category. Diverse dimensions are reduced to the simple form of the production and sale of commodities, where everything only exists to be bought and sold.[8] As Kerruish explains, this becomes the only meaning that can be discussed: 'Fetishism is the substitution of one thing for another, together with a loss or lack of awareness, a forgetting, that the substitution has taken place'.[9] The existence of other meanings, and its own limitations, cannot be acknowledged. Liberating services from GATS fetishism is essential to any meaningful debate that recognises diverse standpoints—indigenous, Southern, feminist, socialist—that reflect different social realities as well as different experiences of the practical activities that are involved.

Market access

The most technical and abstract rules come under Part III Specific Commitments. Article XVI Market Access provides the most explicit expression of services markets, devoid of any social dimension. Four of the six measures it prohibits employ the disembodied terms of 'numerical quotas', 'monopolies', 'exclusive service suppliers' or 'the requirements of an economic needs test'. Because the objective is to open markets, it is presumed that governments should not require firms to show an economic need for them to be established or limit the number of firms who supply a particular service, the amount of the service they supply to local people, how many workers they can employ, their total asset value, whether they should be required to operate through legal forms such as joint ventures and whether there should be limits on foreign shareholdings.

These rules are generic. This ignores the substantive nature of the service and overrides the different considerations that would normally apply to the primary education system, social science and humanities research, tourism, television or electricity supply. They also extend beyond measures targeted at foreign firms to cover any measure that is designed to shape or limit competition in any of these ways. There is no suggestion that governments may have good cause to pursue such measures, even if a predecessor has previously committed not to do so. While governments have the initial right not to schedule a particular service or to list limitations on the extent of access, that is subject to the obligation of progressive liberalisation. Where previous

---

[8] see Collins, H *Marxism and Law* (Oxford, Oxford University Press 1982) p 96.
[9] Kerruish, V *Jurisprudence as Ideology* (London, Routledge 1991), p 166.

governments have scheduled such commitments, their successors find their hands tied unless they offer compensatory liberalisation elsewhere.

Disciplines on Domestic Regulation

In the long term the most far-reaching device in the GATS toolkit may be Article VI on Domestic Regulation within Part II General Obligations and Disciplines. Whereas the Preamble recognises 'the right of Members to regulate, and to introduce new regulations, on the supply of services within their territories in order to meet national policy objectives', this Article potentially negates that right.

Its current scope requires regulations related to licensing and qualification requirements and technical standards to be 'based on objective and transparent criteria, such as competence and the ability to supply the service; and be not more burdensome than necessary to ensure the quality of the service'. Currently this applies only to scheduled services, although a schedule cannot limit the application of Article VI. Contextualised, this could constrain the right of governments to determine appropriate domestic regulations on nursing or teaching qualifications, licensing people or firms to run taxis, casinos, rubbish tips, or to work as a veterinarian, or standards for water purity or construction.

However, Article VI.4 heralds much more significant constraints on domestic regulation. The Council on Trade in Services is required to develop any 'necessary' disciplines 'with a view to ensuring that measures relating to qualification requirements and procedures, technical standards and licensing requirements do not constitute unnecessary barriers to trade in services'. Governments who believe this intrudes on their promised regulatory autonomy have been reduced to arguing that no such disciplines are 'necessary'.

Initially, the process of developing these discipline began on a sectoral basis, although the placement of Article VI and its wording suggest that they are intended to apply across the board and not simply to scheduled services. The Working Party on Professional Services examined licensing requirements, qualification requirements and procedures and technical standards for the accountancy profession, covering accounting, auditing and bookkeeping. This was presumably selected as an uncontroversial commercial activity whose international professional body, backed by the major transnational accountancy/consultancy firms, supported a light-handed global regime.

The Accountancy Disciplines were signed off in December 1998.[10] They require governments to ensure that licensing requirements and procedures, technical standards and qualification requirements and procedures

---

[10] WTO Accountancy Disciplines: http://www.wto.org/english/news_e/pres98_e/pr118_e.htm, accessed 1 November 2003.

are not prepared, adopted or applied with a view to or with the effect of creating unnecessary barriers to trade in accountancy services. Governments must also ensure that measures are not more trade restrictive than necessary to achieve a legitimate objective. Such objectives are described as 'inter alia, the protection of consumers, the quality of the service, professional competence, and the integrity of the profession'. The disciplines do not become operative until current GATS negotiations conclude, but governments are required to apply a standstill that maintains at least current levels of regulatory liberalisation.

Since 1998, the scandals affecting the major accountancy/auditing/consulting firms have shown how deeply embedded even these activities are in social contexts, including pensions, employment, corruption and the stability of the banking system. It is not clear that measures to address such contexts would satisfy the limited market-centred genre of legitimate objectives, and numerous other pro-liberalisation hurdles remain. Was there a less trade restrictive way to achieve those objectives? Might the measures have the unintended effect of creating unnecessary barriers to trade? What would a WTO panel of trade experts consider to be 'necessary' and 'unnecessary'?

That Working Party was succeeded by a broader Working Party on Domestic Regulation mandated to develop generally applicable disciplines. Similar standards could therefore be applied to services like health, education or environment. Proposals tabled by some countries, notably Australia, suggest the current negotiations should go beyond licensing and standards to cover all regulations. In line with the Accountancy Disciplines they should adopt strong necessity, legitimate objectives and least trade restrictive tests. Governments should also be required to notify foreign services firms in advance of any regulations that might adversely affect them. Were this accepted, regulation of every service in every community would need to minimise the interference with the international market and the interests of foreign investors.

Subsidies

The ambiguities affecting subsidies reflect deep underlying sensitivities. 'Non-commercial' objectives such as access to essential services, community cohesion, cultural diversity, regional development or employment have traditionally been supported by subsidies. Subsidies come from taxpayers, directly as government revenue or through servicing public debt, almost always backed by an element of redistribution. They represent a collective investment in people, communities and institutions for the present and the future, although in the neo-liberal era they are increasingly 'transparent' and spread across public and private 'providers'. Even then, payment of subsidies to foreign firms, especially outside the country, is controversial. But the GATS model of competitive global services markets cannot accommodate the denial of public subsidies to foreign firms on the basis that they are qualitatively different from locally embedded services providers.

Application of national treatment (non-discrimination) obligations to subsidies is not addressed in the GATS text. However the negotiating guidelines in 1993 and 2001 make it clear the rule on non-discrimination 'applies to subsidies in the same way that it applies to all other measures ... any subsidy which is a discriminatory measure within the meaning of Article XVII would have to be either scheduled as a limitation on national treatment or brought into conformity with that Article.' A number of country schedules contain such reservations. This makes it difficult for governments to argue that national treatment commitments do not include subsidies, although some governments (such as New Zealand's) cite the opaqueness of the agreement in response to challenges about the implications of commitments in areas like education.

The negotiating guidelines also say 'There is no obligation in the GATS which requires a Member to take measures outside its jurisdiction. It therefore follows that the national treatment obligation in Article XVII does not require a Member to extend such treatment to a service supplier located in the territory of another Member.' But this is only a guideline to negotiators; it is not stated in the Agreement itself, nor in any formal interpretation by the WTO Council for Trade in Services.

There is an Article XV that is explicitly headed 'Subsidies'. But it talks only of developing disciplines on subsidies that have 'distortive effects on trade'. What this involves is not spelt out, although the agricultural equivalent suggests this may mean disciplines on any subsidies that distort the competitive operation of a services market. The text does 'recognize the role of subsidies in relation to the development programmes of developing countries' with a cryptic reference to taking into account 'the needs of Members, particularly developing country Members, for flexibility in this area'. The social ramifications of limiting or possibly prohibiting such subsidies are potentially huge but, of necessity, go unremarked in the Agreement.

Country-specific schedules

The ultimate representation of the desocialised, depoliticised and decontextualised nature of services is the country specific schedule. The complex architecture of separate market access, national treatment and additional commitments in each of four modes of supply across eleven sectors and over 100 subsectors of product classification, supplemented by horizontal commitments and limitations, and a separate schedule for MFN exceptions, is comprehensible only to the initiated. It is not easy to identify the implications of commitments for services 'exporters', even though the terms are intended to reflect their operations. It is extraordinarily difficult to assess the 'import' implications of these constraints for domestic policy decisions. It is incomprehensible to those who perceive services primarily in terms of social relations. Even attempts to preserve social objectives, such as the rights of indigenous peoples, have to be appropriately worded and located within the matrix. Some rules, notably Article VI, cannot be opted out from at all.

Disputes

The WTO's institutional framework limits formal participation to states. In one way, the lack of formal standing and investor-state initiated enforcement, and the economy-wide nature of sanctions, is sub-optimal for individual firms. But it does allow governments to act as proxies for those firms and partisans in the general interest of capital, while appearing simply to enforce international rules. The private nature of the disputes process maintains commercial confidentiality and excludes parties who may raise extraneous issues, such as the social dimensions of the services in issue. Even if those parties gained standing, such arguments would be technically irrelevant as there is no place for them within the rules that the panel of trade experts is tasked to enforce.

CONCLUSION

The GATS presents an image of impenetrable barriers. Its status as an international treaty gives it legitimacy and force. Its form as international law elevates it out of the politico-economic mire in which it was negotiated and transforms it into a normative instrument based on general principles and rules. Those norms establish the market paradigm which the principles and rules develop into singular objectives. Technical definitions, classifications and schedules draw these together in a legal text that purports to provide an operative framework for a liberalised global services market.

Their problem is that the ideology does not describe the social and political reality in which those services are delivered. This contradiction produced an original text which is partial in its coverage, incomplete in its drafting and often opaque in its wording. As awareness of the GATS increases, and international challenges to its paradigm and its implications grow, the prospects for completing that project seem increasingly remote. Attempts to enforce even the existing rules are likely to provoke further antagonism and expose the social realities that rest behind the ideology.

So long as the defenders of the GATS continue to retreat within the terms of the text as a means of deflecting criticism, they will invite further critical scrutiny and blunt their own sword. As this deconstruction has shown, once the norms, principles and technical terms are invested with context the interests of capital and the super-power politics are clearly exposed. The effectiveness of opposition to the GATS therefore rests in large part on the ability to penetrate its ideology and insist that the debate addresses the political economy that lies barely hidden beneath the surface.

8

The Legal Protection of Biotechnological Material: Concord in Discord

MARGARET LLEWELYN

INTRODUCTION

ONE OF THE most controversial aspects of the WTO agenda has been its policy regarding intellectual property rights (IPRs).[1] The Agreement on Trade Related Aspects of Intellectual Property Rights (TRIPs), which was adopted in 1992, seeks to ensure minimum standards of protection in all member states. The objective has been to achieve a degree of harmonisation through the removal of any distortions or impediments which could serve as a barrier to international trade. However, the move to harmonise provision has not met with universal approval. Grave concerns have been voiced over the use of private property rights to protect material involving genetic information (bio-IPRs) and the ability of WTO member states to restrict the availability, and use, of these rights at the national level.[2] At the heart of these concerns lies the view that the TRIPs Agreement compels harmonisation up to the developed country level of protection (the minimum standard being predominantly based on existing provision within developed countries, most notably the United States, Europe and Japan), which operates on the basis of inclusion not exclusion with minimal effect being given to any public interest exclusions or limitations. This attempt to achieve global consensus and coherence appears largely to have failed and whilst the mandate

---

[1] For a more detailed discussion of the background to intellectual property rights within the WTO see Gervais *TRIPs Agreement* 2nd edn, (Sweet and Maxwell, 2003) and *Intellectual Property: Trade, Competition and Sustainable Development* ed Cottier & Mavroidis, *World Trade Forum Series*, (The University of Michigan Press, 2003). This chapter reflects the legal position in 2004.

[2] It is relevant to also note that the focus on the controversy surrounding the patenting of biological material does not mean that the other forms of intellectual property right are without contention. It is not the purpose of this paper to discuss these.

to provide protection remains, the reaction to that mandate has been to further entrench diversity of provision.

OPPOSITION BASED ON ECONOMIC DIFFERENCES?

Before looking at the attempt to harmonise global bio-IPR provision a preliminary point needs to be made. It would be easy to fall into the trap of categorising the debate as one between developed and developing countries[3]—with countries falling into the former group supporting the extension of rights and countries in the latter automatically against. Whilst it is accurate to state that most of the initiatives to extend rights over genetic material have come from within the so-called industrialised nations, it is would be overly simplistic to state that there is uniform agreement within these countries that patent protection should be available over genetic information. An example of this can be seen within the European Union (EU).[4] In 1998 the EU adopted a directive on the Legal Protection of Biotechnological Inventions[5] which requires all member states[6] to provide patent protection for inventions involving genetic material with minimal exclusions from protection. Member states had until 31st July 2000 to implement the provisions of the directive. Almost immediately the Dutch government launched a challenge to its validity on the grounds that it had been invalidly introduced and that it violated certain fundamental principles

---

[3] These are not externally imposed definitions in the sense that, whilst the WTO provisions refer to certain categories of countries (developed, developing and least developed etc), member states of the WTO can decide how to categorise themselves.

[4] It should be noted that for patent law purposes 'Europe' can have two meanings. The first relates to the European Union, and to individual member states of the European Union (EU). The second to the European Patent Convention (EPC) Community. At present the EPC is not an instrument of the EU and as such stands outside the EU. The European Patent Convention is not an instrument of the European Union (EU). It was set up under the auspices of the Council of Europe and is a totally autonomous entity. However there is a loose synergy between the EPC and the EU as all 15 member states of the EU are members of the EPC and the European Patent Office (EPO) has adopted recent EU legislation on the legal protection of biotechnological inventions for the purposes of supplementary interpretation. There is therefore increasing comparability between the law of the EU and that of the EPCC. However, the European Patent Convention community comprises non-EU member states, for example Switzerland. In total the European Patent Convention Community (EPCC) consists of 20 member states with a further 6 countries regarded as extension states likely to join the EPCC in due course.

In order to differentiate between the two meanings this paper will refer to the EU and to the European Patent Convention Community (EPCC).

[5] Council Directive EC4498.

[6] There are currently 15 EU member states, Austria, Belgium, Denmark, Finland, France, Germany, Greece, Ireland, Italy, Luxembourg, the Netherlands, Portugal, Spain, Sweden, United Kingdom.

[7] Action brought on 19 October 1998 by Kingdom of the Netherlands against European Parliament and Council of the European Union (Case C–377/98) OJ C378/13.

[8] http://europa.eu.int/jurisp/cgi-bin/form.pl?lang=en

[9] Denmark, Finland, Ireland, Portugal, Spain, Sweden and the United Kingdom.

such as human dignity.[7] The challenge provided ultimately unsuccessful, and the European Court of Justice rejected the Dutch challenge in 2001.[8] The ECJ decision notwithstanding however, as of February 2004 only seven of the current 15 member states have implemented the directive.[9] Progress on implementation has been delayed in other EU member states due to public consultation exercises and/or discussions with governmental ethics committees. In the case of France and Germany, implementation has been prevented because of concerns that the directive violates certain bioethical and environmental principles and in particular that the directive, which permits the patenting of inventions involving human genetic material, contravened the principles set down in both the UNESCO Declaration on the Human Genome and Human Rights and the Council of Europe's *Convention on Human Rights and Biomedicine* which specify that financial gain should not be made out of the human body or its parts. The EU experience is not an isolated one. Other, non-EU, jurisdictions have also continued to deny patent protection for biotechnological inventions[10] and even where such rights have been granted the use by patent holders of these rights has been severely criticised.[11]

It would be equally incorrect to state that developing countries without exception reject extending patent protection in this way. For those wishing to foster their industrial base, and particularly those which to engage in technology transfer, the move to a more Western notion of intellectual property protection is regarded as being in the national economic interest. Action has been taken therefore to comply with the obligation set down by TRIPs, although in many instances, compliance has not necessarily accorded with the practice of developed countries but has been based on a determination of intellectual property protection suitable for national economic and social needs.[12]

THE TRIPS AGREEMENT

The underlying principle of the TRIPs Agreement is that private property rights are essential in order to support international trade and that any

---

[10] see *Harvard College v Canada (Commissioner of Patents)* 2002 SCC 76.discussed below at

[11] Rimmer Myriad Genetics: Patent Law and Gene Testing [2003] 1 *European Intellectual Property Review* 20.

[12] See for example, the discussions surrounding the amendment of the Chinese Patent Law in 1992 and the legislation adopted by the Andean Pact countries, comprising Bolivia, Columbia, Ecuador, Peru and Venezuela, which in 1996 collectively enacted their *Common System on Access to Genetic Resources*. In respect of plant variety protection the legislative activities of countries such as Thailand and India are interesting, both have introduced legislation using traditional and non-traditional notions of what can and should be protected. For a fuller discussion of this see Correa *Intellectual Property Rights, the WTO and Developing Countries* (London, Zed Books, 2000) and Dutfield *Intellectual Property Rights and the Life Science Industries* (Aldershot, Ashgate, 2003).

[13] Preamble to the Agreement.

differences in provision could form a barrier to that trade and need to be eliminated.[13] The Agreement applies to a range of intellectual property rights (including copyright and trademarks) and contains within its purview enforcement as well as acquisition. Part One of the Agreement sets down some general principles relating to the nature and scope of the right (including the concept of national treatment and equivalence of treatment for non-nationals). For the purposes of this discussion the most relevant sections within Part One are Articles 1, 7 and 8. These permits member states to provide more extensive protection than that set out in the Agreement, 'provided that such protection does not contravene the provisions of the Agreement' (Article 1); that the grant of such rights will be to the advantage of the producers of technological innovation but that they must be 'in a manner conducive to social and economic welfare' (Article 7); and that member states may adopt any necessary measure to protect 'public health and nutrition and to promote the public interest in sectors of vital importance to their socio-economic and technological development, provided that such measures are consistent with the provisions of this Agreement'. The relevance of these provision for the present discussion lies in the extent to which member states may rely on these to mitigate the strength of the rights granted under Part II, V, Patents. These will be discussed further below.

Reading between the lines of the Agreement, and certainly based on responses to non-traditional approaches to complying with its provisions, the expectation was that all member states, irrespective of political or economic background, would bring their national laws into line with those who provide the strongest form of protection.[14] Put bluntly, the TRIPs Agreement could be viewed in terms of both carrot and stick. The carrot, encouraging the introduction of strong rights, being the argument that those with the strongest form of intellectual property rights provision were also economically the strongest—strong intellectual property rights equal economic growth and power. The stick was that unless such rights were available, key innovators from countries with strong rights would not transfer their technology for use in countries where the rights available were not equally strong.

For many member states the fact of the TRIPs Agreement means that they have had (or are trying) to attain a balance between three equally important factors. The first is the provision of rights compliant with the TRIPs obligation—in this the pressure to provide strong rights could, generally speaking, be said to come from the private sector. The second is the provision of appropriate protection which is in the interests of the local community—in industrial terms this often means looking to the public as opposed to private, sector needs. The third and final element is the need to encourage investment and technology transfer at both the national and international levels.

[14] *Supra* Cottier & Mavroidis above n 1.

However, whilst the hope might have been that an equivalence of protection would result the reality was that the Agreement could not enforce this. When these factors are looked at collectively it is easier sometimes to view TRIPs more as a *Dis*agreement on Trade Related Aspects of Intellectual property Rights.

Another reason why the TRIPs Agreement has failed to provide greater conformity and consensus lies in the nature of intellectual property rights.

Traditionally intellectual property rights developed as a result of internal national needs rather than external international pressures. In respect of patent law, the function of the right has been to facilitate the production of inventions at the national level thereby adding to the economic value of that country. Any international agreements, such as the Paris Convention on Industrial Property 1883, were not intended therefore to take away from member states the ability to direct the provision of patent protection other than by putting in place a general framework, predominantly procedural relating to reciprocity, within which the practice of national provision was expected to operate. Even at the European patent organisation, which gives the impression of being a cohesive unity comprising member states of the European Patent Convention (EPC) disparities remain. The effect of a grant under the EPC is to provide a bundle of national patent rights. Once granted, the patent is treated in the same way as a *national* patent in those countries designated by the patent applicant within the application. As a result the patent will be enforced, or litigated, as a national patent, in the national courts of the country concerned. In order to ensure parity of protection the national patent laws of member states equate with the provisions of the EPC but they only do so in the sense of agreeing that for a grant to be made the invention concerned must be novel, involve an inventive step, be sufficiently disclosed and not fall within any of the categories of excluded material. Because the adoption of the European Patent Convention did not remove the right to grant patents at the national level, and because local courts will not necessarily reach identical conclusions on the validity of grants made, decisions of the European Patent Office (EPO) are not binding at the national level. The result is that there are often differences between decisions of the EPO and those at the national level as well as at the national level between different member states.

Because it would have been politically too difficult to prescribe unity of provision, the Agreement was not intended to set up a world-wide system of intellectual property protection. Instead it had to recognise the territorial nature[15] of intellectual property rights with the result that it has to accept the need to maintain appropriate local differences. As a result the Agreement is drafted in very general terms and it is the generality of

[15] These rights being enforceable only in those countries where they are acquired.

the language, together with the fact of local differences, which creates the discord rather than the intended concord.

A particular touchstone for a discussion of the attempts to achieve convergence of protection is the issue of the patentability of inventions involving genetic material. The relevant Articles of the TRIPs Agreement lie within Part Two, section V.

TRIPS PART TWO, SECTION V—PATENTS

Article 27(1) mandates that patent protection *must* be provided for all types of inventions irrespective of the field of technology. The only exceptions to this requirement are contained in paragraphs 2 and 3 which permit the *optional* exclusions of inventions the commercial exploitation of which would be contrary to morality (Article 27(2)), methods of treatments/diagnosis of humans and animals (Article 27(3)(a)), and plants and animals (Article 27(3)(b) first sentence, first half). Patent protection, however, must be provided for micro-organisms and non-biological or microbiological processes (Article 27(3)(a)), and plants and animals (Article 27(3)(b) first sentence, second half), and member states must provide protection for plant varieties using patents and/or an effective *sui generis* system (Article 27(3)(b) second sentence). Exceptions to the right granted are provided that these do not 'unreasonably conflict with a normal exploitation of the patent' (Article 30) or where it is deemed to be in the national interest to do so (Article 31). As will be discussed below, each of these provisions gives rise to uncertainty as to scope. The right granted permits the holder to prevent third parties from making, using, offering for sale or selling the protected product or process or product produced using the patented process (Article 28) and lasts for up to twenty years from filing (Article 33).

This paper will focus on Articles 27, 30 and 31.

Article 27

Article 27 sets down the general principle that patents must be provided for any invention (product or process) from *all* fields of technology. The commonly held view in patent circles is that an invention is patentable unless it does not meet the threshold for protection or it falls within any specified categories of excluded material.[16] In respect of the threshold for protection, Article 27(1) merely states that the invention must be shown to be novel, involve an inventive step (non-obviousness) and be capable of industrial

---

[16] See for example, Grubb *Patents for Chemicals, Pharmaceuticals and Biotechnology* (Oxford, Oxford University Press, 1999.)

application (or have utility). These criteria are not defined leaving it up to member states to invoke their own internal notions of what is novel etc.

Notions of 'Invention'

The absence of a definition of 'invention', beyond that which is novel, inventive, and capable of industrial application, underlines the emphasis on inclusion not exclusion and indicates a presumption of patentability. An example of this presumption of patentability can be seen in the US Patent Offices Guidelines to Examiners which stipulate that:

> An applicant *is* entitled to a patent to the subject matter claimed *unless* the statutory requirements are not met ....When the USPTO denies a patent, the Office *must* set forth at least a *prima facie* case as to why an applicant has not met the statutory requirements (emphasis added).

This assumption of protectability is given further emphasis when determining whether the threshold for protection has been met. In respect of utility, often the most contentious of the granting criteria in respect of bio-science applications, the USPTO states that 'A patent examiner *must accept a utility asserted by an applicant* unless the Office has evidence or sound scientific reasoning to rebut the assertion' (emphasis added).

The American view of protectability is especially important as the US patent system a) has granted the most patents over bio-inventions and b) contains few limitations on the rights granted and virtually no exclusions from protection. It is for this reason that the subsequent paragraphs in Article 27 are couched in optional rather than mandatory terms. For those countries, such as those within the European Patent Organisation, which do maintain categories of excluded material, the overarching presumption of patentability means that any exclusions or limitations are to be given a restrictive application.[17] The premise is clearly inclusion not exclusion and for this reason, the concept of invention increasingly is not defined.

The TRIPs Agreement simply distinguishes between inventions which are patentable (those which are novel, involve an inventive step, are capable of industrial application and sufficiently disclosed) and those which, notwithstanding that they might meet the granting criteria, may not be patentable for, what could be collectively called, reasons of public interest. Member states do not necessarily draw such an apparently straightforward distinction. In Europe, the EPC also draws a distinction between patentable and non-patentable inventions (the categories of excluded material roughly corresponding to those in Article 27(2) and

---

[17] For an example under the EPC see *Novartis/Transgenic plant (G01/98)* [2000] European Patent Office Reports 303.

(3)—the differences will be discussed below). But in addition it specifies material which will not be regarded as inventions for the purposes of patent law (Article 52 EPC). Most of these correspond to material protectable under copyright, but it also specifically excludes discoveries from protection. To demonstrate the lack of consensus even at this apparently fundamental level, a few general points will be made about the notion of invention and also about the application of the granting criteria. These are, however, merely exemplars of the divergences which exist in practice.

Article 27 makes no mention of the exclusion of discoveries from patent protection—the only criteria for determining protectability are the requirements that the invention be novel, inventive and capable of industrial application. These terms are not defined within the TRIPs Agreement, it is left up to national granting offices to determine an appropriate standard for their national purposes. It is important to note that the definitions which are given within national patent laws are *legal* definitions. For the purposes of patent law, a discovery is latent information for which a use has yet to be found. Once a use is found, then provided that use is novel and inventive, the discovered material, as utilised in that novel and inventive manner, may be patentable.[18]

Whilst few would probably argue that a process for producing a new drug involving genetic material should be patentable (and possibly that the new drug itself should be patentable) many would question whether the isolated genetic material itself should be covered by the patent.[19] It is at this point that the issue of legal language becomes critical as it could be argued that the moment at which a discovery becomes a patentable invention occurs when it is described as an invention in the patent specification.

In the United States it is clearly stated that it is possible to patent a discovery, provided the granting criteria are met. The basis for this approach is usually given as Article 1, section 8 of the US Constitution which states that

> [t]he Congress shall have the power...[t]o promote the Progress of Science and useful Arts, by securing for limited Times to Authors and Inventors the exclusive Right to their respective Writings and Discoveries.

35 USC 101 then clarifies this principle by stating that whoever invents or discovers a new and useful composition of matter, process or a new and

---

[18] Concerns over the application of the granting criteria to bio-inventions lead the USPTO in 2001 (US Patent Office Guidelines for Utility. Federal Register/Vol 66 No 4/Friday January 5 2001, 1093), and the UK Patent Office in 2002 (Examination Guidelines for Patent Applications Relating to Biotechnological Inventions in the UK Patent Office, www.patent.gov.uk) to issue new guidelines for examination. Whilst these address some of the concerns raised they still underline the inherent patentability of bio-inventions. In addition these guidelines only have effect within the specific jurisdictions and do not affect the granting practices of other offices, such as the EPO.

[19] For a discussion of this point see the Nuffield Council on Bioethics' discussion paper on *The Ethics of Patenting DNA* Nuffield Council, 2002.

useful improvement to an existing product or process should be able to apply for a patent. In theory, therefore discoveries are patentable under US patent law. However, the fact that the applicant must also demonstrate that the discovery is new and useful together with the requirement that the discovery would not have been obvious to another working in that area means that mere discovery may not be enough to guarantee a patent grant. That said it is widely recognised that is it easier to get patent protection for inventions involving biological material in the US simply because the level of intervention needed by the inventor appears less than under other jurisdictions.[20]

In other countries, including those making up the European Patent Organisation and China, discoveries are explicitly excluded from protection, but these laws invariably ensure that as soon as a novel use for a discovery has been found then it may be patentable. The concept of a 'discovery', therefore, is that of untouched, or unworked, information. Once that material is worked then, provided the working meets the granting criteria, the material in the worked form may be patentable.

In terms of the protectability of inventions (or discoveries) involving living material, up until 1980 the US operated a product of nature exclusion. This meant that many inventions involving genetic material were excluded from protection because their existence or 'manufacture' was not held not to be due to an act of construction by man. In 1980 this changed with the decision in *Chakrabarty*[21] in which the US Supreme Court held that 'anything under the sun manufactured by man' was patentable. The measure for protection was no longer whether nature would, or could, have produced the material, but whether the applicant could show that they had played the principle role in producing that particular manufactured material. This view as to what is meant by the term 'manufacture' can be contrasted with that of the Canadian Supreme Court which in 2002 held that the equivalent provision in the Canadian Patent Act did not apply to a genetically engineered mouse because 'a higher life form is not ... a 'manufacture' or composition of matter' within the meaning of 'invention'.[22]

---

[20] For a discussion of the differences in granting practices see Gitter International Conflicts over Patenting Human DNA Sequences in the United States and the European Union: An Argument for Compulsory Licensing and a Fair Use Exemption *New York University Law Review* December 2001 [Vol 76, 1623], *Guardian Supplement* Who Owns the Genome *The Guardian* November 2000, Llewelyn Industrial Applicability/Utility and Genetic Engineering: Current Practices in Europe and the United States [1994] 11 *European Intellectual Property Review*, 473.

OECD Papers from the Expert Workshop on Genetic Inventions, IPRs and licensing Practices, Berlin 24–25 January 2002 at www.oecd.org, Sulston & Ferry The Common Thread: A Story of Science, Politics, Ethics and the Human Genome (Bantam Press, 2002) Thomas, Hopkins and Brady Shares in the Human Genome—the Future of Patenting DNA *Nature Biotechnology* December 2002, Vol 20, 1185, Andrews Genes and Patent Policy: Rethinking Intellectual Property Rights *Nature* October 2002 Vol 3, 803 and Dutfield *above* n 12.

[21] *Diamond v Chakrabarty* 1980, 206 USPQ 193.

[22] *Harvard College v Canada (Commissioner of Patents* 2002 SCC 76.

In the post *Chakrabarty* era, unsurprisingly, the patent had been granted in the US and, more controversially, by the EPO, but the Canadian Supreme Court was not swayed by either of these two factors. Instead it focused on the meaning of invention within its own law. It said that the Act had to be read in its grammatical and ordinary sense. The term 'manufacture' in section 2 of the Patent Act did not apply to 'anything new and useful made by man' but rather to non-living mechanistic products or processes. To permit the patenting of higher life forms would 'involve a radical departure' from traditional patent law, and the Supreme Court was unconvinced that this was an appropriate departure for it to make.

Clearly in the eyes of the Canadian Supreme Court the obligation under TRIPs to provide patent protection for all inventions irrespective of the field of technology did not apply in this instance as the requirement was to provide patent protection for non-mechanistic products or processes. This obviously was not the view taken either in the US or in Europe although this in itself was not without debate. Whilst in the US the practice of the USPTO has gone largely unchallenged (at least within the US), the decision to include animate material within the definition of a patentable invention in Europe has been more problematic. Notwithstanding the fact that the EPO quickly determined to grant patents over bio-inventions it took legislative action by the European Commission to push this through at the national level. As already mentioned above, the fact of this activity at the EU level has not meant that there has been universal agreement that such 'inventions' are patentable and implementation at the national level has been slow. Problems over the implementation of the EU biotech patenting directive aside, in contrast with the Canadian position the Directive does make it clear that inventions involving biological material are patentable (Article 1) and, once adopted, this principle will be firmly enshrined within all EU national patent laws.

Another example of differences in interpretation can be seen when looking at move to protect material which could be regarded as traditional knowledge or traditional medicines. For many the issue here is not whether such material is an invention, but is rather a question of the proper application of the granting criteria, and in particular the application of the novelty criterion.

Traditional Knowledge

The first thing to note is that there is no agreed definition of what constitutes traditional knowledge (or indeed traditional medicine, the protection of which is another topic of intense debate within intellectual property circles). In 1999 the World Intellectual Property Organisation[23] (WIPO) stated

[23] Report on Fact-Finding Missions on Intellectual Property and Traditional Knowledge (1998–1999) WIPO

that for its purposes it would use a very general definition which would take its start from the collective descriptions used in Article 8j of the Convention on Biological Diversity (CBD). The WIPO definition of traditional knowledge is, therefore, any knowledge, innovations, creations and practices of indigenous and local communities which can be in the field of agriculture, science, technology, ecology, medicine, and includes expressions of folklore (although some regard this term as inappropriate as it implies knowledge set in the past and this belies its ongoing dynamic significance), names, geographical indications, symbols and movable cultural property.

The lack of a definition is important, for whilst it is unclear what can be regarded as the common heritage of any given community those interested in making use of the knowledge, and in particular those who wish to seek private property rights over it, remain relatively free to do so.[24] The question then becomes one of whether such knowledge is capable of attracting protection. In particular, the question is whether the application of the knowledge which the patent refers to is novel and inventive. In respect of the former this is usually a question of whether traditional knowledge is taken to form part of the state of the art.

Generally speaking the state of the art is that information taken to exist at the time the patent application is filed. Anything already known at date of filing is held to be prior art and the applied for invention comprises prior art then it is unlikely to be held to be novel. The issue here is what is meant by the prior art.

Most industrialised countries take account of any prior *use* of material when determining what is the state of the art. In the UK, for example, absolute novelty is required in order for a patent application to succeed. This means that if a plant has been used previously in India or China for a particular medical purpose, then it is unlikely that a company would be able to claim that its use of that plant for the same medical purpose.[25] However, not all industrialised countries operate on this basis, the most notable exception being the US. The US patent system operated a two tiered novelty criterion based on two different notions of when information has been made public. The first tier requires that the information must not have been made known through publication *within* the US— publication in this sense is taken to mean made public through use as well

[24] See in particular Dutfield *Intellectual Property Rights, Trade and Biodiversity* (London, Earthscan 2000 and Correa *above* n 12 also Shiva *Biopiracy* (Green Books, 1998) and Shiva *Protect or Plunder* (Zed Books 2001).

[25] This is not to imply that it is impossible to get patent rights over material which could be regarded as indigenous or traditional. Of great concern to some is the fact that EU biotech patenting directive exlicitly states that patent protection may be sought over 'biological material which is isolated from its natural environment' and that biological material is not exempt from protection 'even if it previously existed in nature' (Article 3(2). The EPO has attracted considerable criticism for patents it has granted such as that over a Neem tree extract amongst others.

as via the printed page. The second tier relates to knowledge of the material *outside* the US. Here the requirement that the information must not have been published only relates to *documented* use. This allows for the possibility of undocumented traditional knowledge to patented by the US patent office.[26] From the perspective of those countries seeking to prevent the propertisation of traditional knowledge the options available are to not provide protection (but this leaves open the possibility of another country providing protection within its jurisdiction),[27] to protect using the existing system of protection (which would have the effect of safeguarding that material from protection in other jurisdictions, the existence of a patent in another country being the most common arbiter of whether material is novel or not, with the country concerned able to choose whether provide protection with or without the optional exclusions) or to protect using a new form of intellectual property right.

The divergence in practice regarding what is an 'invention' for the purposes of Article 27(1) is clear. There is no common ground as to whether 'invention' means a traditional mechanical devise (or process) or if it extends to life forms. There is equally no agreement as to what is the threshold for protection. The same lack of convergence can be seen in respect of the optional exclusions. For reasons of space it is proposed to focus on the exclusion within Article 27(3)(b).

Article 27(3)(b)

Article 27(3)(b) comprises of three elements, the first relates to an apparently broad potential application of the exclusion, with the two successive elements, however, serving to undermine the actual extent to which a member state can exclude genetic material from protection. The Article permits a member state to exclude from patent protection plants, animals and essentially biological processes. However, member states must *not* exclude from patent protection micro-organisms nor non-biological or micro-biological processes. In addition, whilst a member state may exclude plants from patent protection they are required to provide protection for plant varieties. There are a number of questions which this optional exclusion raises each of which again give rise to the potential for ambiguity and divergence in practice.

---

[26] Eg, in 1995, the USPTO granted a patent on the use of turmeric in wound healing despite turmeric having been used for this purpose for generations in India. The patent was revoked not after it had been shown that turmeric had previously been used as a medicine, but only after it had been shown that there was documentary evidence, in both a Sanskrit text and in 1953 article, that turmeric had been used as a medicine.

[27] Contrary to popular myth the existence of a property right in one country does not give the patent holder any right to prevent use in another country. Therefore a US patent granted over rice would not prevent that a farmer in India from growing that rice in India. If the patent was also granted in Indian then there could be infringement.

The first question is to what extent is it possible to differentiate between a plant, an animal and a micro-organism.

The second is what is the difference between an essentially biological process, a non-biological process and a microbiological process.[28]

The third question is what form of protection must a member state provide over plant varieties?

This paper will address the first and third questions.

As will be seen, potentially there are a myriad of different ways in which these questions could be answered—the issue is which, if any, would be regarded as satisfying the TRIPs obligation?

i) Plants, Animals, Micro-organisms.[29]

The language used in Article 27(3)(b) implies that a clear distinction can be drawn between plants and animals on the one hand and micro-organisms on the other. It also implies that there is a common globally accepted definition of the term 'micro-organism'. In fact there is no globally agreed definition of a micro-organism at either the legal or scientific level.

Within scientific communities the term is variously held to include bacteria and cyanobacteria, archaeabacteria, algae, protozoa, slime moulds, fungi (which includes mushrooms), bacteriophages, plasmids and viruses. In many respects it can be seen that the term has become increasingly generic making it difficult to ascribe to it any precise definition.[30] Of particular relevance is the fact that there is increasingly an overlap between the plant, animal and micro-organism kingdoms. This means that at the scientific level it is increasingly difficult to denote clear blue water distinctions between plants, animals and micro-organisms. This blurring of any distinction which might previously have been held to exist, becomes even more apparent when looking at how the concept of a micro-organism is defined in patent law.

Most importantly patent law does not utilise a definitive definition of a micro-organism. The reason being that to do so would close the

---

[28] In Europe and the US the determining factor appears to be the extent of human intervention involved. Art 2(2) of the EU biotech patenting directive states that an essentially biological process is one which consists *entirely* of natural phenomena—the clear implication being that where there is a degree (unspecified) of non-natural phenomena (human intervention) then the process is patentable.

[29] For a more detailed examination of this issue see Adcock & Llewelyn Micro-organisms, Definitions and Options Under TRIPs [2000/2001] 3 *Bioscience Law Review* 91.

[30] For example see *Biology of Micro-organisms*. Hawker, Linton, Folkes and Carlile. (Edward Arnold, London, 1977); *Introduction to Microbiology*. Heritage, Evans and Killington. (Cambridge, Cambridge University Press 1997); *Micro-organisms; function, Form and Environment*. Hawler and Linton. (Edward Arnold, London, 1981); *Biology of Micro-organisms*. Madigan , Martinko and Parker. (Prentise Hall Publishers, 2000); The Giardia Genome Project Database. McArthur *et al* FEMS Microbial Letters. (2000).

opportunities for providing patent protection and as the EPO pointed out in 1988 as part of a Comparative Study undertaken by the World Intellectual Property Organisation 'it does not seem expedient to introduce such a definition as the rapid evolution in the field of microbiology would necessitate its frequent updating'. The emphasis being on the need to provide patent protection and include as much as possible within the ambit of protectable subject matter.

In the absence of any definition of a micro-organism, or clear demarcation between micro-organisms and plants and animals, the only criteria which are relevant for determining protectable are those generally govern the grant of a patent. Provided, therefore, that the micro-organism can be shown to be novel, inventive and capable of industrial application it is patentable. The only material which is excluded is that which falls within the specified categories of excluded material. A country wishing to invoke the exclusion would have to show that the micro-organism is a plant or animal in order for the presumption of protection not to apply.[31]

Grubb[32] states that '[m]ost patent laws do not deal specifically with the question of whether or not a new living strain of micro-organism is itself patentable [and]... the [UK] Patents Act 1977 and the EPC do not exclude such a possibility.' He goes on to state that '[i]t must be remembered that the term 'micro-organism' is interpreted broadly so as to include not only bacteria and fungi but also viruses and animal and plant cells'. This approach corresponds to the practice of granting offices in the USA, Europe and Japan where patents have been granted over plant and animal cells.

The issue which this practice raises is whether a plant or animal cell can be regarded as a plant or animal and therefore if a country not wishing to provide extensive protection of all forms of bio-inventions could exclude such things from protection or whether the mandate in Article 27(3)(b) will prohibit them from so doing. It is also worth noting that the optional exclusion only relates to plants and animals and not to humans. Under existing European law the human body and its simple elements (which means gene sequences for which no use has yet been found) are not regarded as inventions.[33] Processes for cloning human beings are excluded from protection on the basis that these would be contrary to morality.

---

[31] It is perhaps worth stating that not all developing countries have no tradition of protecting pharmaceuticals or indeed an antithesis to providing protection in a post-WTO environment.

[32] *Patents for Chemical, Pharmaceutical and Biotechnology* (Oxford, Oxford University Press 1999) at pp 226 and 227. Grubb is a European Patent Attorney and Intellectual Property Counsel for Novartis International AG in Switzerland.

[33] This is set down in both Article 5 of the EU Biotech patenting Directive and also in Rule 23e of the Implementing Rules of the EPC. For an example of this in operation see the 'Edinburgh University' patent (Patent No 0695351 22/02/2000) as revised in 2002.

The question remains, precisely what can a country wishing to make use of the optional exclusion exclude from protection? Ostensibly they are not bound by the patent practices of other jurisdictions, but it is not clear if these practices will be regarded by the WTO as the benchmark for protection meaning that all member states are expected to provide protection of the kind described by Grubb? The availability of a common definition is particularly critical for those member states which have not previously permitted patent protection for *any* form of biological material, including micro-organisms.

The rationale behind the requirement to provide patent protection for micro-organisms is that these form the basis for most innovative work within the pharmaceutical industry. The absence of protection for these vital components of modern medicaments would mean that not only that expensive to produce pharmaceuticals could be cheaply copied in markets which the pharmaceutical industry would otherwise wish to exploit, but also the cheap copies would make their way back to those jurisdictions where strong patent protection already exists. The effect would be to undermine their market position and possibly lead to a black market in cheap copies.

The counter argument is that allowing patent protection to extend to micro-organisms, broadly defined, will prevent nations from developing their own pharmaceutical industry and they will become increasingly reliant on the external provision of vitally important drugs. Additionally, the expansive definition, to include plant and animal cells, could hamper a local ability to undertake plant and animal genetic research. In an era where it is possible to develop a whole animal (or plant) from a single cell) the implications of the current patent law definition become acute. If member states are obliged to introduce this expansive definition then it could result in a severe restricting of the local animal and plant breeding industries with an increased reliance on externally sourced, but locally protected, material.

In order for the optional exclusion to have meaning it is vital that member states of TRIPs are able to draw distinctions in their national patent laws between that which is a micro-organism (and patentable) and that which is not (excludable). In its report, published in 2002, the UK's Commission on Intellectual Property Rights[34] recommended that member states should be able to introduce their own definitions, but it is not yet clear if this would be acceptable to the WTO.

The Protection of Plant Varieties

The second sentence of Article 27(3)(b) requires member states to provide protection for plant varieties using patent protection and/or an effective

---

[34] www.cipr.org.uk.

sui generis system of protection. Unlike any other provision with section V this is specifically stated to be subject to a review five years after the coming into force of the Agreement.

To return to the issue raised at the beginning of this paper, relating to general distinctions in provision, it is worth mentioning that most developed countries offer a form of plant variety protection using either patent law or a specific form of protection under the auspices of the International Convention for the Protection of New Plant Varieties (UPOV). For the so called 'developed' countries , Article 27 is merely a restatement of existing intellectual property practice. The decision to provide protection, and the form of that protection, has been the result of extensive and exhaustive debate. Within Europe one only has to look at the deliberations which took place during the 1950s on how to protect the results of plant breeding activity[35] and at those which have taken place more recently in respect of the EU Directive on the Legal Protection of Biotechnological Inventions[36] to see the range and scope of arguments.

In contrast, the so-called 'developing' countries have generally had no history of protecting plant material. Prior to joining the WTO they have not had the equivalent opportunity to decide, not only how, but more fundamentally *whether*, to protect plant varieties. As a result of joining the WTO these countries are faced with an immediate obligation to provide protection, the only issue for debate being *how* they should be protected. The issue of whether or not to provide protection is no longer an option for discussion.

The decision for member states is whether they provide protection under patent law, or by the introduction of a specific form of protection (the *sui generis* right) or by a combination of the two rights. What is not clear from the wording of Article 27(3)(b) is what constitutes an *effective sui generis* right. It would seem that member states are not bound by any existing substantive requirements as they would be if they were to provide patent protection. There is no express requirement that the *sui generis* right has to contain specific granting criteria unlike Article 27(1) which mandates that patent protection is granted over inventions which are novel, inventive and industrially applicable. This means that when formulating the right it is possible for member states to seek guidance and/or inspiration from other international agreements including those

---

[35] See Laclaviere The Convention of Paris of December 2, 1961, for the Protection of New Varieties of Plants and the International Union for the Protection of New Varieties of Plants (1965) October, *Industrial Property* 224; Laclaviere A New Intellectual Property Union is Born: The International Union for the Protection of New Plant Varieties (1969) 8 *Industrial Property* 154; UPOV History, Development and Main Provisions of the UPOV Convention (1987) 7/8 *Industrial Property* 320; Greengrass UPOV and the Protection of Plant Breeders—Past Developments, Future Perspectives (1989) IIC 622; Greengrass The 1991 Act of the UPOV Convention [1991] 12 *European Intellectual Property Review* 467.

[36] See for example Llewelyn *The Legal Protection of Biotechnological Inventions: An Alternative Approach* [1997] 3 *European Intellectual Property Review* 115.

not wholly concerned with intellectual property protection. There is scope and flexibility for both imaginative interpretation and application of the requirement. The only proviso is that it must be 'effective'. Once again the opportunity for divergence rather than convergence becomes apparent.

Since the TRIPs Agreement was adopted there have been a number of suggestions as possible *sui generis* right.[37] They include: a right specifically designed to protect plant varieties which takes into account the specific needs of breeders and other end users (this could be said to equate to a UPOV type right—discussed below); the introduction of new forms of intellectual property rights such as a Farmers' Right[38] and a Traditional Resource Rights (TRR) each of which recognises, and protects, the contributions made by the local community; and other mechanisms to avoid biopiracy through, for example, certificate of origin systems, (this latter group would require the patent applicant to i) to present a sworn statement which details the genetic resources, traditional knowledge used and those communities which have been involved in obtaining the information contained in the patent application; and ii) provide evidence of prior informed consent from the peoples concerned to the patent application being filed. Without both these elements the application should fail);[39] and an innovation register or low level patent system. This would take the form of a global database designed to prevent data being misappropriated.[40]

It might be asked why, given the existence of the UPOV Convention, which has provided a form of *sui generis* protection for plant varieties since the 1960s, there is a need, or indeed ability, to look elsewhere. The reason is that the UPOV system, in its various guises, is seen another developed country undertaking which further reinforces the provision of private property rights over genetic material. Since it was first introduced in 1961 the UPOV Convention has been substantively revised twice. Both the 1978 and 1991 UPOV Acts have been sharply criticised—the 1978 Act on the basis that it does not provide sufficiently strong protection for the plant breeders and the 1991 Act on the grounds that it places an unacceptable burden on farmers and breeders.[41]

---

[37] For a more detailed discussion of these see Dutfield n 12.

[38] For a discussion of the Indian legislation see Adcock *Farmers Right or Privilege* [2001/2002] 3 Bioscience Law Review 90.

[39] These options have been exercised by, for example Costa Rica *Ley de Biodiversidad 1998* and the Andean Pact countries which comprise Bolivia, Columbia, Ecuador, Peru and Venezuela. In 1996 they collectively enacted their *Common System on Access to Genetic Resources*.

[40] For a critical analysis of this proposition see Gupta *Suggested Ethical Guidelines for Assessing and Exploring Biodiversity* at wgtrr.ocees@mansfield.ox.ac.uk; For an excellent discussion and analysis of all these issues see Dutfield *Intellectual Property Rights Trade and Biodiversity: the case of seeds and plant varieties* London, International Union for Conservation of Nature and Natural Resources, 2000.

[41] These criticisms have lead to differences even within the European Union—six are members of UPOV 91, 5 of UPOV 78, 2 remain members of UPOV 61 and two are not members of any of the Acts.

In respect of the 1978 Act the criticisms came mostly from the developed world and these was based on the fact that the right only extended to commercial uses of the protected material, that there was a dual protection prohibition (which prohibited the provision of both patents and plant variety rights over the same variety), that not all varieties had to be protected and farmers were permitted to use protected material for subsequent regrowing without payment to the breeder. The 1991 Act, which strengthened the right by removing the dual protection prohibition, requiring protection for all varieties and providing opportunities for member states to restrict limitations to the right, came in for criticism on the grounds that it had shifted too far in the opposite direction and now provided too much protection. In particular, developing countries were concerned that the 1991 Act could be used to restrict the use of protected material by farmers and breeders. Both Acts faced opposition from developing countries on the grounds that they reinforce the view that plant material should be the subject of a private monopoly right and they could help industrialised countries dominate the markets of developing countries thereby taking the concomitant benefit. UPOV responded to these concerns by leaving the 1978 Act open for ratification until 1995.

A key concern voiced was that plant variety protection could lead to a loss of biodiversity. Both patents and plant variety rights are dependent on the plant material protected remaining, to a greater or lesser degree, stable and uniform in order for a right to be granted and to perpetuate. This emphasis on genetic uniformity could encourage a loss of diversity and this again is a key area of concern which could be mitigated by taking a non-traditional approach to plant protection. In addition to these concerns there was also the fact that neither patents nor UPOV type plant variety rights provide for a benefit sharing mechanism which is regarded by many developing countries as a pivotal provision in the CBD. Both the CBD and the International Treaty on Plant Genetic Resources (ITPGR) are commonly held to as setting out international obligations relating to genetic resources which developing countries wish to reflect in the intellectual property provision. In formulating non-traditional protection a common justification given is that the accepted norms of protection, patents and plant variety rights according to UPOV, do not enable a country to meet other commitments relating to genetic resources undertaken through membership of the CBD. In order to meet these commitments it is, therefore, necessary to introduce concepts recognised under the CBD into intellectual property provision.

Because of these concerns, and the fact that the form of the *sui generis* right is not specified in Article 27(3)(b) (there is no mention of the UPOV Convention anywhere in the TRIPs Agreement) has provided Member States, opposed to the current norms of plant intellectual property, with a golden opportunity to develop protection which meets their own local needs. All that they have to demonstrate is that the right is *effective*. The only constraint to this development being that, whilst patent protection or a UPOV right are, presumably, recognised as an 'effective' right and therefore compliant with Article 27(3(b), a new untested right could prove more vulnerable to challenge.

The political sensitivity of the protection of plant varieties has an interesting effect on the interpretation of the form that the stated review should take. The review was due to take place by the end of 1997. The general expectation in developed countries was that it would take the form of seeing which countries had complied with Article 27(3)(b) and taking action against those which had not. Developing countries saw the review as taking the form of a review of the obligation, and lobbied vociferously to have the requirement to protect plant varieties (and microorganisms) removed and replaced with a general exclusion of all living material. The result was impasse. The outcome was that the WTO reconsidered the form of the review and stated that it would comprise an assessment of what had taken place at the national level. Where there was non-compliance (or non-traditional compliance) the WTO would simply assess the effect of this but it would be more inspection than judgement.

It is not only in respect of types of patentable subject matter where continuing divergence in provision can be seen. These also exist in respect of possible limitations to the rights once granted.

Research

The two key articles in TRIPs are Articles 28 and 30. Article 28 outlines the rights conferred and Article 30 provides for a limited restriction of those rights. The rights conferred by a patent conforming to TRIPs relate to the right to make, use, offer for sale, sell and import the patented product or process (where a patent has been granted over a process then the right also extends to any product obtained directly by that process). As can be seen the right is not confined to only commercial uses.

Article 30 allows a member state to 'provide limited exceptions to the exclusive rights conferred by a patent, provided that such exceptions do not unreasonably conflict with a normal exploitation of the patent and do not unreasonably prejudice the legitimate expectations of the patent holder taking account of the legitimate interests of third parties'.

The question which these two Articles raise is to what extent can a member state permit the use of a patented product or process in research without the patent holder claiming that an infringing act has taken place? The answer to this question differs considerably. In some countries a right to use patented material in research is enshrined in statute (eg the UK section 60 Patents Act 1977), whereas in other jurisdiction the right, such as it is, has developed through case law (eg Australia[42] and the US). Where the right to use does exist differences can be seen in the definition of 'research'.

In Europe there has been a tradition of permitting research use where that use is purely non-commercial, this typically has related to work carried out in universities and public institutions where there is no industrial backing. The current position is that two separate notions of non-infringing use are recognised. The first relates to use which is private and non-commercial. The second to experimental use. In respect of the latter, courts across Europe have been increasingly willing to treat experimental research as exempt even where the research has a commercial purpose.[43] On this basis, the experimental use exemption permits research which may modify or improve the patented invention[44] and in some jurisdictions (eg Germany)[45] this use has been held to include use of the patented material in order to provide further information about the properties of the invention, for instance through the use of a patented drug in clinical trials. However, in other jurisdictions, (eg the UK) questions remain as to the actual extent of use in clinical trials where that use is connected with the provision of a service.[46] The law remains uncertain on this matter. There are other important limits.

The exemption does not include research where the patented material is not itself the subject of the experimentation, nor does apply to research which merely replicates the invention, (the best example of the latter is where a company wishes to acquire permission to sell a generic equivalent of a drug which is about to come out of patent. The replication of the patented drug is generally held not to be experimental use).

Even where it is agreed that the use is a commercial one, which strictly speaking falls within the scope of the patent, implications remain.

---

[42] At the end of 2003 the Australian government began a consultation exercise into whether a research exemption should be introduced into patent law. The results of that exercise are expected by the end of 2004.

[43] For the UK, see *Monsanto v Stauffer* [1985] RPC 515. For recent confirmation of the new approach in France, *Wellcome Foundation v Parexel International & Flamel*, Tribunal de Grande Instance de Paris, 20th February 2001: *Intellectual Property News* Issue 17, July 2001.

[44] The exception must also cover experiments to discover whether the invention can be made from its description in the patent specification (essential if the patent is to be challenged).

[45] German Supreme Court, *Klinische Versuche I* [1997] Reports of Patent Cases 623. German Supreme Court, *Klinische Versuche II* [1998] Reports of Patent Cases 423. See similarly *Wellcome Foundation v Parexel International & Flamel*, Tribunal de Grande Instance de Paris, 20th February 2001: *Intellectual Property News* Issue 17, July 2001.

[46] This was one of the issues discussed in respect of the Myriad patent. Myriad Genetics holds a patent over the BRCA1 gene which codes for breast cancer. The patent, which is broadly drafted, covers all uses of the gene. Myriad has taken a robust line in seeking licensing agreements and regards the use of its testing kits, which make use of the BRCA1 gene, in clinical trials as a commercial activity. For a discussion of this see Cornish, Llewelyn & Adcock *Intellectual Property Rights (IPRs) and Genetics: A Study into the Impact and Management of Intellectual Property Rights within the Healthcare Sector:* UK Department of Health 2003.

UPOV specifically permits the use of protected plant varieties in commercial breeding programmes. The practice of free use of material for breeding purposes is therefore well established. With the increased use of patents to protect plant material[47] there is a real concern that the ability of plant breeders to produce new commercial crops will be constrained as patent holders seek licence fees in order to use valuable genetic material.

The lack of clarity over the research exemption is not confined to Europe. In the US, which does not have any statutory basis for a research use, the right is curtailed even further. In *Madey v Duke University*,[48] The Court of Appeals of the Federal Circuit held that the experimental use defence only exists in a 'very narrow and strictly limited' form. The only permitted acts are those which are 'solely for amusement, to satisfy idle curiosity, or for strictly philosophical inquiry ... the profit or non-profit status of the user is not determinative.' The defence, 'if available at all,' must be established by the alleged infringer and the accusing party need not establish as part of its initial claim that use was not experimental. In respect of other uses for research it is permitted, in certain limited instances, for companies to use patented material but only where it is for clearly experimental and non commercial purposes. The Drug Price Competition and Patent Term Restoration Act 1984 (the Hatch-Waxman Act) does permits use for pharmaceutical research purposes (primarily to produce a generic equivalent of a patented drug in order to enter the market upon expiration of the patent). This exemption does not apply to the use of any other type of protected material eg the production agricultural material.

One of the arguments for having a limited research exemption is that the interests of the patent holder are best served by ensuring that the use of patent material is undertaken in the context of a licensing agreement. The limited research exemption ensures licences are sought in all but the least commercially disadvantageous situations. In order to ensure that the patent holder agrees to enter into a licensing agreement, the patent system contains provisions which enable a licence seeking to secure a compulsory licence if it can be shown that the patent holder is unreasonably withholding access to the patented invention.

Compulsory Licensing

It is not proposed to discuss compulsory licensing between individuals in any detail in this paper, but rather to focus on the ability of

---

[47] In Europe it is now established that nearly all aspects of a plant can be protected—any material not taking the form of a plant variety protectable under plant variety rights is patentable, with plant varieties protectable under the *sui generis* right—*Novartis/Transgenic plant (G01/98)* [2000] European Patent Office Reports 303 and Article 4(2) of the EU Biotech Patenting Directive.

[48] *John MJ Madey v Duke University* 2002 No 01–1587, Fed. Cir.

government to secure access to patented material in the interests of public health.[49]

In brief, a number of conditions have to be met before a compulsory
licence can be sought and these are set down in Article 31 of TRIPs. The
first is that it is only possible to seek a compulsory licence *after* a patent
has been granted and decisions are taken on a merit basis. The second is
that a reasonable period must have elapsed before a compulsory licence
can be sought (this provides the patent holder with an opportunity to
exploit the potential for a market lead). This requirement may be waived
in the event of a national emergency. The third is that the applicant has to
show that an attempt has been made to secure a licence from the patent
holder and that the licence sought was on reasonable commercial terms.
Any licence granted will be non-exclusive, non-assignable and subject to
a reasonable royalty. As the Agreement is intended for enforcement at the
national level then the general practice of national offices determining
the grant of a compulsory licence will continue. Article 31 is probably
the most publicly contentious of all the TRIPs provisions and in particular its application where a member state wishes to make use of patented
medicines in order to meet a national emergency. The focus here is on the
relationship between this provision and the general principle set down in
Article 8 which permits member states to adopt measures necessary to
protect 'public health'.

Serving as catalyst for this attention was a well publicised court case in
South Africa which focused attention on the meanings of emergency and
public health. In summary the case, (which polarised governments in
developed and developing countries and within, developed countries,
industry and the general public) concerned a provision on the South
African Medicine and Related Substances Control Act 1999 which permitted the South African to import generic equivalent of drugs patented in
South Africa where the patent holder was abusing the position provided
by holding the patent rights. In the specific instance the Act was being
used to import anti-retroviral drugs for the treatment of HIV/AIDS.
Pharmaceutical companies (predominantly from the US and Europe)
brought legal proceedings on the grounds that the Act contravened
TRIPs. The argument presented was that there was no national emergency, this term only applying to events which were unforeseen (and this
is the argument which the US government was planning to use to support
its decision later in 2001 to grant a licence to a US generic drugs company
to manufacture CIPRO to address the possible anthrax outbreak following 9/11). The action was dropped in 2001 due to the intense international reaction, but whilst public support (and indeed governmental support

---

[49] It is worth noting that it is extremely rare for a compulsory licence to be granted, their
value is instead being thought to lie in serving as a threat bringing the patent holder to the
negotiating table.

in developing countries) was for the South African government, the governments of developed countries (most notably the US and UK) spoke out against the potential circumvention of the pharmaceutical companies patent rights. The sheer volume of concern over when national governments could make use of Article 31 forced the issue onto the agenda for a WTO meeting in Doha in November 2001[50]. The result of this meeting was the so-called 'Doha Statement'.

In brief the Doha Statement says that the TRIPS Agreement does not and should not prevent members from taking measures to protect public health. Accordingly, and that the Agreement can and should be interpreted and implemented in a manner supportive of WTO members' right to protect public health and, in particular, to promote access to medicines for all. The Statement reaffirms the right of WTO members to use, to the full, the provisions in the TRIPS Agreement, which provide flexibility for this purpose. It states that each member has the right to grant compulsory licences and the freedom to determine the grounds upon which such licences are granted. Member states also have the right to determine what constitutes a national emergency or other circumstances of extreme urgency, it being understood that public health crises, including those relating to HIV/AIDS, tuberculosis, malaria and other epidemics, can represent a national emergency or other circumstances of extreme urgency. However, many developing countries remained unconvinced that this meant that they would be able to determine for themselves the precise instances when Article 31 could be applied and the debate resumed in 2002.

In December 2002, the WTO failed to reach agreement on proposals to permit special and differential treatment for developing countries in respect of access to essential medicines. The proposal had been to permit member states each to determine which diseases and medicines should be subject to the special treatment. However, resistance from the USA led to agreement only in respect of tuberculosis, HIV/AIDS, malaria, and other types of infectious epidemics. No agreement was reached on the ability of developing countries without national capacity to produce medicines to grant compulsory licences for the importation of the requisite drugs from other countries. It is worth noting that subsequent to the December 2002 statement, the US has committed itself to making Aids drugs etc. more accessible to developing countries. This unilateral decision does not affect the status of either the Doha statement or the meaning/application of Article 31 TRIPs. However, it is clear from the language used in the Statement that it is primarily directed at developing countries and it is unclear as to the extent to which developed countries will be able to rely on Article 31 to provide healthcare in non-emergency situations. An

[50] For the full text of the Doha Statement see www.WTO.org.

example of how this could be relevant in a developed country context can be seen in respect of the Myriad patent.

As already noted, Myriad Genetics owns a patent over the BRCA1 gene. This gene is extremely useful in the identification of breast cancer and the patent has been the subject of an aggressive licensing campaign by Myriad Genetics in countries such as the UK, Canada and Australia. The question which has been asked in whether any of these countries could rely on Article 31 to seek either a compulsory licence or invoke government (or Crown) use which would permit a government to make use of patented material upon payment of reasonable compensation. The diversity of reactions to this question, as can be seen in the action taken by the Ontario,[51] Dutch[52] and UK Governments.[53]

It is clear that the focus of attention is on *developing* countries and on epidemics. It is unlikely, therefore, in the current political climate that developed countries will be able to rely on the Doha Agreement in order to justify government health policies in respect of non-population-endemic diseases. There may however be a shift in perceptions and sympathies at the national level which would make reliance on existing legal powers acceptable at the bar of public opinion.

CONCLUSION

The responses of the member states of WTO, to the obligation set down in TRIPs has been diverse and often non-conformist ranging from the adoption of full-blown patent protection (based on either the US or Europe models), with such protection often being complemented by a co-existing plant variety rights system based on the International Convention on the Legal Protection of New Plant Varieties (UPOV) to providing no protection at all (see for example the statements of the Organisation of African Unity). The most common response has been to minimise the use of the patent system, in so far as the TRIPs Agreement permits and to look to formulations of plant variety protection which may, or may, not follow the UPOV model.

Where the invention in question has taken the form of a pharmaceutical product (which TRIPs requires to be protected under patent law) then

---

[51] The Government of Ontario, Canada is currently taking action against Myriad's BRCA 1 and BRCA 2 patents on grounds including breadth of claim, reach through claims and access to healthcare. For a comprehensive discussion of the *Myriad* patent see Rimmer Myriad Genetics: Patent Law and Genetic Testing [2003] *European Intellectual Property Review* 20.

[52] The Dutch Government is lending support to the opposition to Myriad Genetics' BRCA 1 patent currently being led by the Dutch Association of Clinical Genetics. In respect of the BRCA 2 patent, the Dutch Government is itself the opponent. The Dutch Government is also considering an opposition to the grant of a third breast cancer patent to Myriad and is conducting a broad study of gene patenting.

[53] See Cornish *et al above* n 46.

member states have to looked to, what they believe to be, the overarching principles of public health and morality to justify a less rigorous approach to provision of protection. In respect of plant inventions the optional exclusion of plants from patent protection has generally been relied upon and the requirement to protect varieties via a *sui generis* system interpreted in ways which enable countries to develop locally appropriate protection—such new rights not necessarily mirroring UPOV. In some instances, most notably in respect of the countries which comprise the Organisation of African Unity, the decision has been taken not to provide any protection of any kind for living material. These responses have resulted in a number of developed countries, most specifically the United States, calling into question whether there is actual compliance with the TRIPs obligation as there is an apparent lack of parity between provision. There are moves to sanction non-compliance countries through the WTO. In return those members states of the WTO who have not adopted the model of protection available in the US (or Europe) are claiming that they are entitled to develop their own models of protection and that the language of the TRIPs Agreement is such that it enables them so to do. Instances such as the South African Aids case and the patenting of indigenous medicines and plant material by multi-national companies has lead to growing public sympathy for the position of developing nations. In turn governments are attempting to reflect this concern whilst at the same time refusing to accept any diminution of the strength of intellectual property rights because of their perceived economic importance.

The TRIPs Agreement, and the responses to it, provide a clear example of how attempts to establish a global framework of protection can rebound when the economic and political motives of those primarily responsible for determining the standards within the framework differ from those required to make significant legal changes in order to comply with that framework.

By way of anecdote, the following events (which took place in the UK at around the same time as the conference from which this series of papers emanated) indicate the complex and often contradictory factors which continue to dominate bio-IPRs.

In April 2003, Paula Radcliffe broke her own world record for the women's marathon in London. The week previously she has had an accident when she collided with a bicycle—she dislocated her jaw, and badly grazed her arms and legs. Many commentators cast doubt as to whether she would be able to race the following week. She did and the rest is now marathon history. Not surprisingly she was asked how she was able to race given the severity of her injuries incurred just the week before—her secret, emu oil. She had been told of this miracle cure by Kathy Freeman, her fellow track runner who knew of the oil through its use in her Aboriginal community and who herself relied upon the oil to speed up recovery from injury. There is immense interest in the emu oil and many pharmaceutical companies are vying to be able to produce a mass market version, its use by Paula Radcliffe will only serve to make this quest more determined.

The very next day, the final complete draft of the human genome was published coinciding not only with the 50th Anniversary of Crick and Watson's discovery of the structure of DNA but also with the publication of the Royal Society's long awaited report on the patenting of genetic material.[54] The Report expressed grave concern over the possible impact of the race to patent on research and on access to new products. At the same time the Patent Office published a practice note stating that human stem cells are patentable provided that they meet the usual grounds for patentability—there is no presumption in patent law that human stem cells should be treated any differently from other types of genetic material.[55] This notice was published just days after the European Parliament voted to ban stem cell research (although this decision was later reversed).

By coincidence or design, one does not know, that same week the British Broadcasting Corporation decided to have as its Book at Bedtime Huxley's Brave New World. The response to the TRIPs requirement clearly shows there is no singular new world resulting from genetics, but many worlds with diverse responses. Those who embrace or who seek a new way depends on where, and to what extent, these worlds should depart or converge.

---

[54] The Royal Society *Keeping science open: the effects of intellectual property policy on the conduct of science* 2003.
[55] www.patent.gov.uk

9

CARICOM and the Role of Regional Organisations in the Global Legal Order

RICHARD KIRKHAM

O VER THE LAST few decades the global legal order has changed beyond all recognition with the result, amongst other things, that the role and impact of the nation state in that legal order has been significantly altered. One of the many outcomes of this new situation is that observers of global politics have been forced to become more sophisticated in their analysis of the distribution of political power.

> In some instances, governments are simply impotent to press their preferred policies in the face of the new global order; in others they can only do so through extensive partnerships with a wide variety of other players, and in yet others they are tasked to trace the outline shape of developments and seek ways of influencing them, either directly or through membership of a considerable number of organisations, some competing, at least on individual issues.[1]

The task for the public lawyer is to chart these new institutions and networks of governance and work assiduously for the inclusion within them of appropriate constitutional values and safeguards. One such form of governance that looks set to become a permanent and powerful influence in the new global order is that of regional organisations. This piece looks in some detail at one particular attempt at regional integration, the Caribbean Community and Common Market (CARICOM), and assesses to what extent there are lessons to be learned from its developmental experience.

THE IMPORTANCE OF REGIONAL ORGANISATIONS

The range of regional organisations that now exist in the modern global order is both impressive and bewildering. There is by no means a single

---

[1] ND Lewis, *Law and Governance* (London, Cavendish, 2001), at 221.

format for regional organisations to follow, still less a uniformity of purpose. Some regional organisations exist to pursue an issue of joint concern to all the member states. For instance, the Arctic Council is an intergovernmental body within which all the arctic nations are members, together with six international organisations who represent the various indigenous peoples who live in the region. Such bodies may have little independent power, but they can establish a constructive forum within which members can discuss and elaborate upon potential solutions to shared problems. Other regional groups are more powerful in their own right and more often than not have been built up around the trade agenda—ASEAN, Mercosur and NAFTA to name but a few. One of the key features of these organisations is that they provide the basis for wider international negotiation and spin off into additional fora such as ASEM or ASEAN + 3. Meanwhile one group, the EU, has taken the project of regionalisation much further, by aspiring to integrate a significant range of governance functions and develop a shared social agenda. Moving into the twenty first century, there are signs that other groups are attempting to follow this lead.

Regardless of their exact format, regional organisations can be viewed as an intelligent response to the new and old challenges that confront societies and governments alike. They also represent a reassertion of influence and control on behalf of their members over the global market place. But it is noticeable that, in what is in effect a second wave of regionalisation,[2] this is not about turning the clock back and denying the process of globalisation.[3] What we are witnessing here are various players on the international stage restructuring the forms of governance which bind them, in order to improve their ability to face up to the challenge of globalisation.[4]

Towards the achievement of their goals, properly constructed schemes of regional integration have much potential although the hurdles that need to be overcome are many, as are the pitfalls. For instance, new layers of governance bring with them additional administrative costs and are susceptible to the vices of unaccountable governance. They can also result in delayed decision-making and may only succeed in raising the expectations of citizens, thus sowing the seeds for future disillusionment with governments. Indeed, it is a common concern with regional organisations that they are another example of power being taken away from the people and vested in systems of governance that provide indirect accountability at best. There is also the fear that they could predominantly operate

---

[2] Eg B Hettne, 'The New Regionalism: a Prologue' in B Hettne, A Inotai and O Sunkel (eds), *The New Regionalism and the Future of Security and Development* (Basingstoke, Macmillan, 2000), at xix.

[3] Eg P Mistry, 'Regional Integration and Economic Development' in B Hettne, A Inotai and O Sunkel (eds), *The New Regionalism and the Future of Security and Development* (Basingstoke, Macmillan, 2000).

[4] ND Lewis, 'Law and Globalization: An Opportunity for Europe' *European Public Law* [2002] 219, at 235.

so as to favour the richer nations at the expense of the less influential. Thus one of the most important tasks ahead for public lawyers is to prompt all regional organisations in the direction of good governance.

As for the makeup of regional organisations, from the point of view of theory it is difficult to offer too much by way of prescription. Ultimately, the location of government is contextually dependent on the circumstances and, more importantly still, should be seen as an exercise of the political right of its constituent members. Nevertheless, there are some common factors that can provide us with clues as to the long-term viability of regional organisations.

An essential prerequisite of any form of supranational organisation that aspires to govern effectively must be that the various countries involved possess a shared vision of its core terms of reference. More than this, for the organisation to be successful, there must be some genuine desire for shared governance amongst governments and citizens alike, and a willingness to work with the new arrangements. An absence of such willingness at either level will lead to weaker results and, as history has demonstrated, frequently the demise of the organisation.[5]

Of the practical circumstances that drive forward regionalisation, there are many. The economic advantages of regional integration are well known, but another common factor is the desire to pool diplomatic strength. Regional organisations raise the possibility of establishing a voice that can sit at the negotiation tables of the world and speak with an effective amount of power. There is also evidence to suggest that successful regional governance is more than just a self-interested exercise in commercial advantage.[6] On occasion, regional organisations possess a wider vision of governance that will respect the different stages of development of its members through the deliberate redistribution of funds, or by allowing for favourable economic conditions. On other occasions the motivation for collective governance may be more fundamental, such as the desire to achieve military security or to guarantee democracy.

Finally, there is another factor that needs to be taken into account when considering the potential for regional governance. That is, the countries involved must possess the practical capacity to carry the project through. Partly this is about popular acceptance of the regional scheme and the need for leadership skills, but it is also a question of physical capacity in terms of governance. Given the complexity of the project and the need for regional organisations to come to terms with the varying viewpoints of the member states involved, a strong tradition amongst member states in

---

[5] Eg FC Wheare, *Federal Government* (London, Oxford University Press, 1963). Wheare was writing about federal governance, but many of the questions that he asked are of equal relevance to regional organisations.

[6] Above n 3.

democracy, good governance and respect for the rule of law would appear to be highly advantageous if the regional scheme is to succeed.[7]

With these background ideas in mind, this piece will look at CARICOM as an example of one of the many organisations around the world that are currently seeking to find a way to tap into the lucrative benefits that can be achieved through regionalisation.

CARICOM: A MODEL FOR THE FUTURE?

As an object of study, CARICOM is informative to a debate on regionalism for two main reasons. First, it provides us with a revealing insight into the motivations that lie behind the regional integration of sovereign nations. This is all the more interesting in the case of CARICOM because the scale of ambition contained within the project reflects a deep-rooted belief in regional integration. CARICOM has three main objectives: to establish a common market and single economy; to pursue a coordinated foreign policy; and to pool scarce resources in a number of key areas of governance, such as health, education and the environment.

The second reason to take note of CARICOM is that the history of the organisation provides an example of the problems faced when it comes to implementing the objectives of regional integration. The truth is that for all the tradition and fine words that have come out of CARICOM, in terms of tangible results the organisation still has much to prove. A study of the CARICOM project is particularly opportune at this moment in time as its future success is very much on a knife-edge. There is a very real likelihood that in a few years time the group will represent just another footnote in the history of the Caribbean as it becomes swamped by the larger aspirations of the FTAA. However, it is also just possible that before the decade is out we could be referring to CARICOM as a model for future integration schemes.

The background

Founded in 1973, CARICOM is one of the oldest of all efforts at regional integration and has claims to be one of the most ambitious and advanced of its type ever attempted. Moreover, the group is made up of more member states than most efforts at regional integration, a factor which has caused it considerable political and constitutional difficulties. As compared to other regional schemes there are similarities and differences in equal measure. The most obvious difference is that CARICOM is probably the smallest of all such schemes, both in terms of economic and geographical size. Today

---

[7] Above n 3, at 33.

it is made up of fifteen member states[8] and five associated members,[9] most of which are small island nations with small populations. This means that on the global economic stage the impact of CARICOM is minimal, with the group being the home to only thirteen million people[10] and responsible for 0.27 per cent of global output. It is though an organisation that is heavily integrated into the world trading system with 42 per cent of its trade being undertaken with countries from outside the community.[11] This is an unusually large amount and makes the region peculiarly vulnerable to shocks within the global economy.[12] It is hardly surprising then, that the desire to protect the region against such vulnerability has become a recurring theme in the efforts to develop the integration agenda.

As with other such groups, in terms of geographical location and history the member states have a considerable degree of commonality. Not only do all the member states share a close affiliation with the Caribbean Sea, the impact of colonial history and a common culture provide the source of an obvious bond. But in other respects, such as size, wealth, economies and language spoken, the diversity within the group is impressive.

Despite this degree of diversity, a shared approach towards governance has long been a goal in the region. The first attempt was based upon the ten-nation West Indian Federation. It lasted only four years and dissolved in 1962, largely because of the contradictory desire for independence amongst some of its members.[13] Nevertheless, around this time concrete steps were made in the direction of establishing shared programmes of governance, steps which have set in train a process that has never gone away. For instance, the University of the West Indies was founded in 1948, the Regional Shipping Services in 1962, and the Caribbean Meteorological Service in 1963. These were all bodies which were designed to operate in areas which were, and still are, considered to be fundamental to the region as a whole and would have been relatively ineffective and prohibitively expensive to operate within the nation state

[8] Antigua and Barbuda, Barbados, Belize, Dominica, Grenada, Guyana, Jamaica, Montserrat, St. Kitts and Nevis, Saint Lucia, St. Vincent and the Grenadines, and Trinidad and Tobago, all of which were members from the beginning. The Bahamas joined in July 4 1983 although is not a member of the Common Market, Suriname on July 4 1995, and Haiti on July 3 2002.

[9] Anguilla, Bermuda, the British Virgin Islands, the Turks and Caicos Islands, and the Cayman Islands.

[10] Six million if you exclude currently its most troublesome member state, Haiti.

[11] Figures taken from A Peters, *The Fiscal effects of tariff reduction in the Caribbean Community* (Washington, Inter-American Development Bank, 2002, available at: http://www.iadb.org, accessed 1 March 2004), at 6–10.

[12] V Jordan, *The Caribbean Court of Justice as part of a wider integration movement*, Development Strategy Forum, University of West Indies, 15–17 January 2003 (Barbados, Caribbean Development Bank, available at: http://www.caribank.org/, accessed 1 March 2004), at 2.

[13] Above n 5, at 28.

alone. The continuing strength of this logic is supported by the fact that till this day there has been a considerable degree of success in terms of functional co-operation across the ordinary boundaries of sovereignty, particularly in areas such as education and foreign policy.[14]

After the demise of the Federation, a more prolonged effort at regionalism in the Caribbean began in 1963 with the first of what became known as the 'Heads of Government Conferences'. This led in 1965 to tentative moves towards a common market and eventually in 1973 to the Treaty of Chaguaramas (the Treaty), which established CARICOM. But 30 years later the ideals of the Treaty have yet to be delivered even after a series of attempts to revamp the process. Even so, one thing that remains striking is the continued belief of its members in the potential contained within the project. This is a belief that is shared by external investors in the region such as the Inter-American Bank.[15]

Within CARICOM there are almost certainly considerable opportunities to be had in regional integration. Unlike other regional groups, in terms of inter-regional trade the potential boon does not appear to be enormous given the problems of communication and the relatively small size of CARICOM's market. But in other respects there is much similarity with other regional projects. In particular, within the integration and cooperation agenda it is hoped that considerable *internal* institutional efficiencies can be achieved, while *externally* the main goal is the potential for more effective inclusion in the international arena. These gains should result in more efficient use of scarce human resources and improved economies of scale, leading to enhanced bargaining power and competitiveness abroad.[16]

In short, interregional cooperation is seen as the catalyst required to help overcome the severe handicaps involved in being countries in possession of small and undiversified markets trying to compete on the international stage. Through such a process, it is hoped that the region can avoid dependency on external countries and organisations. In the words of the Prime Minister of Jamaica:

> We see CARICOM as a collective instrument for mitigating the vulnerability of our individual small states: vulnerability to political pressures from powerful interests in the wider world; vulnerability to trade, economic and financial shocks from the global market-place; vulnerability to the impact of natural and man-made disasters.[17]

[14] Above n 12, at 3.

[15] A Jessen and E Rodriguez, *The Caribbean Community: Facing the Challenges of Regional and Global Integration*, Occasional Paper INTAL–ITD 2 (Buenos Aires, The Inter-American Bank, 1999), at 19.

[16] *Ibid* at 44.

[17] P Patterson, *CARICOM beyond thirty: Connecting with the Diaspora* (CARICOM 30th Anniversary Lecture, Brooklyn, New York, 2 October 2003, available at: www.caricom.org/, accessed 1 March 2004), at 9.

Implementation of the single market and economy

Despite the attractiveness of these goals, in its first 15–20 years CARICOM failed to secure the common market that was the key objective of the Treaty. A major difficulty was the nationalistic approach adopted by some of its member states who were accused of using the organisation as a tool for protectionism.[18] But the end vision never entirely disappeared, and if anything was made more essential by the growth in global trade during the eighties.

The nineties saw renewed energy in the project and a series of protocols were added to the Treaty, culminating in the signing of a revised version in 2001 (the Revised Treaty).[19] In a further development, the 'Rose Hall Declaration on Regional Governance and Integrated Development',[20] the member states agreed in principle to an overhaul of CARICOM's institutional arrangements. Taken together, these documents represent an extremely ambitious statement of intent for the future of CARICOM. If the Revised Treaty is successfully implemented what we will be left with in the Caribbean is a Common Market and Single Economy (CSME), within which there will be no tariff or non-tariff barriers to lawful trade, no barriers to the provision of services across CARICOM and a significant degree of freedom of movement for workers.[21] Furthermore, there will be no obstacles to the movement of capital from one member state to another, the ability to invest across borders will be made easier and in the long term there are even proposals in place for a unified currency.

However, all of this remains a big if. Deadlines and timetables have been set for progress on the implementation of the CSME but serious doubts have been expressed as to whether the proposed date of introduction, the end of 2005, will be achieved. One study conducted in 2002 found that none of the Revised Treaty provisions on competition law had been implemented and that harmonisation of company law was a long way off given the differences contained within the various legal systems in CARICOM. In the field of financial services, harmonisation had only reached the stage of identifying the differences that would need to be overcome, while in the area of customs law it would seem that the model proposed in the Revised Treaty was close to be being abandoned altogether. In addition, CARICOM still had not successfully implemented a

---

[18] Above n 15, at 19.

[19] The Revised Treaty of Chaguaramas establishing the Caribbean Community including the Caricom Single Market and Economy.

[20] Rose Hall Declaration on Regional Governance and Integrated Development, signed 4 July 2003.

[21] In the first stage of liberalisation this freedom of movement is to be restricted to defined categories of skilled workers.

common external tariff making it difficult for the group to develop a coherent external trade policy.[22]

In terms of the free movement of goods there is better news as it is estimated that some 95 per cent of intra-regional trade is compliant. Likewise, progress has been made on the free movement of persons although full implementation is still some way off. With regards to free movement of capital and services, little concrete action has yet to be undertaken and as for the single economy, this too is an aspiration well behind schedule with, for instance, monetary union an objective that remains a distant dream.[23]

Creating a sense of community

There is still time for the member states of CARICOM to catch up and transpose the detail of the Revised Treaty into legislation and action on the ground. But in the absence of such action CARICOM stands accused of being little more than a talking shop. In this respect, CARICOM is experiencing a classic problem that most efforts at regional integration seem to be beset by at one time or another: the conversion of aspirations and goals into meaningful action.

One particular hurdle that has to be overcome is that of national sovereignty. Nation states remain the focus of legitimate power in the global legal order. Therefore, ultimately for an international treaty to be operational on the ground and to have an effective impact on the citizens of the signatories to the treaty, it must be converted into law and practice by the member states themselves. Certainly in the areas normally covered by regional integration schemes, without that initial step then an international agreement to coordinate the economies of member states comes to very little. In this regard, it is noticeable that Article 10 of the EC Treaty has been copied virtually word for word in the Revised Treaty. In theory, this commits the member states of CARICOM to meet any obligations arising out of the Revised Treaty.[24] However, unlike the EC Treaty, there is an absence of any mechanism by which the member states can be sanctioned for failure to meet those obligations. Furthermore, the member states of CARICOM remain wedded to a strong view of national sovereignty. Evidence for this can be seen in the recent Rose Hall Declaration in which it was felt necessary to reaffirm 'that CARICOM is a Community of Sovereign States, and of Territories able and willing to exercise the rights

---

[22] HR Brewster, *The Caribbean Single Market and Economy: is it realistic without commitment to political unity?* (Georgetown, Guyana, CARICOM Secretariat, 2003, available at: http://www.caricom.org/speeches/csme-politicalunity-brewster.htm, accessed 1 March 2004).
[23] *Ibid.*
[24] Above n 19, Art. 9.

and assume the obligations of membership of the Community'.[25] For what is an otherwise radical document, this is a revealingly defensive statement that may be a reflection of the group's colonial past.

That as may be, but if CARICOM is to succeed, at some stage the member states will have to act and demonstrate a genuine desire and willingness to make the concessions required to move the project forward.[26] This reluctance to sacrifice national sovereignty is thoroughly understandable. Yet the problem for regional integration is that if national sovereignty is allowed to hold sway, large chunks of the original scheme could stay underdeveloped because one or more of the member states have chosen to stall on action. The frustration with such self-interest is clear amongst those who monitor the progress of CARICOM.

> So far, some of the CARICOM members resemble players involved in the prisoner's dilemma, in which an individual betrays his comrades in order to better his own situation. Such behaviour by CARICOM members undermines the authority of the organization by destroying the trust underlying such multilateral agreements, endangering the fulfilment of the group's common goals.[27]

Evidence for this self-defeating behaviour within CARICOM can be seen in Jamaica's signing of an air services agreement with the US Federal Aviation Administration outside of CARICOM's collective negotiation on this issue. Meanwhile, the Bahamas will not agree to the free movement of labour because it would have a disproportionate effect on its economy, whilst Trinidad and Barbados find themselves incapable of concluding a fishing agreement.[28]

All of this is undoubtedly worrying for those who would like to see the project succeed, but the fact that it takes time for member states to come to terms with the balancing act that is implied by membership of a regional group does not necessarily entail the ultimate failure of the project. But more worryingly still, there is evidence to suggest that the real causes of difficulty within the organisation are more fundamental than simple national pride and rivalry. Foremost amongst the problems faced by all the member states within CARICOM is a lack of administrative resources to push the project through. Much of the work that needs to be completed involves the drafting of complex legislation and the establishment of new administrative agencies which the member states have little experience of operating. At present, much of this work would appear to involve

---

[25] Above n 20, at para A1.
[26] Above n 3, at 32.
[27] A Cordova. and J Vance, 'Will the Caribbean take the leap of faith?' in The Panama News (vol 9, no 15, 3–16 August, 2003, available at: http://www.thepanamanews.com/pn/v_09/issue_15/opinion_04.html, accessed 1 March 2004).
[28] *Ibid.*

a duplication of effort between CARICOM and the member states, and between member states themselves. This is work that the member states are ill equipped to perform. Hence, if the member states really want to see the CSME put in place, there is a strong argument for more effort being put into sharing bureaucratic energy and knowledge.[29]

Introducing a commission and developing community law

If this is a correct analysis, then the time has come for the member states to take the plunge and cede to the larger community a significant degree of decision-making power. Without this, the process of implementation will continue to be tortuous, prone to set backs, and ultimately liable to be overtaken by events. Thus it is the structure of CARICOM and the method used to introduce the CSME that is the inherent problem.

> The method decided on was to amend the Treaty of Chaguaranus by a series of nine Protocols. Each of these is required to give effect to different aspects of the CSME. Each requires signature and ratification by CARICOM's member states. And each requires legislation and administrative action in the member states for it to be effectively implemented. A tall order indeed. According to a recent report coming out of the CSME unit based in the Government of Barbados, there are several hundred different actions required among the 14 member states. With a severe shortage of legal drafting skills, legislative time and administrative personnel; it is little wonder that many countries are behind the task.[30]

On this topic, many feel that there are lessons to be drawn from the European experience.[31] When the EEC was first introduced, bureaucratic capacity was a smaller part of the problem in its development than with CARICOM. Even so, what was of great assistance to the organisation was the fact that from the outset it was possible, through its Council, for the EEC to make Community law outside the treaty making process. By doing so it enabled all parties involved to speed up the introduction of the common market. Furthermore, although the seventies and eighties were periods of relatively slow development, after a period of fierce internal debate a solution to the impasse was found in the endowment of enhanced powers on the Community institutions.[32] As a result, within the Council it became possible and commonplace to make Community legislation in circumstances where unanimous voting was not required. This

---

[29] See also H Brewster, T Dolan and T Stewart, *Implementation of the Caribbean Single Market and Economy*, (Washington, World Bank, 2002).

[30] N Girvan, 'CARICOM's Governance: no time for inaction' in The Guyana Chronicle, 6 July 2003.

[31] Eg above n 28 and n 29.

[32] Single European Act 1986.

allowed the Community to take on board a degree of control which result-ed in much improved progress on the single market.

If efficient and practical decision-making are so important is there the willpower within CARICOM to do something similar to the EU? At present CARICOM is governed, or at least advised, by four Ministerial Councils supported administratively by a CARICOM Secretariat. These Ministerial Councils have broad responsibility for the key areas of the CARICOM project. The Ministerial Councils make recommendations to the Community Council of Ministers who in turn are responsible to the Conference Heads of Government. This set-up means that in practice the output of the Ministerial Councils amount to recommendations which could lead to treaties and declarations. In reality, however, even if a decision is made at the level of the Heads of Government, the will of CARICOM only comes into effect once it has been acted upon domestically by the member states. It is true that CARICOM breaks down the political day-to-day responsibility for moving forward the agenda of CARICOM into a series of portfolios, with each member state being responsible for one portfolio. Nevertheless, through such a varied distribution of responsibilities, although there is created plenty of scope for debate and interaction, there is also generated a perfect scenario for large-scale duplication of work, delay and obfuscation.

The dangers inherent in this constitutional set up have long been appreciated within CARICOM itself. With a view to preparing for the future, in the late eighties the group began to look seriously at the alternatives. The major contribution to the debate of this period was a seminal report produced in 1992 by the West Indian Commission called *Time for Action*.[33] Central to the proposals contained within that report was the idea of a CARICOM commission which would be empowered to act upon the decisions of CARICOM by introducing community legislation and enforcing them through the use of its legal powers. At the time, CARICOM decided not to take on board these ideas and instead chose to pursue to the full the existing arrangements by which maximum control of the organisation was retained by the member states. Over the following decade efforts were made to streamline the process by which CARICOM operated but the fundamentals of the distribution of power remained the same. As a consequence, the resulting progress of the introduction of the CSME remained unimpressive.[34]

There are though signs that the time has finally come when a different approach will be considered by the member states and acted upon. In July

[33] West Indian Commission, *Time for Action-The Report of the West Indian Commission* (Black Rock, Barbados, 1992).
[34] JJ Taccone and U Nogueira, CARICOM Report INTAL–ITD 1 (Inter-American Bank, Buenos Aires, 2002), at ch 7.

2003 the member states signed up to the Rose Hall Declaration, inclusive within which was the following aspiration:

> The establishment of a CARICOM Commission or other executive mechanism, whose purpose will be to facilitate the deepening of regional integration in the areas of responsibility specified ... [by Heads of Government]. The Commission's function will be to exercise full time executive responsibility for furthering implementation of Community decisions in such areas as well as to initiate proposals for Community action in any such area.[35]

The stated aim would appear to be to create a structure of governance capable of spearheading CARICOM into the future, but at this stage many questions remain unanswered. While the introduction of a body with an independent mandate to bring forward proposals for legislation is a significant step forward, it is not the main part of the solution. With the EU, for instance, it could be argued that of more importance to the ultimate success of the organisation has been the fact that there is a mechanism by which the Commission's proposals are acted upon at the 'supranational level'. Furthermore, this process is more effective in practice because of the considerable powers of qualified majority voting possessed by the Council.

There is at yet no equivalent arrangement within CARICOM. All the main decisions of the organisation require unanimity amongst the member states.[36] The only exception to this rule is with regard to the decisions made by the various organs of the community. But even here, the member states reserve the right, by a vote of two-thirds, to declare an issue to be of critical importance to the national well-being and hence subject to unanimous voting.[37]

Yet the concept of a body of community law within CARICOM seems inevitable. Within the Rose Hall Declaration there is reference to:

> The development of a system of mature regionalism in which critical policy decisions of the Community taken by Heads of Government, or by other Organs of the Community, will have the force of law throughout the Region as a result of the operation of domestic legislation and the Treaty of Chaguaramas appropriately revised.[38]

Following the Declaration a 'technical group' was set up within the Secretariat to look at the options for advance in this area, albeit within a tight remit that required it to retain respect for national sovereignty in any

---

[35] Above n 20, at para A3.
[36] Above n 19, Art. 28(1).
[37] Above n 19, Art. 27(6).
[38] Above n 20, at para A2.

solution. The proposal submitted by the technical group includes the introduction of the capacity to make community law to implement the objectives of the Revised Treaty. However, this will be achieved through a multi stage process. First, it is envisaged that member states will be required to introduce domestic legislation that will allow for the direct applicability of so-called 'instruments of implementation' when they are passed at the community level. 'Instruments of implementation' would be proposed and drafted by the commission but will require the approval of all member states before they take the force of law.[39] If these proposals are accepted and acted upon then they will represent another breakthrough for CARICOM. But it could turn out to be a source of regret that the organisation is not looking to be more radical as these proposals do not even take CARICOM as far as the original EC Treaty, an arrangement that had later to be amended in order to speed up the decision-making process.

Enforcing community law

Another key area which has been left unresolved by the Rose Hall Declaration is the enforcement of the Revised Treaty, even though Chapter Nine of that Treaty describes a number of alternatives by which disputes can be resolved. There are two main flaws with the Revised Treaty as it stands: the absence of a community institution to bring proceedings against member states who commit a breach of the Revised Treaty; and the silence within the Revised Treaty as to how rulings and agreed settlements are to be enforced.

On the first point, the Revised Treaty leaves it to the member states themselves to pursue grievances. But such an arrangement could be extremely problematic in an organisation such as CARICOM where there is a significant disparity in economic and political clout between the respective member states. The risk is that by leaving it to the member states to initiate complaints the smaller nations might be intimidated from taking the required action.[40] These fears are exacerbated by the absence from the Revised Treaty of enforcement mechanisms. Article 207 of the Revised Treaty states that 'decisions of the arbitral tribunal ... shall be binding on the Member States parties to the dispute' and Article 215 that 'the Member States ... shall comply with [the judgment of the court] promptly'. Again, fine words, but nowhere is there provision to deal with the situation where a member state refuses or fails to comply. Nor is this scenario addressed in the Rose Hall Declaration which has proposed a commission

---

[39] Initial Report of the Expert Group of Heads of Government, 'Carrying the Process Forward', CARICOM Secretariat: Geargetown, Guyana (2003).
[40] Above n 12, at 5.

for CARICOM. Here it should be noted that the Article 226 and 228[41] powers of the European Commission have played an important part in the progress of the EU and given a real meaning to its role as the 'Guardian of the Treaty'. Accordingly, if the idea of the CARICOM commission is not to become a white elephant then it should be granted similar powers.

But an even more elemental point that needs to be addressed before a commission with enforcement powers can become reality is the need for the member states of CARICOM to recognise the competence of a community court. In this respect, one key component of the potential new CARICOM structure is now very close to coming to fruition, that is the establishment of the Caribbean Court of Justice (the Court).[42] This could be truly significant because for many writers it was not the Commission that was the real driving force behind the EEC in its formative years, but the Court of Justice of the European Community.

The Caribbean Court of Justice

The process by which the Court has been set up provides another example of the political difficulties that bedevil any attempt at regional integration on an international scale. One problem that has slowed the project down has been the fact that the Court is to be more than just a supreme court for CARICOM, as it is also to be an appellate court for the English speaking member states of the group. Another issue that has needed resolving is the extent of the Court's powers of adjudication over the Revised Treaty.[43] However, not only is it an axiomatic requirement of modern systems of governance that there should be recourse to an authoritative independent arbiter, but within the regional system the danger of leaving such decisions to national courts is that those courts would come up with 'a Pandora's box of interpretations' which would not necessarily be consistent with one another.[44] Thus it must be that in the interpretation of the Revised Treaty, in the name of legal certainty and uniformity, a community court has exclusive jurisdiction. This was all foreseen by the authors of a much earlier drive for constitutional reform.

> Integration in its broadest economic sense ... must have the underpinning of Community law. Integration rests on rights and duties; it requires the

---

[41] The EC Treaty.

[42] As of February 2004 sufficient progress had been made to bring into force the Caribbean Court of Justice Trust Fund, CARICOM Secretariat, *Caribbean Court of Justice Trust Fund Agreement enters into force—Court arrangements advance*, Press release 17/2004, 11 February 2004.

[43] D Pollard, The Caribbean Court of Justice: Challenge and Response (Georgetown, Guyana, CARICOM Secretariat, 2000, available at: http://www.caricom.org/, accessed 1 March 2004), at 2.

[44] *Ibid* at 6.

support of the rule of law applied regionally and uniformly. A CARICOM Supreme Court interpreting the Treaty of Chaguaramas, resolving disputes arising under it, including disputes between Government parties to the Treaty, declaring and enforcing Community law ...—all by way of the exercise of an original jurisdiction—is absolutely essential to the integration process. It represents ... one of the pillars of the CARICOM structures of unity.[45]

Within the Revised Treaty these key principles seem to have been secured and accepted[46] and if and when the Court finally does come into operation, it will be fascinating to see when it first has to affirm its authority as the supreme court within CARICOM and deliver its version of *Marbury v Madison*[47] or *Costa v ENEL*.[48]

The Court's successful introduction is going to be something of a litmus test for CARICOM but, on paper at least, it possesses many positive features. For instance, it is encouraging to see that the appointment of judges to the Court will not be left to the politicians but made the responsibility of the newly created Regional Judicial and Legal Services Commission.[49] Similarly, the fact that the funding of the Court has been safeguarded through the establishment of a Trust Fund is important.[50] Interestingly, this is one of the few aspects of the CARICOM arrangements where agreement has been arrived at regarding sanctions for noncompliance. Non-payment of contributions to the budget of the Court will result in member states being denied access to it so long as the member state remains in arrears.[51] But to safeguard further the Court, it is also hoped that its long term funding will be secured through contributions from such donors as the EU, the US and Canada.[52]

Ideally then, through the introduction of the Court we should see the evolution of three critical aspects to governance in CARICOM. There will thereafter be uniformity in the interpretation of the Revised Treaty; there will be rights of access to the courts for an interpretation of the Revised Treaty; and a jurisprudence will develop alongside the Revised Treaty.[53] In short, CARICOM will become bound by the rule of law.

There are though several riders to this optimistic vision. First, as it stands the implementation of the CSME is entirely dependent upon the

---

[45] Above n 33, at 500.
[46] Above 19, Art. 211.
[47] (1803) 5 US 1 Crunch 137.
[48] Case T–6/64 [1964] ECR 585.
[49] Agreement Establishing the Caribbean Court of Justice, Art. V(3)(1). The exception is the President of the Court who will have to be approved by the Contracting Parties to the Treaty, Art. IV(6).
[50] Financial Protocol to the Agreement Establishing the Caribbean Court of Justice, Art. 8.
[51] Although not citizens of that member state, *ibid* Art. 7.
[52] Above n 42, at 5.
[53] The Member States have accepted that the decisions of the Court will create legally binding precedents, above n 19, Art. 221.

member states passing domestic laws. Until, and if, the new proposals for a commission and 'instruments of implementation' are introduced, there will be no equivalent to the European principle of direct applicability of community law. This implies that for the foreseeable future, references to a body of community law being formed need to be couched with the qualification that CARICOM remains 'an association of sovereign states and not a supranational entity'.[54] Second, there is still no sign of any enforcement mechanism to implement the rulings of the Court or the law of CARICOM generally. Third, individual citizens will not have direct rights of standing in the Court. They will though, have indirect rights in that it will be at the Court's discretion to allow them to appear in Court where the case being heard involves a determination of whether or not the law confers a benefit upon them.[55] The most likely scenario where this might happen is where a member state court has had cause to refer a case to the Court for the determination of an issue under the Revised Treaty.[56] Here, the parallels with the Court of Justice of the European Communities are noticeable and deliberate. Nevertheless, given the overall structure of CARICOM, by itself it is unlikely that the Caribbean Court of Justice will have the same impact that its European counterpart had within the EEC during that organisation's early years.

Democracy and civil society

There has been no mention in this analysis so far of the means by which CARICOM provides for the inclusion of local voices in its decision making process. This is an extremely important issue as the temptation to ignore civil society and the rights of citizens are all too evident within regional institutions. Indeed, already within the Caribbean there are considerable concerns that CARICOM is an elitist project being introduced by administrators and politicians far removed from popular opinion.[57] Here we confront familiar difficulties with engaging the people in the political process. Clearly, there is a need to improve the explanation of the project to the electorate and to find ways to incorporate them into the process. Ideally, referendums would be passed preceding the radical shake-ups that could be about to hit the region, but none are on offer at this stage or even being talked about.

However, work is being carried out in this area. Once more contained within the Rose Hall Declaration can be found a positive statement of

---

[54] D Pollard, The Original Jurisdiction of the Caribbean Court of Justice, (Georgetown, Guyana, CARICOM Secretariat, 2003 available at: http://www.caricom.org/, accessed 1 March 2004), at 3, fn 2.

[55] Above n 19, Art. 222.

[56] Above n 19, Art. 214.

[57] S Ryan, 'Rose Hall's well kept secret', in Trinidad Express, 16 November 2003.

intent, this time to strengthen the role of the Assembly of Caribbean Community Parliamentarians. At present this representative element to CARICOM resembles that of the old EEC Assembly.[58] The Assembly of Caribbean Community Parliamentarians has no powers other than those of debate and recommendation, and is made up of representatives of the member state parliaments. It is likely, however, that if the process of incremental reform witnessed in CARICOM's progress so far is anything to go by, then out of the current deliberations on the future of the Assembly some form of addition to its role will be considered. If we look to the European model again then if a commission is introduced the Assembly could be granted powers of scrutiny over that body, as well as a say in its appointment and approval for its budget.

Perhaps a bigger role still that the Assembly has to play is in raising the awareness of the work of CARICOM. The comment has been frequently made that the public of CARICOM are ignorant of the purpose of the organisation, to the extent that even members of the private sector seem to be unaware of their rights and obligations under the new single market framework.[59] There must also be potential for greater use of civil society organisations. Here too the foundations are there as there is a clear recognition of the need for more comprehensive programs of participation with, and support for, civil society.[60] As yet though, this is another area where concrete progress is awaited.

The complexity of regionalism

Before coming to any conclusions as to the lessons that can be learned from the CARICOM experience, another feature of governance in the Caribbean should be noted. CARICOM provides us with an interesting example of the complexities involved in international negotiation. In the case of CARICOM, the situation is made even more confusing than normal because the organisation negotiates with other regional bodies both internally and externally.

Internally, the body that CARICOM has to work with is the Organisation of Eastern Caribbean States (OECS). The OECS was established in 1981, partly in recognition of the problems and stagnation within CARICOM itself. The group is made up of seven of the smaller islands within CARICOM and in terms of economic influence is too small to have any real impact. But in terms of ideas the organisation has made some very positive contributions and can claim to have acted as something of a motivating force for the larger CARICOM project. Since its formation, the

---

[58] Established in 1989.
[59] Above n 34, at 48.
[60] The Liliendaal Statement of Principles on 'Forward Together', 2–3 July 2002.

OECS has had considerable success in establishing the institutions necessary to develop the agendas of regional governance. Thus within the OECS there is now in place a common judiciary, a central bank and currency, a common civil aviation administration, a common telecommunications authority and a common tourism promotion organisation. Quite apart from increasing the capacity of the member states to govern efficiently and effectively, this arrangement has enabled the member states to overcome the particular problems faced by small nations in establishing the requisite checks and balances required of healthy constitutions.[61]

The continuing problems faced by the organisation should not be underestimated, which is no doubt why the OECS continues to play an active part within CARICOM. But its member states do so knowing that they have a stronger voice as a group than they would have as individual member states. It could be likewise with the relationship of CARICOM externally with other regional organisations in the Americas. Should the project of CARICOM succeed, this organisation could become a source of inspiration.

For fear of being overwhelmed, at an earlier point in time CARICOM declined to consider the inclusion of larger nation states in the region. But in view of the global realities CARICOM does now seek to work together on a number of issues with neighbouring states and the other regional organisations in the Caribbean, the Andean Community and the Central American Integration System. One forum within which they have sought to interact is the Association of Caribbean States (ACS), established in 1994 and which takes in 220 million people. As yet the ACS has enjoyed only limited success, particularly in relation to trade negotiations. In the long term, it is hoped that improved cooperation amongst ACS states can be achieved. For the time being though, what the ACS does provide is an active forum through which all Caribbean states can explore ways of achieving improved functional co-operation.[62]

As for trade negotiation, CARICOM negotiates regionally and globally on behalf of its members.[63] This approach is vital to the interests of the CARICOM member states given their current fears as to the impact that WTO rules will have on small nations and the imminent reduction in preferential treatment from the EU.

---

[61] KD Venner, Sub-Regional Governance—the OECS experience (St Kitts, West Indies, Eastern Caribbean Central Bank, 2002, available at: http://www.eccb-centralbank.org/PDF/governor%20speech-1-9-2002.pdf, accessed 1 March 2004), at 6.

[62] N Girvan, Notes on CARICOM, the ACS, and Caribbean Survival, Conference on Caribbean Survival, University of West Indies, 20–22 March 2000, available at: http://www.geocities.com/CollegePark/Library/3954/caribbeansurvival.pdf, accessed 1 March 2004.

[63] Above n 20, at para B13.

CONCLUSIONS

For CARICOM the future is uncertain. On the one hand complaints persist that progress is slow and there is a fear that the Rose Hall Declaration will become just another chapter in a long line of fine words which come to nothing.[64] Yet paradoxically, there are some signs of a twin track approach developing within CARICOM with some member states eager to look for ways to move forward faster.[65] Hence, it is probably far too early to write off CARICOM, particularly as bit-by-bit the member states do appear to be acting.[66]

Assuming CARICOM does succeed in implementing the CSME, how much deeper could the organisation expand in terms of governance? There are certainly some who would have the organisation take on a wider range of functions, and within the Rose Hall Declaration there is a specific reference to a regional task force on crime and security.[67] But here we return to the need to secure legitimate government for there are risks in attempting too much without the corresponding support of the electorate.

> As has become evident in recent years, globalisation is increasingly placing limits on the room for maneuver of individual nation states; to some extent, a process of erosion of sovereignty is already underway. Redefining sovereignty at the community level may be an effective means to improve economic governance within CARICOM. In a region in which sovereignty is relatively recent, however, the process of regional institution-building must proceed with great caution and only if all parties involved agree. Joint and/or coordinated action must, therefore, be carefully chosen in areas where there is consensus (involving civil society) and a greater chance of success.[68]

It will be fascinating to see how this project continues into the future. But however far it goes, what does appear apparent from the CARICOM experience is the continuing belief in the idea of regionalism as one way to tackle the realities of the globablised world. If it is to be accepted that the free trade agenda is here to stay, then the smaller countries of the world need to seek new ways to secure their future.

---

[64] M La Rose, 'CARICOM policies fail to reach the people', in Stabroek News, 2 December 2003.

[65] Stabroek News, 'Editorial', in Stabroek News, 23 July 2003.

[66] For instance, in February 2004 the Jamaican Parliament began to debate new legislation which will make it easier for the Jamaican Government to comply with its duties under CARICOM. Under the new Act, the Jamaican Government will be granted the power to amend Jamaican law in order to allow it to provide for the implementation of Jamaica's obligations under the Revised Treaty, Jamaican Information Service Caribbean Community and Common Market Act to be Repealed, 26 February 2004.

[67] Above n 20, at para B16.

[68] Above n 15, at 45.

Despite the obvious challenges which the free movement of goods and services, labor and capital may pose to CARICOM, it is imperative that the community surges forward. If countries concentrated on their singular needs
then the region would comprise small vulnerable economies, which do not
commandeer much voice. Given the new global marketplace, CARICOM
must harmonize its productive capacity to take advantage of the opportunities being presented.[69]

More forthright still, the Prime Minister of Jamaica has said:

What remains incontrovertible is that if regional integration was an option
three decades ago, there is absolutely no valid alternative today.[70]

What then does the CARICOM experience tell us, if anything, about
regional integration generally? A number of observations can be made. A
preliminary point is that it is essential that schemes implementing regional integration find ways to establish their legitimacy and to incorporate
fundamental constitutional values. This represents an even more serious
challenge at the supranational level than in the nation state given the relative isolation of such bodies from citizens. But although not perfect, as a
standard bearer for this form of governance the EU has demonstrated that
such things as the rule of law, political accountability and reliable
accounting and audit procedures can be achieved at this level. This will
be one of the major challenges that CARICOM will have to face up to over
the next decade, however, the introduction of a Caribbean Court of Justice
is a mightily exciting move in the right direction. In terms of democracy
and openness, more work needs to be done but CARICOM is at least
exploring the possibilities for enhanced interaction with the people. This
is an important issue, as it is probable that CARICOM will achieve its
goals much quicker if it can secure popular support. Furthermore, in the
long term there is an elusive vision that should regional organisations
find a solution to the conundrum of political participation, we will be
much closer to establishing a constitutionally legitimate means by which
to regulate globalisation.

But constitutional law is not just about promoting accountability and
the rights of individuals, it is also about establishing workable government. In this respect a study of CARICOM is most beneficial. The member states of CARICOM have chosen as an objective to move beyond the
facilitation of discussion, advice and consultation, and have sought to
integrate a whole raft of government functions. However, what the

---

[69] First Citizens Bank, Economic Newsletter, *Towards the implementation of the CARICOM single market*, vol 6 no 5, March 2003, available at: http://www.caricom.org/, accessed 1 March
2004.
[70] Above n 17, at 3.

CARICOM project seems to be proving is that if regional integration is to aspire to significant economic and social objectives, then a precursor to success is the establishment of an appropriate institutional infrastructure.[71] At the forefront of this process is the need for member states to come to terms with the idea that this involves a degree of sovereignty being, if not sacrificed, then at least entrusted to the regional scheme. Within CARICOM, not only does the Court of Justice depend upon this delegation of sovereignty, but there are a whole raft of other community agencies required that will not work effectively if concessions are not forthcoming. Given that globalisation has already entailed the loss of sovereignty, then this should be a step that can be negotiated, particularly as within regional schemes it is possible to include significant checks and balances to safeguard against disadvantage. However, as the CARICOM story shows, notions of sovereignty are deep rooted within most nation-states, particularly ones that have fought so long to secure that goal. Furthermore, once a regional group has solved the sovereignty problem, the next one to deal with is funding. This is an issue that CARICOM has only just started to tackle.[72]

Concessions on funding and sovereignty will be easier to secure where member states can be convinced that they will gain from the overall enterprise. To help achieve this, safeguards that provide guarantees that both the stronger and weaker members of the scheme stand to benefit would appear to be essential for successful regional schemes if they are not to implode when put under pressure.[73] Within CARICOM this requirement is presently dealt with by granting certain member states special status and through the work of the Caribbean Development Bank.[74] The strength of these arrangements will be one of the keys to the long term health of CARICOM.

One important lesson that CARICOM does appear to have learnt is that regional schemes should not be seen by member states as a space within which to hide from the global economy. There is more than a suggestion that members of CARICOM adopted this insular approach in the past and it did not work. Today if regionalism is to have any part to play in the global legal order such projects cannot afford to be based on isolationist policies.[75] Hence, it is significant that within the Rose Hall Declaration it is recognised that far from looking inward, CARICOM needs to strengthen its 'relations with other countries in the wider Caribbean, Latin America, Africa, Asia and the Pacific, and in particular to contribute to increased solidarity within the Non-Aligned Movement and the Group of 77'.[76]

---

[71] Above n 29.
[72] Above n 29.
[73] Eg above n 3, at 30.
[74] Above n 19, Art 4.
[75] *Ibid.*
[76] Above n 20, at para C2.

If the present reform package is implemented successfully, CARICOM could become an example of how, given time and space, member states can get used to the commitments required of cooperative schemes and in so doing are capable of developing the institutional capacity to make the project work. It may be that given the inherent hurdles that need to be overcome, all regional schemes will require patience and a reasonably long gestation period before they become effective. If this is the case, then regional groups should not be stretched too far, particularly whilst new systems of governance are bedding down. Thus to ease the path of progress, it is important from the outset to consider who should be members of regional initiatives.[77] Where there are potential members who are troublesome, whether it be in terms of size, internal difficulties or the relative underdevelopment of their economies and political structures, then perhaps it is wiser to integrate these states at a later date from a position of strength rather than from the outset. In this respect, CARICOM's decision not to include the likes of Venezuela in its original scheme was probably a wise one, whilst the inclusion of Haiti may yet prove to be the group's achilles heel.

The extent to which such conclusions can be inferred from the CARICOM story we will only really be capable of determining in a few years time, but one conclusion that can be drawn now is the pervading rationality and purpose behind the idea of regionalism. There remain fundamentally sound economic and logistical reasons for embarking on regional integration schemes and in the era of globalisation these are supported by wider political considerations as well. On many occasions schemes of regional integration will be wholly inappropriate but on others the logic of cooperation will be overwhelming. The simple truth is that there is no one ideal solution to the design of governance but regional integration is one viable alternative.

---

[77] Eg above n 3, at 27.

10

Globalisation and Global Justice in Competition Law

A DEFINITION OF GLOBALISATION?

G LOBALISATION IS A word that carries highly pejorative implications. It is an extremely polarising concept that is applied to many
spheres. There is no agreed definition of globalisation and it is not
the place of this chapter to attempt to find such a definition. However, in
order to give this paper some context, the sense in which globalisation is
to be understood is as follows:

> ... globalisation is many faceted and multidimensional. And it involves
> ideas, images, symbols, music, fashions and a variety of tastes and represen-
> tations of identity and community. Yet such diversity and complexity can
> not obscure the fact that the world's productive assets and the world trade
> and financial markets are now dominated by large institutional investors
> and transnational firms.[1]

It is with this suggestion of one definition of globalisation in mind that the
milieu in which the impact of globalisation should be received. This chapter will seek to address the issue of first whether there is a globalisation of
competition law and if so, whether having a global system of competition
law can be achieved in the context of delivering global justice.

---

* Senior Lecturer in Law at the University of Westminster. I am indebted to Paul Hughes
of the University of Westminster for further comments on this paper and David Tonkinson
of the Basingstoke, Andover & North Hampshire Industrial Mission for assistance with
sourcing materials. Any errors remain my own. The law is stated as I understand to be at 4
July 2005.
   [1] JA Camilleri, in JA Camilleri *et al* (eds) *Reimagining the Future: Towards Democratic
Governance* (La Trobe University, Melbourne, 2000), preface at xviii.

THE GROUNDS FOR INDICATING THAT THERE IS
A GLOBALISATION OF COMPETITION LAW

It is commonly acknowledged that there is a globalisation of markets[2], resulting in corporations having to act globally, which is driving the move towards the globalisation of competition law. There is an arguable case for consistency in the enforcement of competition decisions on pure econom-ic grounds as it would enable businesses to keep their costs down in terms of meeting the local competition rules. From that perspective business, at least, is arguing, albeit indirectly, for globalisation. The evidence that is usually cited to support the idea of globalisation is the notion of conver-gence. Questions of convergence were addressed in very broad terms by JHH Weiler in *The EU, The WTO and the NAFTA -Towards a Common Law of International Trade*. Although Weiler is presenting his argument from the perspective of the beginning of a 'Common Law of International Trade'[3] the principles can still be applied to the development of a common law of competition as he examines the issues of convergence and divergence on a global basis. Jenny takes a similar view of the inter-relationship between trade policy, regulatory reform and competition policy. He describes them as being:

> complementary because whereas trade policy eliminates governmental bar-riers to international trade, deregulation aims at getting rid of domestic reg-ulations which serve no useful purpose and limits potential competition as well as market access, and competition policy tries to eliminate business barriers which could defeat the objective of market access underlying trade liberalization or deregulatory efforts by governments.[4]

Weiler's evidence for there being a commonality of law is based on three grounds. Firstly he states that 'the same regulatory measure may come simultaneously within the jurisdictional reach of more than one trade regime and may even be adjudicated simultaneously.'[5] In the case of EU countries this is true as there is the overarching reach of the EU legal order. Weiler further opines that '...in the material law of disparate inter-national trade regimes we can see considerable convergence.'[6] The truth of this statement in the field of competition law is disputable as although it is possible to see considerable convergence, equally there have been

---

[2] There is a plethora of material on globalisation. A very readable introduction to the his-torical development of globalisation and the growth of global markets by M Mussa, *Factors Driving Global Economic Integration* can be found at http://www.imf.org/external/np/speeches/2000/082500.htm (last accessed 5 July 2005).

[3] JHH Weiler, *The EU, the WTO and the NAFTA*, (Oxford, OUP, 2000), 3.

[4] F Jenny, Globalization, Competition and Trade Policy: Issues and Challenges in R Zach, (ed) *Towards WTO Competition Rules*, (Kluwer, London, 1999), 13.

[5] JHH Weiler, *The EU, the WTO and the NAFTA* , (Oxford OUP 2000) 3.

[6] *Ibid* at 4.

some bitter disputes between competing enforcement bodies.[7] The final ground Weiler offers in support of his thesis is that there is 'the strengthening of private parties in all regimes.'[8] This position presupposes firstly that there is a mature legal system that is accessible to all. Second, the premise rests on remedies being available to private parties. This is not always the case in the application of competition laws on an international basis.[9] Third, for private parties to benefit from the law it has to be enforced. There are jurisdictions with competition systems that have not always looked to their statute book.[10]

It should be noted that the most obvious candidate for implementing and policing a global competition law regime at the time of publication of Weiler's book was the World Trade Organisation (WTO).[11] The Ministerial Declaration at Doha[12] had set out a framework for competition law. In the Declaration it was recognised that '...the majority of WTO Members are developing countries. [The WTO sought] to place their needs and interests at the heart of the work programme adopted in this declaration.'[13] These were bold words which were eventually shown to be hollow with Framework Agreement of July 2004.[14]

Weiler saw the rationale behind convergence as being due to:

> ... an increase in the pressure on WTO bodies or WTO-approved bodies to adopt international standards which private operators in the Global marketplace could adopt as a way to ensure the access of their products to national markets.[15] The WTO may not call this Harmonization but it will be the functional equivalent. Indeed, the most intriguing development in this respect will be the convergence of national regulatory regimes among the large trading blocs (USA, EU, Canada, etc.) as a means of ensuring smooth operation of 'their' corporations and then the internationalization of such harmonized standards.[16]

---

[7] Usually it appears to be the EU and the US competition authorities that are at loggerheads.

[8] JHH Weiler, n 5 above at 4.

[9] WTO rules at the time of writing do not allow for remedies for private individuals.

[10] For example, the Japanese Fair Trade Commission has been criticised for its ability to act against foreign undertakings that may have infringed competition rules but not domestic ones.

[11] Many writers have supported the idea of the WTO as the global competition enforcer, such as Fox and Jenny.

[12] DOHA MINISTERIAL DECLARATION WT/MIN(01)/DEC/1 20 November 2001 at http://www.wto.org/english/thewto_e/minist_e/min01_e/mindecl_e.htm (last accessed 4 July 2005).

[13] Paragraph 2 Doha Declaration available at http://www.wto.org/english/thewto_e/minist_e/min01_e/mindecl_e.htm (last accessed 4 July 2005).

[14] This compromise agreement has also demonstrated how problematic the ability of the WTO to actually implement a unified strategy for competition law was.

[15] Why Weiler feels that this is the most appropriate method of enforcement is curious bearing in mind that only sovereign states can bring actions at WTO level.

[16] JHH Weiler, n 6 above at 231.

Weiler is, therefore, highlighting the question of 'harmonisation' or 'convergence'. Leaving aside the question of whether harmonisation and convergence are the same thing,[17] the idea of whether convergence is taking place needs to be addressed. It is the generally received wisdom that convergence is happening[18] and on that note, it is apposite to discuss how widespread is this convergence process.

THE CONVERGENCE OF COMPETITION SYSTEMS

This is probably best illustrated by looking at some case examples of how independent competition systems react to the same facts to discover whether convergence is more apparent than real. It is usual to look towards the treatment of merger cases by the US and EU authorities to analyse the occurrence of convergence, but it is also possible to consider convergence in other circumstances.

The history of relations between the airlines Virgin Atlantic and British Airways is not only littered with public media spats, but also the occasional lawsuit. In the 1990s Virgin lodged complaints about BA's alleged anti-competitive practices in both the US and the EU. The basis of both claims was that BA had offered incentives to travel agents and corporate customers to grant either special commission payments or discounts when reaching given targets. In the EU Commission decision'[19] BA was found to have infringed Article 82 and was fined 6.8 m Euros. However, in the New York District Court' Virgin's claim was dismissed for failing to show that the 'challenged incentive agreements have had an actual adverse effect on competition as a whole in the relevant market.'[20] It is the definition of the relevant market that demonstrates why contrary decisions were reached in these cases which were based on very similar facts. In the case decided by the Commission the definition of the relevant market was that of the market for air travel agency services in the UK, which

---

[17] It is submitted that they are not. The use of the term 'convergence' implies that there is a coming-together of legal systems but it is not necessarily planned. 'Harmonisation' suggests a more deliberate process. It is convergence that will be the focus of concentration in this paper.

[18] The question of convergence was dealt with very succinctly in a 1999 ABA Report on coordination and convergence with the comment 'the competition laws of the various nations generally have tended to become more alike over time. This natural convergence is to be expected. Laws tend to converge as nations learn from one another, and as more nations become industrialized or seek partnership in the world trading system, and thus support similar goals.' *Report of the ABA sections of antitrust law and international law and practice on the internationalization of competition law rules: coordination and convergence, Part II Driving Forces Towards Harmonization in the Global Economy*, (ABA, December, 1999), 16.

[19] *Virgin/British Airways* 2000/74 (2000) OJ L30/1.

[20] *Virgin Atlantic Airways Limited v British Airways plc* 93 Civ 7270 (MGC) 28 available at http://www.nysd.uscourts.gov/courtweb/public.htm (accessed 4 July 2005).

was found to be a substantial part of the Common Market as this is clearly explained in the opinion.[21] Judge Cederbaum in the US litigation defined the market as that for passenger air travel between Heathrow and New York, Los Angeles, San Francisco, Washington or Chicago.[22]

In the *Gencor/Lonhro*[23]case, it was proposed to merge the South African platinum mining operations of both companies. Although the South African authorities did not find any problem with the proposed new concentration, the EU Commission was of the opinion that, despite their being no part of the operations taking place within the territory of the EU, this merger would fall within the jurisdiction of Commission. Its decision was that the merger, despite referring to 'activities outside the Community [would] have the effect of creating or strengthening a dominant position as a result of which competition in the Common Market is significantly impeded.'[24] In an article for the *European Competition Law Review* Fox asked some challenging questions about these contrary outcomes.[25] One of the comparisons that Fox drew on was that of the outcome in *Boeing/McDonnell Douglas* merger.[26] As in *Gencor*, neither of the parties involved had any assets or facilities in the EU, but the Commission still had jurisdiction because the proposed concentration had a community dimension. Boeing was contentious as the merger would result in there being only two manufacturers of large commercial aircraft—Boeing of the US and the European-based Airbus Industrie—and that Boeing's dominant position would be strengthened. The Federal Trade Commission cleared the merger in July 1997 and took the attitude that Commission should clear it as well but the Commission, possibly mindful of the impact on the European manufacturer, refused clearance until Boeing gave a series of undertakings, which it has been suggested were principally to protect Airbus.[27]

The differential approach to Microsoft's pre-eminence in the computer operating systems market continues to splutter onwards. Despite the agreement by the Bush Administration to settle the US claims against the

---

[21] *Virgin/British Airways* above n 20 at paras 69–85.

[22] *Virgin Atlantic Airways Limited* v *British Airways plc* n 21 above. In the copy of the judgment available to the writer no explicit evidence for this definition of the market was found.

[23] *Gencor/Lonhro* (97/26 (1997) OJ L11/30). On appeal *Gencor* v *Commission* case T-102/96 [1999] 4 CMLR 971.

[24] *Gencor* v *Commission* n 24 above at para 82.

[25] E Fox, *The Merger Regulation and its Territorial Reach* [1999] ECLR 334 at 336. Unfortunately Fox does not answer those questions.

[26] *Boeing/McDonnell Douglas* Case No IV/M.877 OJ [1997] L 336/16. It should also be borne in mind that the US had threatened a trade war unless the merger was cleared.

[27] For further details on the merger see B Bishop, Editorial, The Boeing/McDonnell Douglas Merger [1997] ECLR 417 and J Faull, International Antitrust Takes Flight: a Review of Jurisdictional and Substantive Law Conflicts in the Boeing-McDonnell Douglas Merger, ABA International Committee Spring 1998 Meeting, Washington DC, 2 April 1998.

company, the EU Commission announced in March 2004 that they had found that anti-competitive practices were being used by the company.[28] An appeal by Microsoft against that decision is pending.

A further case to consider in the context of the convergence argument was the proposed *GE/Honeywell* merger.[29] This case demonstrated the fragility of the convergence argument. Writing in the *European Competition Law Review* in 2002, Alec Burnside commented on the superficiality of the claims[30] by regulators in the EU and the US that there is convergence in their thinking on mergers. He describes these claims as 'over-hyped' and goes onto state that:

> past alignment, may have been more a matter of convenience and coinci-
> dence than inevitability. It had become the conventional wisdom of the
> antitrust conference circuit that convergence on substance had de facto been
> achieved, despite the formal difference between the European Union's dom-
> inance test and the United States' 'substantial lessening' standard. Instead,
> the conventional wisdom ran, the main challenge was to align procedures.
> Certainly GE/Honeywell confirms the procedural difficulty, but it gives the
> lie to the happy assumption of convergence on substance.[31]

Certainly an examination of the treatment meted out in the parallel cases involving Virgin and BA substantiate Burnside's opinion that conver-gence is over-hyped by showing up this disparity very clearly.

If the 'conventional wisdom' is not followed, then the results in cases such as *GE/Honeywell* and *Gencor* have tended to be dismissed as simply

---

[28] EU Commission Press Release IP/03/1150, 6/8/03, *Commission gives Microsoft last oppor-tunity to comment before concluding its antitrust probe* at http://europa.eu.int/rapid/start/cgi/guesten.ksh?reslist

[29] GE/Honeywell COMP/M2220 [2001] OJ C046/03.

[30] For the official view on the EU failure to clear the GE/Honeywell merge 'there are sev-eral speeches by Monti.' Two that particularly address the issues raised and comment very gingerly on the perceived lack of convergence between the EU and US authorities are SPEECH/01/340, *The Future for Competition Policy in the European Union*, Merchant Taylor's Hall, London, 9 July 2001 at http://europa.eu.int/rapid/start/cgi/guesten.ksh?p_action.gettxt=gt&doc=SPEECH/01/340|0|RAPID&lg=EN (last accessed 4 July 2005) and SPEECH/01/540, *Antitrust in the US and Europe: a History of Convergence*, General Counsel Roundtable American Bar Association, Washington DC, 14 November 2001 at http://europa.eu.int/rapid/start/cgi/guesten.ksh?p_action.gettxt=gt&doc=SPEECH/01/540|0|RAPID&lg=EN (last accessed 4 July 2005). These can be contrasted with the more critical approach taken by the DOJ as exemplified by *Conglomerate Mergers and Range Effects: It's a Long Way from Chicago to Brussels* by William J Kolasky, Deputy Assistant Attorney-General, Anti-Trust Division, US Department of Justice, George Mason University Symposium, Washington, DC, November 9 2001 at http://www.usdoj.gov/atr/public/speeches/9536.pdf (last accessed 4 July 2005). Kolasky refers to the 'firestorm of criticism, not just from the US anti-trust agencies and senior administration officials' and recognises the decision as a 'sharp divergence' in the application of merger policy between the EU and the US.

[31] A Burnside, *GE, Honey, I Sunk the Merger* [2002] *ECLR* 107 at 108.

the results of applying two different competition systems.[32] Burnside acknowledges this view in his remarks that 'as to procedure, no amount of strategic planning by companies can compel the authorities to fall in line with each other.'[33] He further refers to the 'inconsistent procedure' of the jurisdictions, but that is a natural consequence of variant jurisdictions.

The consequences of *GE/Honeywell* et al may be helpful in assessing the practicality and value of a global competition forum. Much has been made to date of the 'success' in co-operation between the US and EU, such as the *Boeing/McDonnell Douglas* merger[34] and the Bilateral Agreement,[35] however, it can not cover up, as shown by *GE/Honeywell* or *Virgin/BA*, the fundamental problem of the different bases that competition systems are founded on and the variance in aims of those systems.

MODELS OF COMPETITION LAW

The next consideration is that of the different bases and rationales for competition systems and then to examine how far there can be convergence and divergence of these different types of competition systems. In this section 'competition' is being used as a very loose and general term to take account of different economic bases.

A general definition of competition law can be found in any textbook,[36] but most writers agree that there are aims and values of particular countries or trading blocs that will colour the concerns that a competition law system is expected to address.[37]

A selection[38] of divergent models of state 'competition' law are:

---

[32] For example see A Schaub, International Co-operation in Antitrust Matters: Making the Point in the Wake of the Boeing/MDD Proceedings [1998] Competition Policy Newsletter nos. 1, 2, 3–4.

[33] One of the consequences of this is the growth of forum shopping.

[34] Case No IV/M.877 OJ [1997] L 336/16. Boeing was eventually cleared by the EU Commission, but the decision was contingent on many conditions, and it should also be borne in mind that the US had threatened a trade war unless the merger was cleared.

[35] Agreement between the European Communities and the Government of the United States of America regarding the application of their competition laws [1995] OJ L95/47.

[36] For example, Furse states that the primary purpose of competition law is to remedy some of the situations in which the free market system breaks down. (M Furse, *Competition Law of the UK and the EU*, 4th ed, (Oxford, OUP, 2004), 1. However, this is not the only purpose.

[37] For example, see R Whish, *Competition Law* 5th ed. (Butterworth's London, 2003), ch 1 or A Jones, and B Sufrin, *EC Competition Law: Text, Cases and Materials*, 2nd ed. (Oxford, OUP, 2004), ch 1 for a further discussion on the aims and objectives of variant types of competition law systems.

[38] The categories are loosely based on the definitions of models of competition law identified by the ABA in their paper on Coordination and Convergence and those presented by Professor Beth Farmer of Dickinson Law School in a paper given at the Institute of Advanced Legal Studies on the Globalization of the Enforcement of Competition law on 24 March 2003. The commentary on the classifications is by the writer.

1) The capitalist system.

   The rationale here is that the market will be left to its own operations and the role of the regulators is to not interfere unless firms engage in conduct that harms competition. This is essentially the American system[39] as developed from the Sherman Act 1890.[40] 'Under US law, a monopolist has the right to compete and to compete hard, even if the competition hurts smaller firms.'[41]

2) The EU model.

   Despite the superficial similarities, it has to be noted that the purposes of the EU competition system are very different to that of the anti-trust regime in the US.[42] The EU system of competition law is there to facilitate the Single Market,[43] prohibit the use of State Aids and enable small and medium size enterprises to compete. This system of competition law is highly regulatory.

3) Competition law as part of industrial policy.

   This is the type of system used in Japan where competition is intended to 'effectuate' the economic goals of society. As with Germany a system of competition law was imposed on Japan after the Second World War. Audretsch describes '...the most distinguishing feature of traditional Japanese competition policy in comparison with American and European models [is] "its immersion in overall industrial policy"'.[44] However, the external perception of the enforcement of competition law by the Japan Fair Trade Commission was that it was minimal. Policy was driven by the Ministry of International Trade and Industry which encouraged the practice of business organising into groupings known as 'keiretsu' which hampered the opening up of the Japanese markets to non-Japanese enterprises. South Korea is a further example of a

---

[39] More precisely, it is the Chicago School of anti-trust thinking.

[40] The use of 'developed' is deliberate as many of the terms used in the Sherman Act were undefined. Jones and Sufrin describe it as 'law without a discernible policy behind it. Policies .... emerged later.' A Jones, and B Sufrin, *EC Competition Law: Text, Cases and Materials*, (Oxford, OUP, 2001), 19.

[41] *Report of the ABA sections of antitrust law and international law and practice on the internationalization of competition law rules: coordination and convergence, Part III The Current Stage of Convergence* (ABA 'December' 1999), 23.

[42] The similarities arise owing to the influence of German law on the development of the EU canon of competition. German competition law was heavily influenced towards the US model following the Second World War.

[43] Gerber argues that for 'both [the Commission and the ECJ] competition law has been a source of power because it has been instrumental in the integration process. The Commission has often enjoyed political support for its competition law initiatives because they have been perceived as necessary to dismantle barriers to trade among the Member States, an overriding goal of all institutions within the European Union.' D Gerber, *Modernising Competition Law: A Developmental Perspective* [2001] ECLR 122 at 126.

[44] D Audretsch, The Market and the State: Government Policy Towards Business in Europe, Japan and the United States, (New York, New York University Press, 1989), 115.

country which maintained a 'managed economy' and only adopted a competition law when the economy had matured.

4) The 'Pure Statist' or communist model.

This is the system formerly used in the Soviet bloc countries and still widely employed in China, where nearly all businesses are state owned. However, most former Soviet bloc countries are attempting to join the EU or have bilateral trading agreements with it that require the adoption some form of competition law. China is gradually allowing competition into its domestic markets and a consideration of a new Chinese competition system is underway[45].

5) Restrictive practices law.

This is the preferred model of many developing countries who wish to protect and grow their small local industries and keep out the multi-nationals. It is a pattern particularly used by East Asian economies where it was believed that it would be more beneficial to develop domestic industries for the long-term rather than take the immediate benefits offered by multi-nationals.[46] Additionally there is much suspicion of the motives of the developed countries who are promoting the virtues of 'their' style of competition law as it could be 'a tool of the industrialized nations to exploit the economies of the less developed countries at the latters' expense.'[47]

Note that not all the economic models of trade necessarily have a role for 'competition' as it is used in the western sense. And it can be asked, why should they? This differentiation as to the perception of need for a competition law is likely to be the main barrier to a model of global competition law, without even starting a discussion of global justice.

One of the conclusions that can be drawn from the existence of these disparate models is that local conditions will influence the development or lack of a competition law system. Despite the incursions of the supranational regulatory bodies such as the WTO and the OECD into the field of competition law, a small but important point appears to be forgotten. It is one of different norms and values. Economic systems are being used to achieve different ends. For example, the pre-requisite for membership of the WTO and thus access to the benefits that it affords, such as greater access to markets, is the acceptance of WTO norms. These may not

---

[45] At the time of writing it was not clear what form this competition regime would take.

[46] For a more in-depth consideration of this please refer to Ha-Joon Chang, *Industrial Policy and East Asia – the Miracle, the Crisis, and the Future,* a revised version of the paper presented at the World Bank Workshop on "Rethinking the East Asian Miracle", San Francisco 16–7 (sic) February 1999 at http://www.econ.cam.ac.uk/faculty/chang/wbip-pdf.pdf (last accessed 4 July 2005).

[47] *Report of the ABA sections of antitrust law and international law and practice on the internationalization of competition law rules: coordination and convergence, Part III The Current State of Convergence* (ABA, December, 1999), 35.

be the most appropriate for developing economies. It should be noted that the expectations of an ability to compete and adapt to the conditions of competition for developing and least developed countries are different to those of the developed world. Many countries that are now the main industrial economies achieved their pre-eminence prior to the development of competition rules, eg, the UK and the US. Possibly only West Germany could be cited as an economy that grew under a strict competition law discipline, but the German economy foundered on reunification in 1991 and has been hamstrung by the introduction of the Single European Currency.

A GLOBAL COMPETITION AUTHORITY

The ideal of an international body to oversee adherence to competition rules is not a new one. It was proposed in the draft Havana Charter of 1948. The scope of the body's powers was to be far wider than is likely to be permitted to any body created now as:

> the international organization was to receive and winnow complaints from governments and private interested persons, investigate them, decide whether or not practices had harmful effects, recommend remedial action to member states, and publish reports of its decisions and recommendations and the actions taken.[48]

There are already linkages between various of the national and transnational competition authorities such as those agreements between the US and the EU, but overarching the sphere of trade although not yet, competition law, is the WTO. Any global body would be expected to enforce its rules across the board for all countries, no matter whether they are developed or least developed. However, to take this position as the starting point is to begin with a proposition that superficially appears fair, but in reality means starting with an unlevel playing field. It was said by Dr Robert Aboagye-Mensah, General Secretary Christian Council of Ghana, that:

> international trade between my country and the West is like an antelope and a giraffe competing for food which is at the top of a tree. You can make the ground beneath their feet level but the contest will still not be fair.[49]

---

[48] C Edwards, *Control of Cartels and Monopolies: An International Comparison*, (Oceania Publications Inc, Dobbs Ferry New York, 1967), 230–1.
[49] *Trade Justice, a Campaign Handbook*, a joint publication of the Methodist Relief and Development Fund, Speak, Traidcraft and Christian Aid, 2002 at 8.

The UK government has expressed the view that:

developing countries also need laws to deal with such things as monopolies and mergers and restrictive business practices. We are working within international organisations to develop the best way of putting these in place.[50]

There is no explanation of why it is so important for developing countries to have these laws when it took until 1998 for the UK to pass the Competition Act in 1998 and 2002 for the Enterprise Act. In a paper presented to UNCTAD the economic case against the necessity for competition rules for developing countries was cogently argued by Professor Ajit Singh suggesting that a case by case basis was a more appropriate method of assessing a country's need for a competition law rather than the proposed 'one size fits all' idea.[51]

It has been suggested that the WTO is best placed to act as the forum for any progress on global competition talks as it has the largest membership at 148 countries of any trade forum and because the veto accorded to all countries no matter what their size means that the voice of developing countries can be heard. However, it is usually the US that uses the veto. Conversely, the WTO has also been seen as the least bad alternative. Among the many factors that would have made the WTO unsuitable as a forum for the enforcement of a global system of competition law was the inequity of representation. Rich countries or trading blocs such as the EU or the US maintain a permanent presence at the WTO, who can lobby consistently for their interests, whereas the least developed countries such as Malawi[52] simply do not have the resources to compete, and the voices that most need to be heard are not. There are often suggestions that despite formal decisions been taken on a one-country-one-vote system, much of the real bargaining is done at a bilateral level from which developing countries are excluded. However, with the admission of China as a member of the WTO, it has been speculated that the developing world may have a champion, in concert with India, to put a case that is more likely to be listened to, even if not immediately acted upon.

Writing from the EU perspective, Brittan and Van Miert[53] suggested that the steps to follow in order to achieve the prerequisite minimum for a competition framework to operate successfully were:

---

[50] *Eliminating World Poverty: A Challenge for the 21st Century-A Summary*, (Department for International Development, London, 1997), 15.

[51] M Khor, Expert at UNCTAD competition meeting warns that a WTO competition agreement will undermine developing countries' development efforts at http://www.twnside.org.sg/title/twninfo42.htm (last accessed 4 July 2005).

[52] J Stanhope, *teartimes*, Autumn 2003, 20.

[53] L Brittan, and K Van Miert, *Towards an International Framework of Competition Rules*, Com (96) 284 at http://europa.eu.int/comm/competition/international/com284.html (last accessed 4 July 2005).

1) The adoption of domestic competition structures
The core minimum put forward by Brittan and Van Miert that is recommended to put basic competition rules in place is to have regulations such as those on 'anti-competitive practices, outlawing restrictive agreements, preventing the abuse of a dominant position and mergers.'[54] Additionally, there should be an enforcement mechanism and finally there should be access to the domestic enforcement authorities for private parties.

Theoretically this sounded feasible but developing and least developed economies have expressed their opposition to the development of domestic competition law systems as a priority when there are still many other issues in relation to social inequalities to be solved. It has been noted in several articles[55] examining the development of competition systems in the former Soviet bloc countries that wish to accede to the EU, that problems arose because of lack of resources, training and the lack of a competition culture. If there are problems for the central European countries which have an industrial base, then how much more so for the least developed countries?

2) The adoption of common rules
Brittan and Van Miert claim that the benefits of having a common core of principles would be to facilitate the growth of competition world-wide, would lead to a greater convergence between competition laws and result in closer co-operation between competition authorities. For those countries with competition systems and Trans-National Corporations this can be accepted as beneficial as for them the more consistency there is in the rules, the easier and cheaper it becomes to comply with them. However, for those countries who do not have competition laws, the argument is irrelevant. Also, as seen with the GE/Honeywell merger debacle, the question of convergence can be illusory. Co-operation is fine until the 'national' interest is under threat, as in *Boeing*.

3) The establishment of an instrument of co-operation between competition authorities
This has occurred without the need for a global authority with the proliferation of the many bilateral agreements that exist between developed countries. However the system is cumbersome and lacks consistency. Again, it does little to assist the developing and least developed countries.

4) Dispute settlement
In relation to dispute settlement the WTO is only a useful forum between countries in its current format, and then only to a limited extent. There are no remedies available to private parties. It is arguable that as it is

---

[54] *Ibid.*
[55] For examples, see A Stobiecka, Polish Competition Law Update, [2002] ECLR 92, M Kalaus, Estonia: the New Competition Act Introduces Full Merger Control, [2002] ECLR 304, T Fiala, The New Competition Act in the Czech Republic, [2002] ECLR 400.

between private parties that most of the enforcement actions will be needed, it is likely that there will be no role for the WTO as an enforcement mechanism.[56]

An examination of the proposals put forward by Brittan and Van Miert leads to the conclusion that these suggestions do not appear to solve the jurisdictional issues that have been referred to earlier, eg, the conflict between the US and the EU as to when their respective competition bodies should be allowed to act. In addition, the proposals are manifestly unsuitable for use by developing and least developed countries.

The conclusions of Brittan[57] and Van Miert were very strongly in favour of global enforcement. Their argument as to why international rules are needed is based on a quartet of reasons:

1) 'Multilateral rules would promote more equal conditions of competition world-wide.'[58]

However, this does not automatically mean that countries would be able to compete more equally.

2) 'To avoid conflicts of law and jurisdiction between countries and to promote a gradual convergence of competition laws.'[59]

Burnside has previously identified that this is false. The conventional wisdom of the 'conference talking shop' has already agreed that gradual convergence is happening without the international rules. It has also been demonstrated how effective it is.[60]

3) 'To increase the effectiveness and coherence of the community's own competition policy enforcement.'[61]

Historically the EU's competition enforcement policy has lacked coherence, particularly in the field of mergers.[62]

---

[56] The dispute between Kodak and Fuji had to be dealt with by complaints at the international level heard by the WTO as there was no alternative method of recourse for Kodak to have the case heard at the time.

[57] Brittan and Van Miert, *Towards an international framework of competition rules,* Com(96) 284 at http://europa.eu.int/comm/competition/international/com284.html (accessed 4 July 2005).

[58] *Ibid.*

[59] *Ibid.*

[60] Monti attempted to rebut criticism of the convergence track record between the EU and the US in his speech at Merchant Taylor's Hall where he states that only one other merger had been prohibited by the Commission.

[61] Brittan and Van Miert, n 57 above.

[62] The Commission's guidance on mergers has been criticised for its lack of clarity by Freshfields Bruckhaus Deringer at http://europa.eu.int/comm/competition/mergers/review/contributions/ref048_freshfields_en.pdf (last accessed 4 July 2005). The grounds for the recent slew of Commission decisions that have been overturned by the CFI have underlined the lack of explicit and coherent guidance available to those seeking to apply the merger guidelines, for example, *Airtours Plc* v *Commission* (Case T-342/99) [2002] ECR II-2585, *Schneider Electric SA* v *Commission* (Case T-77/2002) [2002] ECR II-4201, *Lagardere SCA V Canal + SA* v *Commission* (Case T- 251/2000) [2002] ECR II-4825, *Tetra Laval BV* v *Commission* (Case T-80/02) [2002] ECR II-4519.

4) 'Enhanced commitment to competition policy enforcement would strengthen the trading system along the lines of our legal systems and market economies, of which competition law is a basic feature.'[63]

This demonstrates the Eurocentric nature of the proposals and conclusions by emphasising the importance and the role of competition law within the EU. However, it fails to acknowledge that competition law does not hold the same primacy in other jurisdictions.

THE CURRENT ALTERNATIVES FOR STRUCTURING COMPETITION RULES

Bi-lateral agreements

Bi-lateralism has a large following among the G8 and there is a framework laid own by the OECD for the format of such agreements, but its 'success' is exemplified by cases such as *GE/Honeywell*. These types of agreements are usually pitched at a low level of convergence such as information-sharing but not much more. The problems that are not dealt with by the use of bi-lateral agreements include the mismatch of legal bases, the practicality of all trading countries entering into bilateral agreements and on what model, and there remains the question of inconsistency in decision-making. Additionally, it is suggested that bi-lateralism will lead to distortionsof competition since not all countries will participate in this type of agreement. However, the principle driving force behind bi-lateralism is that it is the US administration's preferred option.

One of the leading authorities and supporters of greater harmonisation is Professor Eleanor Fox of NYU Law School. In an article from 1997 she proposes that global competition law should take the form of a

> liberal antitrust to fit the worldview of liberal trade; not without derogations, but with a framework for permissible derogations...work on the ground up infrastructure of antitrust agency co-operation, liberal regional co-operation and sectoral agreements.[64]

However despite being an argument for a global antitrust Fox's proposals look suspiciously like the preferred model of international antitrust from the US perspective of bilateral agreements rather than a workable multilateral proposal. Fox does not explain how the bilateral structure becomes multilateral. Fox's thinking becomes more understandable when she uses the EU framework of Directives as her exemplar for these agreements.

---

[63] Brittan and Van Miert, n 57 above.
[64] E Fox, *Towards World Antitrust and Market Access, The American Journal of International Law*, Vol 91, No. 1 (Jan 1997) 1–25 at 2.

However, it has to be stated 'with respect' that to suggest that the EU's competition policy is complete and unitary in quality is to misunderstand the functioning of the EU.

Multi-lateralism

Multi-lateralism has many proponents and this route leads to the standardisation of rules, but still does not overcome the basic problems of the fundamental differences in the legal bases. It equally has many opponents, but the growth of mega-mergers and the economic strength of trans-national corporations across many jurisdictions may result in this option being taken up by default.

There are various bodies that have been proposed as potential candidates for the role of global authority. The WTO attempted to take on this mantel, and the progress made on this front will be assessed later in this article. However the alternatives include the Organisation for Economic Co-operation and Development (OECD), the United Nations Conference on Trade and Development (UNCTAD) and what used to be described as the 'Stand Alone' Option.

The OECD has a track record in competition issues and has established multi-lateral agreements with other supranational bodies, but it does not have the capacity for binding agreements and has a limited membership, although there is the OECD global forum. UNCTAD does have a Competition Code, but it is not binding. The 'Stand Alone' option appears to have been ruled out by the creation of the International Competition Network (ICN), despite its self-imposed limitations. The ICN has at this time explicitly ruled itself out of being an enforcement body. It is, by its own admission, a 'talking shop'. However, this organisation could be a better option as the global enforcement mechanism if its remit were to be re-examined and expanded. Farmer is mildly supportive of this option,[65] but when the membership of the ICN is considered it presents the same problem as using the WTO. It is the G8 countries that are the major players, who already have mature competition systems. Is it best practice[66] as Von Meibom and Geiger claim? Or is there something less savoury going on?

The situation remains that, at present, there is a lack of legal certainty at many levels. Von Meibom and Geiger suggest that there is the creation of 'a uniform world Competition Law.'[67] They describe this move as both simple and radical. However, achieving it will be neither. They fail to specify whose rules should be adapted and from whence will come the

---

[65] Opinion expressed at the Institute of Advanced of Legal Studies' 25 March 2003.

[66] W Von Meibom and A Geiger, *A World Competition Law as an Ultima Ratio*, ECLR 9 [2002] 445 at 452.

[67] W Von Meibom and A Geiger, n 66 above, 445 at 446.

enforcement? Von Meibom and Geiger also suggest an entirely new structure[68] for competition rules but do not follow up on the practicalities.

The Doha Declaration—the Attempt to Find Global Competition Rules

The great hope for universal competition rules came with the general principles contained in the early part of the Doha Declaration. These principles set out the underlying position of the WTO as to the direction that it was hoped international trade rules would take. The background for the Doha Round was that of September 11. Countries tended to be in more conciliatory mood. There was a strong, but somewhat superficial stress on the special status of the developing and least developed countries. However, it remained clear that the vision of the WTO was of an organisation that wanted as many members as possible and all of those members to have the same rights and obligations, no matter what their state of development. This was the main source of conflict between the developed and developing countries.

The basic statement of intent in paragraph 1 reinforced the attitude that it is possible for trade to resolve economic problems.

> The multilateral trading system embodied in the World Trade Organization has contributed significantly to economic growth, development and employment throughout the past fifty years. We are determined, particularly in the light of the global economic slowdown, to maintain the process of reform and liberalization of trade policies, thus ensuring that the system plays its full part in promoting recovery, growth and development. We strongly reaffirm the principles and objectives set out in the Marrakesh Agreement Establishing the World Trade Organization, and pledge to reduce the use of protectionism.[69]

The stance adopted was squarely one of 'liberalisation is good and protectionism is bad'—when it is utilised by developing countries. This is too starkly delineated a position, and not indicative of the true nature of the use that the developed countries make of protectionist measures. Oxfam cites the example of trade taxes paid on Bangledeshi exports to the US as 14 times higher than those paid by the French.[70] The development of many of the East-Asian economies in the 1970s and 1980s was underpinned by protection of domestic industries until they were able to compete internationally.

---

[68] It is based on the idea of a world competition law monitored by a world competition court in W Von Meibom, and A Geiger, n 66 above, 445 at 448.

[69] Doha Declaration, paragraph 1 at http://www.wto.org/english/thewto_e/minist_e/min01_e/mindecl_e.htm (last accessed 5 July 2005).

[70] *Stitched Up*, Oxfam Briefing Paper April 2004 at p13 Available at http://www.oxfam.org.uk/what_we_do/issues/trade/downloads/bp60_textiles.pdf (last accessed 4 July 2005)

Paragraph 2 continued this theme.

> International trade can play a major role in the promotion of economic
> development and the alleviation of poverty. We recognize the need for all
> our peoples to benefit from increased opportunities and welfare gains that
> the multilateral trading system generates. The majority of WTO Members
> are developing countries. We seek to place their needs and interests at the
> heart of the work programme adopted in this declaration, ...we shall contin-
> ue to make positive efforts designed to ensure that developing countries,
> and especially the least-developed among them, secure a share in the
> growth of world trade commensurate with the needs of their economic
> development. In this context, enhanced market access, balanced rules, and
> well targeted, sustainable financed technical assistance and capacity build-
> ing programmes have important roles to play.[71]

The striking point about this statement was the recognition of the stage of
economic development of the majority of members, but the aims of the
Declaration were not in the majority's interest. It has been shown that the
imposition of the developed world's economic policy on developing and
least developed countries can be catastrophic. For many developing countries, particularly in Africa, the trade-off for loans from the World Bank or
International Monetary Fund was the imposition of a Structural
Adjustment Programme, which was always tied to 'liberalisation' of the
economy.[72] It should also be pointed out that 'balanced rules' are not automatically fair rules.

Paragraph 3 recognised 'the particular vulnerability of the least-
developed countries and the special structural difficulties they face in
the global economy'[73] but refuses to make any concessions owing to
those difficulties.

Paragraph 6 again reiterated that all members would be expected to
participate on the same basis of '...an open and non-discriminatory multilateral trading system, and acting for the protection of the environment
and the promotion of sustainable development can and must be mutually supportive.'[74] An open system is not necessarily appropriate for the
least developed countries.[75] Oxfam cites the statistics that the high income

---

[71] Doha Declaration, paragraph 2 at http://www.wto.org/english/thewto_e/minist_e/
min01_e/mindecl_e.htm (last accessed 4 July 2005).

[72] 'In Mozambique prices tripled in the first year of the adjustment programme' per J
Hanlon, *Mozambique: Who Calls the Shots*, (London, James Currey, 1990) cited in M Curtis,
Trade for Life, Making Trade Work for Poor People, (London, Christian Aid, 2001).

[73] Doha Declaration, paragraph 3 at http://www.wto.org/english/thewto_e/minist_e/
min01_e/mindecl_e.htm (last accessed 4 July 2005).

[74] Doha Declaration, paragraph 6 at http://www.wto.org/english/thewto_e/minist_e/
min01_e/mindecl_e.htm (last accessed 4 July 2005).

[75] Organisations such as Christian Aid point to the need for poor countries to 'have the
right to intervene in their own economies and develop trade policies which suit their own
development needs.' Available at http://www.christian-aid.org.uk/campaign/trade/
0303govt.htm (last accessed 4 July 2005).

developed countries account for 14 percent of the population but 75 percent of world exports. Low income developing countries 'which account for 40 percent of the population' have only a 3 percent share of world trade.[76]

Paragraph 9 appears to welcome the southern countries, stating that '...we are committed to accelerating the accession of least-developed countries.'[77] However, this is without any conciliation on the question of suitability of the rules for these economies, and is predicated on the basis of acceptance of developed world norms and values.

The statements on the interaction between trade and competition policy were contained in paragraphs 23, 24 and 25 of the Declaration. These three short paragraphs set out the basis upon which the WTO intended to build a competition framework. However, despite all the excitement and froth over Doha, successive deadlines for negotiations were missed due to the blocking tactics of the developed countries.[78] When the crucial opportunity came at Cancun to advance the talks on a global competition strategy, it was due to the repeated blocking of any progress by the G21 and a group of mainly African countries that it became clear that there was no basis of an agreement and the moderator, Luis Ernesto Derbez the Mexican Foreign Minister, terminated all discussion.

Following the failure of talks at Cancun and subsequent meetings the WTO agreed that the

issues, mentioned in the Doha Ministerial Declaration in paragraphs 20–22, 23–25 and 26 respectively, will not form part of the Work Programme set out in that Declaration and therefore no work towards negotiations on any of these issues will take place within the WTO during the Doha Round[79].

Although it was implicit in the Doha declaration that the WTO was seeking a level playing field, there was recognition of the fact that it

---

[76] Available at www.oxfam.org.uk (last accessed 4 July 2005).

[77] Doha Declaration, paragraph 9 at http://www.wto.org/english/thewto_e/minist_e/min01_e/mindecl_e.htm (last accessed 4 July 2005).

[78] For example, see http://www.christian-aid.org.uk/campaign/trade/0303govt.htm (last accessed 4 July 2005).

[79] At http://www.wto.org/english/tratop_e/dda_e/draft_text_gc_dg_31july04_e.htm (last accessed 4 July 2005). The issue of global competition rules is therefore not ruled out but will have to wait until the end of the Doha Round. It is hoped that the WTO will take account of the alternatives suggested from the EU such as the suggestion for the possible content of a global competition agreement. A WTO competition agreement could be based on the following elements: a domestic legislative framework to be based on the principle of non-discrimination; transparency, regarding laws, regulation and guidelines of general application; guarantees of "procedural fairness" in competition investigations (including protection of confidential information) and the right of petition to competition authorities and/or the judiciary; administrative competition decisions subject to judicial review. *New Round Negotiations on Trade and Competition* at http://europa.eu.int/comm/trade/issues/sectoral/competition/index_en.htm (last accessed 4 July 2005).

would be harder for the developing and least developed countries to participate in the proposed multilateral agreement without assistance and flexibility, particularly in terms of resources and training.[80]

To demonstrate the gap in perspective on this issue between the North and South, it is worth considering the standpoint of the EU on the benefits of the Doha Declaration, which was relentlessly optimistic.[81] This was much at variance with the scepticism expressed by developing and least developing countries. This can be illustrated by the reaction of Devellennes and Kiriazis from D-G Competition[82] who suggested that the Doha Declaration was 'quite satisfactory' for the following four reasons:

1) The general recognition of the benefits of an overarching competition framework appeared to have been accepted by all the signatories to the Declaration.

   However, there was a sense that they are not completely confident that this was the case. There were often suggestions that developing and least developed countries were subjected to behind-the-scenes pressure to accept the decisions that the developed countries wanted.[83] Devellenes and Kiriazis further suggested that there would be a trickle-down benefit as a consequence of the wider acceptance of competition regimes. The question as always with this argument is how much is left from the trickle?

2) Despite the time lag between Doha and any likely actual policy at Cancun, the time should have been profitably used to draft the basis of a policy.

   Obviously this did not happen. However, there may have been a subconscious recognition of the complexity of the issues and likelihood that an agreement would not be reached, as implicit in the

---

[80] A statement from the EU recognised that any agreement at Cancun would have to have been adaptable in its application. 'Any multilateral framework agreement in the WTO must take into account the specific needs of developing countries. There must be flexibility in the ways they co-operate, and they must be allowed to introduce a competition agreement step-by-step in realistic transition periods. Competition authorities in developing countries must benefit from better co-ordinated technical assistance and capacity-building activities.' *New Round Negotiations on trade and competition* at http://europa.eu.int/comm/trade/issues/sectoral/competition/index_en.htm (last accessed 4 July 2005).

[81] See, for example, Cancun Special: Advancing the Doha Development Agenda *Council Conclusions on the Preparation of the WTO 5th Ministerial Conference, Cancún 10-14 September 2003* Brussels, 21 July 2003 at http://europa.eu.int/comm/trade/issues/newround/doha_da/cancun/cc210703_en.htm (last accessed 4 July 2005).

[82] Y Devellennes, and G Kiriazis, *Competition Policy Makes it into the Doha Agenda*, Network Competition policy newsletter Number 1 February 2002 27–28 at 27 http://www.europa.eu.int./comm/competition/publications/cpn/cpn2002_1.pdf (last accessed 4 July 2005).

[83] For example, see *Trade Justice, a Campaign Handbook*, a joint publication of the Methodist Relief and Development Fund, Speak, Traidcraft and Christian Aid, 2002, pp10, 19 and 27 and the Third World Network websites which give examples of the deal making in the run up to Cancun, for example, *Non-transparent, manipulative processes underway at WTO* at http://www.twnside.org.sg/title/5400a.htm (last accessed 4 July 2005).

commentary was the feeling that perhaps the strategy needed a rethink or refining before the real negotiation started.

3) The EU deserved recognition for it role in competition being part of the Doha Round as it had been 'driving this issue for some time.'[84]

A less charitable view would be that this is evidence that this was a policy to benefit 'the haves' of the EU, and not 'the have nots' of the developing and least developed countries. This returns to the fact that competition policy is fundamental to the EU for the success of the Single Market and this is a specific end in the EU of having competition rules. Again there were suggestions that there was a good opportunity for the policy-makers at the EU to position themselves so that they could continue to drive the issue. But this was unlikely to be of much benefit to developing and least developed countries who had no, or only a very immature set of, competition rules. These countries are still thinking in terms of trying to establish industries internally, let alone compete on the international stage in the same way as undertakings in the EU and US. When these local companies contemplate entering into markets they have to contend with the power of Trans-National Corporations (TNCs). It has to be acknowledged that TNCs have the capacity to do much good in developing and least developed countries by introducing new technologies, better labour practices, new jobs, higher environmental standards and stimulating competition which can enhance the domestic market. However, too often TNCs are associated with abuses of developing and least developed countries and instead of helping markets to open up they tend to destroy the local competition by unfair practices and exploiting the local labour forces, for example, the Bhopal disaster, the workers in South Africa subjected to illness created by Asbestos by Cape or the frequent citations of Nike as a poor employer. TNCs follow capital and although competition rules may make entry to markets easier for a TNC there is no guarantee that the TNC will remain if there is a more favourable regime elsewhere. This could be an argument for the introduction of consistency in competition rules, but this is predominantly a benefit for those TNCs outside developing and least developed countries. Nascent economies still need protection to grow to be able to compete equally.

4) The existing bilateral and multilateral agreements should be examined to assist in the process of deciding how the framework will operate.

---

[84] Y Devellennes, and G Kiriazis, *Competition Policy Makes it into the Doha Agenda*, Network Competition policy newsletter Number 1 February 2002 27–28 at 27 http://www.europa.eu.int./comm/competition/publications/cpn/cpn2002_1.pdf (last accessed 4 July 2005).

The opinion was expressed that

> ...members of the Working Group will be able to go beyond the examination of abstract principle and focus on the drafting of a detailed negotiation agenda that will lead in future to the adoption of rules of a binding nature. The envisaged multilateral rules will certainly influence both the legislative activity and the enforcement practice of many members of the WTO.[85]

For many countries this simply means that they will have to draft a set of competition rules. For example, China is currently developing ideas on how competition is to be administered but it is proving difficult to accommodate the variety of thinking available on competition into the framework.

As has been seen, the WTO will not, for the foreseeable future, have a role as the global enforcer of competition rules. Whether there is any organisation that could fulfil the role of global competition policeman, will it be done it in a way that will ensure global justice? And whose definition of justice is to be used?

The Brittan/Van Miert model acknowledges the flaws implicit in the arguments for an overarching competition body. On the one hand they state that

> an international agreement on competition rules would bring benefits to nations of the trading community. All countries could participate in an agreement to incorporate competition law provisions in their domestic law.[86]

This definition refers to the 'trading community', which may not include all nations. Also note the 'could.' Perhaps not all countries would actually be able to achieve this type of participation. However, the major drawback in the concept of a 'one size fits all' competition regime is highlighted by the comment that

> At the same time the application of the co-operation and enforcement provisions would require, of participating countries, that they have a sophisticated administration capable of handling sensitive information and of assessing commercial practices in a dynamic context. Many developing countries do not yet have this administrative machinery.[87]

---

[85] Y Devellennes, and G Kiriazis, *Competition Policy Makes it into the Doha Agenda*, Network Competition policy newsletter Number 1 February 2002 27–28 at 28 http://www.europa.eu.int./comm/competition/publications/cpn/cpn2002_1.pdf (last accessed 4 July 2005).

[86] Brittan and Van Miert, *Towards an international framework of competition rules*, Com(96) 284 at http://europa.eu.int/comm/competition/international/com284.html (last accessed 4 July 2005).

[87] Brittan and Van Miert, n 86 above. D-G competition has demonstrated frequently that it cannot do this, particularly as mentioned earlier in the context of mergers where it doesn't appear to understand its own regulations.

Why should they? Why should competition be a priority for developing economies? It can be seen in the European context that many countries that recently joined the EU would fall into the classification of developing countries as they have had to graft a system of competition law onto their legal system as a prerequisite for membership of the EU. If a developing country does not have a system of competition law in place, then where is it going to get its model from? Predictably the mature anti-trust regimes will be held up as exemplars and then the choice has to be made as to which of those models will be selected. It can also be asked whether the help a developing country will get will be dependent on the model for which they opt.

There is an argument for adopting the EU system of competition rules because of its scope and that it is being made manageable for a growing number of countries. However, due to the aims underlying the EU's arrangements it is questionable as to whether the system could be appropriate for general application. It has been said that

> Within the community the elimination of trade barriers and the application of competition law have gone hand in hand. This approach is unique in the world. The competition policy of the community has...grown to full maturity and is rigorous and neutral in its application.[88]

This underlines the problem with a global system of competition rules—the time that it has taken for competition systems to mature as economies mature. It is unlikely that developing and least developed countries will have the luxury of time.

Brittan and Van Miert demonstrated a sense of realism in relation to the process of establishing a global approach to competition law by accepting that

> if adopted co-operation provisions would, in a first stage, apply only between a limited number of signatories with mature antitrust agencies. Provisions could group together developed and advanced developing countries to start with, and gradually come to include more countries.[89]

Although this is to be commended as a wholly sensible approach, it underlines the problems of trying to get all countries to accept and compete on the same terms and that it is not a practicality, at least in the short term. The major failing of this view is that it fails to recognise that some countries, despite their good intentions will never be able to 'shoulder the obligations of the agreement' and thus be 'eligible to participate.'[90]

---

[88] Brittan and Van Miert, n 86 above.
[89] *Ibid*.
[90] *Ibid*.

The turnover of many multinationals is now greater than that of many developing countries. The control of private anti-competitive practices is what is important. Will the WTO make provision for that or will it just allow for state action against other states?

CONCLUSIONS

Under the Doha Declaration the basis of a workable strategy was laid down for competition law, but in reality this could not be translated into a truly workable system which afforded equal treatment to all the members of the WTO. A 'one size fits all' approach has not worked. The Doha agreement stated that 'full account shall be taken of the needs of developing and least developed country participants and appropriate flexibility provided to address them.'[91] However, the WTO failed to encompass the diversity of the economic systems and could not ensure that developing countries can trade fairly and on an equal footing with the major industrialised economies. At this juncture Doha cannot be described as a pattern for a fair trade system for the future, merely another talking shop which the G8 wanted to endorse and adhere to only when it suited them. Witness the US which has the most protectionist system in existence.

As has been noted earlier, many writers have commented on the 'convergence trend between the EU and the WTO.'[92] As the jurisdictions of the EU have had many years over which to develop both their competition law systems and jurisprudence it is unsurprising that, despite the Doha assurances, those younger economies decided against competition rules, as there was no chance for them to compete fairly. There is a lack of technical knowledge and resources. The influence exercised by developed nations needs to be countered. Practices such as tying co-operation to aid packages and the intimidation of poorer countries need to be stopped. If the WTO remains serious about becoming a global enforcement mechanism and taking on that role on an equitable basis, then questions of cost and penalties need to be addressed. At present if a poorer country wishes to bring an action against a richer country, then apart from the cost, the result if successful is sanctions, not fines!

It has been said that 'updating the world trade rulebook is a pre-condition for a fair, predictable and transparent rules-based system to govern world trade and investment and is a priority for many WTO Members.'[93]

---

[91] Doha Declaration at http://www.wto.org/english/thewto_e/minist_e/min01_e/min-decl_e.htm (last accessed 4 July 2005).

[92] JHH Weiler, 'Epilogue: Towards a Common Law of International Trade' in Weiler (ed), *The EU, The WTO and the NAFTA* (Oxford, OUP, 2000) 202.

[93] The Doha Development Agenda, Principles for the Doha Development Agenda at http://europa.eu.int/comm/trade/issues/newround/doha_da/index_en.htm (last accessed 4 July 2005).

This sentiment is in accord with the view of many third world countries who do not want negotiations on competition law until the current system is reformed on a fairer basis[94]. The issue of competition rules is being driven by rich countries, which is exemplified by the attitude of the EU towards the competition agenda.

Critics of the current system include groups such as the Trade Justice Campaign. Their premise is a very simple one that 'it is morally wrong to expect the poorest to compete with wealthy and well established international traders.'[95] They further argue that it is not merely a question of trying to establish a level playing field but because of the inequity between the rich and the poor 'the international rules and practices that govern trade (and thus competition) must give the weakest and most vulnerable special help until they are strong enough to compete without it.'[96] Instead of a uniform system of competition rules, there should be a graduated scheme of special treatment to enable this development to take place.

'The international trading system was devised by the rich to suit their needs; it ignores the needs of the poor.'[97] This exploitation of the trading system in favour of the developed countries is not a new phenomenon. Although the view is commonly expressed that the countries of the South will not develop unless those countries utilise trade liberalisation, history demonstrates that the proponents of this standpoint are perpetuating a fallacy.

> For centuries England has relied on protection, has carried it to extremes and has obtained satisfactory results from it. There is no doubt that it is to this system that it owes its present strength. After two centuries, England had found it convenient to adopt free trade because it thinks that protection can no longer offer it anything. Very well then, Gentlemen, my knowledge of our country leads me to believe that within 200 years, when America has gotten out of protection all that it can offer, it too will adopt free trade.[98]

Following the debacle at Cancun the developing and least developed countries have cleared stated that there is no need for a global authority.[99] However, if there were a global competition law, implementation at

---

[94] See *Trade Justice, a Campaign Handbook*, a joint publication of the Methodist Relief and Development Fund, Speak, Traidcraft and Christian Aid, 2002 at 31 and BL Das, *Dangers of negotiating Investment and Competition Rules in the WTO*, Trade and Development Series No. 16, (Penang TWN 2001).

[95] *Trade Justice, a Campaign Handbook*, above n 94 at 3.

[96] *Trade Justice, a Campaign Handbook, ibid.*

[97] Pope Paul VI, quoted in *Trade Justice, a Campaign Handbook*, above n 94 at 5.

[98] Ulysess S. Grant, US President 1868–76, cited in AG Frank, *Capitalism and Underdevelopment in Latin America*, (New York, Monthly Review Press, 1967), 164.

[99] The ABA has expressed reservations as to the appositeness of a global competition code enforced by a central body. Report of the ABA sections of antitrust law and international law and practice on the internationalization of competition law rules: coordination and convergence, Part III The Current State of Convergence (ABA December 1999) 61.

national level would lead to the potential for inconsistent interpretation. This problem would be circumvented by the creation of a global authority.

The development of a global competition law system is a moral and ethical issue, not just an economic and legal one. However, despite many misgivings it is not the position of the paper to argue for the abolition of the WTO or any other body which may have a potential role as forum for competition law. Rather what is hoped for is, as the Campaign for Trade Justice suggests, a shift in the emphasis of the proposed rules so that poor countries can benefit in the same way as developed countries. At present the position remains as explained by South African Competition Commission and Competition Tribunal Minister Alec Erwin, who referred to

> this apprehension on the part of the developing countries that they are having something imposed upon them and the desire of the developed countries to get international regulation as quickly as possible, but because they are moving from a position of strength, the inevitable tendency to push their own laws forward.[100]

However, it appears unlikely due to the variance in the aims and objectives underlying the different systems of competition law that the future development of a global system of competition law is problematic. It was one of the 'Singapore' issues that were imposed on trade discussions in 1996. Third World countries do not see competition as a priority and forcibly argue against any further implementation of any type of global competition system. The developed countries take the contrary view of there being a role for competition. They just fail to agree on exactly what that role is and how it should best be regulated. The US has pushed ahead with its bilateral agreements and these will have the effect of skewing the market system. There will be the trading blocs which have bilateral agreements and those that do not. Those that do not will be denied access to markets. Already the US has rewarded those countries that co-operated at Cancun and punished those that did not.[101] The situation is that the current US administration simply cannot appreciate that there is another viewpoint on the impact of a global trading system and thus global competition rules. As far as they are concerned everyone should adopt free trade, as long as the Americans are allowed to protect

---

[100] A Erwin, *The Impact of Globalisation and New Technology on Competition: The Role of the Competition Authority in a Developing Country,* Speech 29/03/01 at http://www.compcom. co.za/events/Presentations%20&%20Speeches/competition_commission_and_erwin.htm (last accessed 4 July 2005).

[101] Shortly after Cancun, the US Trade Representative pushed forward the establishment of an Andean Free Trade association and concluded a Central American Free Trade Association with El Salvador, Guatemala, Honduras and Nicaragua. Further information available at http://www.ustr.gov (last accessed 4 July 2005).

their industry.[102] They cannot see why the countries of the South are so vehemently against 'free trade'. It genuinely baffles them.[103]

At the time of the Cancun Ministerial commentators identified a move amongst the Third World countries to try to resurrect the talks in some form as the adverse effects of being outside a multi-lateral agreement were starting to impact. However, as Bush remains in office attempts to pursue a multilateralist solution are likely to fail because of the US's preferred option of bi-lateral agreements. Bilateralism gives less power to poor countries in negotiations. 'American legislators prefer such deals. America has pursued a regional trade agreement for the Americas, has signed bilateral deals with Chile and Singapore, has begun bilateral talks with 14 other countries, and promises many more.'[104] While it is clear why America wants bilateral deals, it is an impoverished alternative for developing countries compared to what they could have negotiated under a multilateral system. With the Americans leading down the bilateral route, other trade blocs are following. The EU is also looking at bilateralism and it is becoming the norm in Asia.

At the present it is difficult to evaluate where, if anywhere, the globalisation of competition law is heading. As the political status quo continued with a Bush re-election in 2004, then there is no real mileage in examining the potentiality for a global enforcer of competition law as this is not the preferred option of the Bush administration. It should be remembered that the impetus behind the issue is very much a European one and the key moves in recent years have been due to the insistence of the EU negotiators. IF the EU has lost interest, or confidence as appears to be demonstrated by Lamy's abject performance at Cancun, then a global system of competition law is unlikely to happen. However, it may be that a more realistic view of the need for one global system is taken and instead of placing all hopes on the WTO with the inherent flaws that the one-member-one-vote system has, then greater and more practicable use may be made of the ICN. With its admitted limited aims the ICN may prove to be the forum whereby greater co-operation and thus greater harmony, if not convergence, may be achieved leading to a globalisation of sorts of competition law. Whether the global enforcer of competition rules, whatever shape it takes, will be able to dispense global justice while administering global competition law is unlikely. There is a lack of political will to achieve either end.

---

[102] The WTO has frequently found the US to be in violation of rules on subsidies given to both the cotton and steel industries. For a commentary on the more recent decisions against the US please see for example, http://www.oxfam.org.uk/press/releases/cotton030305.htm (last accessed 4 July 2005).

[103] See for example, http://www.ustr.gov/Document_Library/Op-eds/2003/America_will_not_wait_for_the_won't-do_countries.html?ht=(last accessed 4 July 2005). This typifies the position of the US Trade Representative Robert B Zoellick.

[104] *Cancun's charming outcome,* The Economist September 20, 2003 at 13.

To conclude, as the paper started, with a quote from *Re-imagining the Future*:

> [T]he globalization of economic, social and cultural life is a continuous process and future generations will have to come to terms with it even more than the present generation. Our responsibility is to look beyond the crises of the moment and to help prepare the world community for the problems and opportunities of the future.[105]

And on that basis it would be preferable to see global justice than any of the current suggestions for a system of global competition law.

---

[105] B Boutros-Ghali, foreword in J Camilleri *et al*, *Reimagining the Future—Towards Democratic Governance* (Victoria, La Trobe University, 2000), xi.

11

From Constitutions to Constitutionalism: A Constitutional Approach for Global Governance

MIGUEL POIARES MADURO

P ROCESSES OF GLOBAL governance, I will argue, change the forms and locus of power. They also challenge the conditions of national constitutionalism and with it they require a rethinking of constitutionalism itself. Such rethinking must depart from two practical questions: what are the consequences of global governance for national constitutionalism? Can global governance be moulded by a form of global constitutionalism? These two questions embody tremendous normative challenges, requiring us to revisit the basic ideals of constitutionalism and to discuss its different possible forms: what are the normative ideals of constitutionalism? Can they be pursued outside the conditions secured by national constitutionalism? If they can, what are the requirements to be secured by global constitutionalism? And what ought to regulate the relationship between such form of constitutionalism and national constitutionalism?

In this paper I will argue that constitutionalism is required as the form of power in global governance. But I will also recognise that national political communities still provide the best proxy for constitutionalism. This apparent conundrum is solved by distinguishing constitutions (constitutionalism in the context of political communities) from constitutionalism (as a theory of power or social decision making). How such constitutionalism can have a global form and how is it to be related to constitutions will be linked to a constitutional approach based on comparative institutional analysis and a vision of constitutionalism as a set of paradoxes involving two balances: a procedural balance between inclusion and intensity of participation and a substantive balance between individual autonomy and civic solidarity. These balances are, in turn, instrumental to the constitutional ideals of freedom and full participation and representation. The character of the constitutionalism argued for in here has, as a consequence, that no single constitutional model is adopted and no across the board solution is put forward. Instead, this paper argues, what we can identify is a series of constitutional choices and what we can provide is a set of constitutional criteria. But even the latter, it is argued, do not provide us with indisputable or easy answers. That is so because the ideals of constitutionalism embody, in themselves, permanent paradoxes and tensions that never provide a final answer but simply a context for legitimating that answer. What we can try is to place global governance at the core of such paradoxes and tensions. It is in that way that we can transform it into a tool, and not an obstacle, of constitutionalism.

I start by reviewing the impact of global governance on the form and locus of power. In section 2, I explain how such processes challenge national constitutionalism. I then discuss the relation between constitutionalism and national constitutionalism: in section 3, I argue that national constitutionalism is simply a contextual representation of constitutionalism; in section 4, I argue that national constitutionalism is however the best proxy for constitutionalism we have so far. Section 5 is devoted to an analysis of different current constitutional perspectives on global governance (pro and against global constitutionalism). I will point to the limits of these approaches by referring to what I call their single constitutional character.[1] The final section discusses what an alternative approach may look like.

GLOBAL GOVERNANCE AND THE FORM AND LOCUS OF POWER

In 1993 the Spanish constitutional scholar Francisco Rubio Llorente published a remarkable book called *La Forma del Poder*[2] (The Form of Power). For Rubio Llorente, the Constitution is the form of power. In here, I will depart from a similar perception of constitutionalism as a set of processes and rules that allocate, discipline and govern power in such a way as to maximise the constitutional ideals of freedom and full participation and representation.[3] It does not follow from this perspective that wherever there is power there must be a Constitution. It does however require any exercise of power to be traced back and ultimately legitimised by reference to some constitutional authority. Moreover, this entails that any independent power must be the subject of constitutionalism. It further requires that any conflict between different constitutional authorities must itself be regulated by constitutionalism.

---

[1] It is a broader conception of the idea of single institutionalism argued by Neil Komesar *Imperfect Alternatives, Choosing Institutions in Law, Economics, and Public Policy* (Illinois, University of Chicago Press, 1997).

[2] Rubio Llorente, Francisco. *La Forma del Poder*, (Centro de Estudios Constitucionales, Madrid, 1993.)

[3] I explain in more detail somewhere else this point of departure and its underlying assumptions. See Miguel Poiares Maduro, 'Europe and the Constitution: What if this is as good as in acts', in writer and wind (eds), *Constitutionalism Beyond the State* (Cambridge, CUP, 1949).

Traditionally, the form of power has been the Constitution of the Nation State. The States were the holders of the ultimate authority and of a monopoly over power (encapsulated in the traditional conception of sovereignty); others could exercise such power but either in the form of a delegation or authorisation from the State (regulated, in turn, by its Constitution). Constitution and power coincided in the same *locus:* the State. The idea of global governance reflects a perception of change in the locus and form of power. There is a transfer of power to global sites of varying degrees of institutionalisation. And there is also a substantial change in the mechanisms that determine the exercise of such power. Both the allocation of authority and the forms of participation and representation are impacted by those changes. In some instances such power can no longer be traced back and legitimated through the State Constitution, in other instances such power alters the national constitutional form of power.

In this way, the idea of global governance can be seen as including a variety of different phenomena that have, as their common element, a change in the locus and form of power. We can easily identify some of these phenomena in various current international trends of which one can give some examples: Judicialisation refering to the growth in third party dispute resolution in international law (of which the WTO is the strongest example), the international courts of humanitarian law, and the role of courts in regional integration regimes; The supra-nationalisation of policy-making that takes place, in various degrees, mainly in the context of regional regimes of integration (such as the EU, NAFTA, MERCOSUL etc.); Standardisation and its associated technocratic international bodies and agencies; Transnational political action, expressed in the increased networks that cut across national States and create political and power links between both private actors (with increased transnational coalitions promoted, in a more or less institutionalised form, by such things as the internet or ONGs forums) and public actors (such as is the case with networks of members of the national administrations or judges);[4] 'Privatisation' of international law through the increased role of private actors both on its litigation (either directly, by being given a right of access to international courts, or indirectly, by influencing the judicial actions brought by States) and its law-making activities; Economic liberalisation and the increased role it allocates to the global market in shaping the regulation of economic activity.

As it may already have become clear, global governance will not be taken to include, in here, only centralised forms of decision making but, instead, any form of social decision making that takes place at the transnational level expressing a use of power that can no longer be legitimised by

---

[4] Rev Anne-Marie Slaughter, 'Squaring the Circle'. Reconciling Sovereignty and Global Governance Through Global Government Networks? (Review of Anne-Marie Slaughter, *A New World Order*) 2005 *Harvard Law Review* Vol.118. pp. 1255–1312.

reference to the Constitutions of the States. Rules, dispute resolution and political deliberation may be the 'stars' of global governance but the processes of power transfer are broader. There are less formalised and even atomistic forms of decision making at the global level that have, in effect, taken over some of State's governmental functions. These processes (such as the market) have embedded certain mechanisms of representation and participation that produce social decisions, requiring them to be subject to constitutional analysis.[5] In the following examples I will highlight these changes in the *locus* and form of power raised by the processes of global governance.

International Organisations and Power Changes

Traditionally, international organisations were not conceived as affecting the conditions for the domestic political definition of policy-making. International organisations were mainly set up to reduce information and transaction costs and to provide the necessary framework for viable cooperation among States since this would be difficult to achieve without the institutionalised processes provided for by those international organisations. The application of this classical conception of international organisations has, however, become increasingly highly problematic. Regional integration systems are the most obvious example. But that is also the case with international organisations such as the WTO or the ILO for example. In the case of the WTO, its legal norms and judicial power end up attributing to it independent normative authority. That is the case even at the political level. Once international organisations are perceived by the different social actors as emerging forms of independent power, they will attempt to profit from these organisations to pursue their different agendas. As a result, international organisations will tend to develop political and social goals that may diverge from those of its initial masters (the States). There is a circular dynamic between the spill-over of the power initially attributed to the WTO, which raises the interest of social actors for political action in this institution, and the reinforcement of the institution's power precisely by virtue of the political dynamic promoted by the action of those social actors. This cycling dynamic promotes the overall power of the WTO and its role as a global political arena. In the process, the control of social decision-making by traditional national political processes decreases.

---

[5] In reality, much of the economic analysis of the market is, effect, constitutional analysis: issues such as externalities or information and transaction costs are simply economic jargon for problems of participation in the market and, as I will discuss below, this is both the core of constitutionalism and the currency for the transdisciplinary discourse that is required by the current global processes.

The WTO and the ILO are good best examples of international institutions that, more than simply coordinating the policies of different States, promote independent political and social goals which are determined by a constituency of social actors which goes beyond the States and participates in manners different from those occurring in domestic political processes. The consequence, of constitutional and social relevance is that the actors that participate and dominate in these emerging political arenas are not necessarily the same that have participated in the drafting of public policies at the national level. Some actors are disempowered while others are empowered and it is this that explains the scepticism with which some social groups see international trade and globalisation: the constitutional balances of representation and participation established by national constitutions are altered. At the same time, these new centres of decision-making assume certain functions of governance that have traditionally been subject to the democratic standards of the State. This raises claims of a democratic deficit.

The Transfer of Power to the Market

One of the consequences of the legal and economic processes of regulatory competition arising from international trade is a reduction in the political control over the economic sphere. Liberalisation of trade generates competition among the products and services of different polities which, in turns, leads to a competition between the different regulatory frameworks to which those products and services are subject therein. Political communities have to determine their policies not only on the basis of their internal preferences but also taking into account the need for their products and services to be competitive in the global market. The consequence is a transfer of power from political processes to the global market. It is the 'market'[6] that will choose between competing regulatory policies. Again, it becomes crucial to assess the 'constitutional quality' of representation and participation in such a market and to assess the consequences of such changes.

Technocratic Forms of Global Regulation

A similar change in power occurs when, instead of trusting the regulation of international trade to the market, we decide to subject it to international

---

[6] This is a broader market than the simple market of business transactions: it includes, for example, the mobility of market participants (companies, consumers, workers) as a form of influencing decisions.

standards set by international technocratic bodies. Both markets and these technocratic bodies have an inherent rationality and a set of normative values which is not subject to a traditional form of political discourse and its patterns of participation and representation. To put it differently, these institutions decide on the basis of a community of participation and representation that is different from that of political processes. Once again, the democratic and constitutional question arises.

Changing the Domestic Patterns of Representation and Participation in Public Policies

There are many instances where we can continue to link the determination of specific policies at the global level to an agreement among the more traditional participants in the international community (States). However, the simple fact that the State's decisions will be decided in the framework of a different State policy sphere means that representation and participation in the drafting of those policies will change. The coordination of domestic policies at the international level means that many of the State determinations of those policies are, at least in part, brought into the realm of foreign or commercial policy. Once we accept that States do not have an homogeneous national interest and that there are different mechanisms and forms of participation involved in different areas of domestic policy-making, one of the consequences of the increased number of policies that are 'appropriated' by foreign and commercial policies is that the relevant participants in the framing of those policies change. The most obvious example of this is the empowerment of executives at the expense of parliaments that occurs as a consequence of these processes.

In addition, the international and regional arenas have increasingly become an instrument for certain domestic actors to challenge the deliberations of national political processes in the definition of the social good. The emerging global decision-making processes can be used by different social actors to challenge a particular domestic political outcome that they did not favour. In some cases, this promotes the re-deliberation of democratically agreed national policies. In other cases, it may even be said to offer to some citizens the option of exit with regard to the decisions of their political community. That challenges that political community balance of representation and participation.

All these changes, allocate the exercise of power to different institutional alternatives from those that are traditionally entrusted with such power by national constitutionalism. With it, they change the patterns of representation and participation defined by national constitutionalism and it is this that explains the tremendous suspicion with which such processes are seen by some social groups (particularly, those that see themselves disempowered by such processes). The question that arises, therefore, is

whether demands for constitutional legitimacy should only follow institutionalised political arrangements that coincide with the States or if they
should follow power in general. When States cannot constitutionally control global governance what ought to?

THE CHALLENGE TO NATIONAL CONSTITUTIONALISM

From what has been said so far, it has already become clear that the constitutional claim over global governance arises from two sources: first,
there is an increased number of global 'sites' of independent power that
require a form of constitutional governance; second, there is a challenge
to national constitutionalism that, itself, requires constitutional analysis.
National constitutions as the form of power guaranteed the constitutional self-determination of their respective political communities. That was
grounded in three pillars: the definition of the ultimate authority; self-
government; and democratic autonomy. All these pillars are affected by
the processes of global governance.

The first pillar is that of the Constitution as the ultimate criteria of
validity of a legal system and, therefore, as the criterion of ultimate authority. The Constitution was the utmost expression of sovereignty as the
ultimate source of power in the political and legal organisation of society.
Even the claim of authority that has always been made by international
rules under international monist theories of international law supremacy
was not conceived as challenging the fundamentals of national constitutional sovereignty since that supremacy was traditionally legitimised
through reference to a previous self-binding commitment of the States
supported by *pacta sunt servanda*.[7] In this case, international instances of
shared, pooled or even limited State sovereignty do not really challenged
State sovereignty since those exercises of international sovereignty are
delegated from the States and limited by the strict mandates of that delegation. However it has increasingly become the case that the new forms
of regional and global governance claim normative authority independent from the States. In some cases, the extent of this claim is such that
the supranational power is, in effect, backed up by a claim of constitutional supremacy. This challenges the traditional conception of sovereignty and requires us to embrace a notion of competing sovereignties.
Whatever the different degrees of challenge, what is clear is that the role
of National Constitutions as the determinants of an ultimate authority is

---

[7] It can be said that such principle even if creating an higher norm than national constitutional norms was mainly an operative principle that safeguarded in all other respects the
notion of national constitutional sovereignty. Moreover, such conception, itself, reflected the
same idea of sovereignty as definition of an ultimate authority.

under challenge. The trend towards a framework of constitutional pluralism is an answer to that challenge.[8]

The second affected pillar of national constitutional self-determination
is embodied by the idea of self-government. The narrative of this challenge
is well known: States are increasingly affected in their capacity to
autonomously determine their domestic policies due to external constraints derived from both international organisations, competition with
other States, and the extra-territorial effects of other State's policies. The
question of policy autonomy is also a question of participation. This is so
for two reasons: first, national political communities perceive an 'intrusion' (or inclusion ...) of 'outsiders' in what they have decided; second, less
policy autonomy entails a reduction in the relative power of the voice of
each citizen of that polity. Their relative power in participation decreases
as the scope of the participants is increased by the participation of others.

The third pillar is also linked to participation but in a different manner.
When I refer to the democratic autonomy of national political communities
protected by national constitutions I am thinking, in this case, of the autonomy of the members of such political communities to define the balances of
participation and representation in those political communities. In other
words, their power to structure the mechanisms of representation and participation of different members of the political community in different institutions and their policies. As already mentioned, global governance changes
such domestic patterns of representation and participation in public policies.

The challenge brought by global governance to these three pillars of
national constitutions can however become a broader challenge to national constitutionalism. In this case, national constitutionalism is not simply
a national expression of constitutionalism but embodies a certain dominant conception of constitutionalism. It identifies constitutionalism with
the borders and conditions offered by national political communities.
Such challenge is evident when we confront the foundations of national
constitutionalism with the ideals of constitutionalism. Can such challenge
have any normative foundation? In other words, how can such challenge
not be seen simply as erosion of constitutionalism? That is what I discussed else where and summarise in the next section.

NATIONAL CONSTITUTIONALISM AS A CONTEXTUAL
REPRESENTATION OF CONSTITUTIONALISM

In a previous work I have argued that constitutionalism is related to three
paradoxes: the paradox of the polity; the fear of the few and the fear of the

---

[8] Miguel Poiares Maduro,'Contrapunctual Laws; Europe's Constitutional Pluralism in
Action' in Neil Walker (ed) *Sovereignty in Transition* (Hart Publishing, Oxford, 2003).

many;[9] and the question of who decides who decides. They are paradoxical because they simultaneously embrace conflicting values in an attempt to reconcile them that is at the core of constitutionalism. With respect to all of them, national constitutionalism can be seen as both a promoter of and a limit to constitutionalism.

The polity is the basic assumption of a Constitution. Constitutional questions have always been addressed within a pre-existing polity (normally the Nation State). It is that polity that has served as the yardstick of constitutionalism. Relations within the polity are regulated by constitutional law. Relations among polities, instead, have been dominated by a different set of actors (the States) and a different set of rules (international law). The Constitution both defines and presupposes a polity or political community whose members are bound by such constitution. It is from this political community and its people that the democratic process draws its legitimacy and that of the majority decisions reached in the democratic representative process. The basis of the polity is normally referred to as 'the people'. Constitutional and democratic theory scholars normally presuppose that 'a people' already exists.[10] But what makes a people? And who has the right to be considered as part of the people? And why should participation and representation be limited by the requirement of belongingness to such a polity? It is the paradox of the concept of polity in its relation with constitutionalism and democracy. Isn't a national demos a limit to democracy and constitutionalism? In fact, participation in national democracies is not granted to all those affected by the decisions of the national political process but only to those affected which are considered as citizens of the national polity. It is not the existence of democracy at national level that is contested but the extent of that democracy.[11] There is problem of inclusion faced by national polities.[12] Such problem of inclusion does not exist simply by not taking the others into account in decisions that affect them. National polities are also not open to all those which would accept their political contract. National polities tend to exclude many which would accept their political contract and are affected by their policies simply because they are not part of the *demos* as understood in a certain ethno, cultural or historical sense. In this way, if national polities can be seen as an instrument of constitutionalism, they also limit its ambitions of full representation and participation.

---

[9]   An expression originally crafted by Neil Komesar, see n 1 above.

[10]   Robert Daw, *Democracy and its Critics* (Conn, Yale University Press, 1989) at p. 3.

[11]   The different between the existence of democracy and the extent of democracy is highlighted by Jon Elster, 'Deliberation and Constitution Making'in Elster (ed) *Deliberative Democracy* (Canbridge, CUP, 1998) at pp. 97–122.

[12]   Dahl points out that polities have a twofold problem: '1—The problem of inclusion: What persons have a rightful claim to be included in the demos; 2—The scope of its authority: What rightful limits are there on the control of a demos', n..., at 119. See also David Held, *Democracy and the Global Order* (Cambridge and Oxford, Polity Press, 1995) mainly chapters 1 and 10.

The same occurs with the paradox of the fear of the few and the fear of the many. All major constitutional arguments and doctrines gravitate around a complex system of countervailing forces set up by constitutional law to promote the democratic exercise of power (assure that the few do not rule over the many) but, at the same time, to limit that power (assuring that the many will not abuse of their power over the few). There are two basic fears underlying constitutional discourse and organisation: the fear of the many and fear of the few. Such fears translate into two biases in decision-making: majoritarian and minoritarian biases. The core of constitutional law is the balance between the fear of the many and the fear of the few. Constitutional law sets up the mechanisms through which the many can rule but, at the same time, creates rights and processes to the protection of the few. Separation of powers, fundamental rights, parliamentary representation are all expressions of these fears.[13] Traditionally, the many have been associated with the decisions taken by the majority through the political process while the protection of the few is associated with individual rights. The function of judicial review of legislation has frequently been argued on substantive or procedural conceptions of minority protection.[14] This classical picture of constitutional law has been challenged by the multiplication of social decision-making forums and the insights brought by new institutional analyses. Interest group theories of the political process have demonstrated, for example, how democratic decision-making may, in effect, be controlled by a few against the interests of the many.[15] This has helped to challenge idealised visions of the workings of national democratic institutions. In this light, and as I have tried to demonstrate in detail else where and will also address below, there is no reason why instances of supra-national and global governance cannot be seen as correcting instances of majoritarian or minoritarian biases in national institutions that national constitutionalism has not adequately addressed.

The final paradox is that of who decides who decides? National constitutions have always been conceived as holding the answer to that question. In its relationship with the notion of State sovereignty highlighted

---

[13] Bellamy 'The Political Form of the Constitution: the Separation of Powers, Rights and Representative Democracy' in Bellamy and Castiglione (eds.) *Constitutionalism in Transformation: European and Theoretical Perespectives*, (Oxford, Blackwells, 1996), highlights three principles that have defined constitutionalism: rights, separation of powers and representative government. However, in his view, the first has come to predominate in recent years: 'Rights, upheld by judicial review, are said to comprise the prime component of constitutionalism, providing a normative legal framework within which politics operate', at 24.

[14] For the first see Ronald Dworkin, *Taking Rights Seriously*, (Cambridge, Harvard University Press, 1977.) For second see John Ely, *Democracy and Distrust: A Theory of Judicial Review*, (Cambridge, Harvard University Press, 1980.)

[15] Other theories have contributed in same sense. Ackerman's 'dualist democracy', for example, equates both the political process and the courts with the promotion and/or protection of democratic decisions. See, Bruce Ackerman, *We The People; Vol. 1 Foundations* (Mass, Harvard University Press, 1991).

above, natiotial constitutions have usually been considered as the higher degree and ultimate source of legitimacy of the legal system and its rules. Independently of one's conception of constitutional law as a 'grundnorm', a set of rules of recognition, positivised natural law, an higher command of a sovereign supported by an habit of obedience, or other, constitutional law has always been conceived as the higher law of the legal system, criterion of legitimacy and validity of other sources of the law. The new sites of power of global governance challenge that authority of national constitutions and require a pluralist conception of power that is in contradiction with proving the question of who decides who decides with a single answer. This may appear to challenge national constitutions but it does not challenge constitutionalism. In reality, the question of 'who decides who decides' has long been around in constitutionalism. It is a normal consequence of the divided powers system inherent in constitutionalism. In fact, it can be considered as an expected result of the Madisonian view of separation of powers as creating a mechanism of checks and balances. Though national constitutions may have developed historical answers to that question they are a contextual product of certain constitutional regimes and not a systemic feature of constitutionalism. On the contrary, the nature of the organisation of power inherent in constitutionalism requires the question to be permanently open and frequently reassessed. In this way, the pluralist relations of power brought forward by global governance may challenge national constitutions but may also serve to promote the ideals of constitutionalism.

Once we understand the paradoxical character of constitutionalism we can free ourselves from the boundaries of national constitutionalism. There is nothing in constitutionalism that makes of national polities the natural jurisdiction for full representation and participation. There is nothing that imposes that the fear of the few and the fear of the many must be addressed within a national polity and, in fact, the control of such fears may require us to move beyond national jurisdictions. Finally, it is artificial to think that national constitutionalism can allocate a final authority on who decides who decides when constitutionalism is precisely about dividing (and, in this way, limiting) authority. Seen in this light, national constitutions become a simple contextual expression of constitutionalism.

Constitutionalism is therefore both possible and necessary outside the State. But what does this mean for national constitutionalism? And what claims can the latter have with regard to an emerging global constitutionalism? And can global constitutionalism simply overcome national constitutionalism by either assuming or rising above the characteristics of national constitutionalism? The fact that national constitutionalism is simply a contextual representation of constitutionalism does not mean that it is no longer the best representation of constitutionalism. National political communities may still provide the best context on which constitutional ideals can be promoted. If that is the case, national constitutionalism should still be considered as the preferred form of constitutionalism and this would impact on the way we can currently constitutionalise global governance.

NATIONAL CONSTITUTIONS AS A PROXY FOR CONSTITUTIONALISM

As we have seen constitutionalism is all about establishing difficult balances between values or institutions that it, simultaneously, advances and fears: the balance between the common values of the polity and the individual preferences of its members; the balance between the democratic will of the majority and the rights of the minority; the balance between the intensity and the scope of participation. These balances and the inherent paradoxes in which they are reflected are aimed at promoting the ideals of freedom and full participation and representation that dominate constitutionalism. At the same time, national constitutionalism has developed a series of instruments to promote such balances, in the form of the doctrines of fundamental rights, separation of powers, democratic decision making through representation etc. The political contracts of national constitutionalism are composed as a set of inter-dependent doctrines and institutional frameworks that aim at preserving the tensions of constitutionalism without letting the balance tilt to either side. May be we can talk in this respect about a procedural and a substantive balance in constitutionalism.

The procedural balance of constitutionalism regards the balance between intensity and inclusion in promoting participation in the deliberative process. This has a two-fold dimension: in the first place, deliberative processes should not only promote equal participation but ought also to reflect the intensity of the impacts in the different affected interests; in the second place, deliberative processes are faced with the dilemma arising from the fact that the relative participation and representation of each individual decreases the higher the scope of the participants included in deliberation.

The substantive balance of constitutionalism regards the balance between individual autonomy and civic solidarity. Constitutionalism is about safeguarding a society of equal and free individuals. But it has also become clearer that such a society requires both mechanisms to manage the conflicts of interests between those individuals and the provision to all members of that society of equal instruments to pursue happiness in the exercise of their freedom. Needless to say how contested are some of the underlying assumptions or even the way to achieve these goals. But it is true that in all modern societies it is generally recognised that constitutionalism must also embrace a principle of distributive justice in the pursuit of its ideals. The commitment towards both the common resolution of societal disputes and a principle of distributive justice is what composes the idea of civic solidarity. This tension between individual autonomy and civic solidarity also underlies much of constitutionalism.

National constitutions, with national political communities and their artificial borders, offer a particularly favourable framework to manage such tensions and implement those two balances of constitutionalism. They are, in this sense, a good proxy for constitutionalism. This is so because of the conditions provided for by the existence of a political community and its underlying long-term political contract. What allows for the trade-offs necessary to such constitutional balances to operate is the long term perspective introduced by the political contracts underlying national political communities. Majoritarian democracy, for example, is necessary in the context of massive and complex societies both to make deliberation possible and, in some cases, to promote redistributive policies.[16] But such majoritarian democracy means that some will loose in certain circumstances and others will not even see the intensity of their interests really taken into account. In this respect, a political community brings back the balances between the scope and intensity of participation and individual autonomy and civic solidarity. First, it assures the loosing side that their loss in one instance can become a victory in another (there are no absolute looser and winners).[17] Second, it avoids zero-sum decisions: those winning, knowing they may loose in the future, have an interest in taking all interests into account in all decisions and in trading-off participation for intensity of impacts. Third, it authorises for other long-term agreements to derogate from democratic decisions in order to safeguard values such as individual autonomy or distributive justice (this is the role of fundamental rights). The full development of constitutional ideals and their trade-offs require a context of application that is not dominated by one-shot decisions but is, instead, grounded on the stable framework provided by a political community. Communities are not, in this sense, contrary to a liberal perspective. In many respect, an appropriate theory of liberalism must make room for communities in the pursuit of individual autonomy. This is so for three sets of reasons: first, communities provide the deliberative space and institutions necessary for the pursuit of individual autonomy (without participation in deliberative processes there is not true individual autonomy and without the democratically organised institutions of political communities there is no form

---

[16] Whether or not majoritarian democracy is the natural form of democracy is more debatable. See James M Buchanan and Gordon Tullock, The Calculus of Content-Logical Foundations of Constitutional Democracy (Ann Arbor, University of Michigan Press, 1962). The same on whether majoritarian democracies provide more efficient decisions. It depends on the concept of efficiency and on the measurement of impacts.

[17] There can be risks of more insulated groups being subject to majoritarian bias and that is why national constitutionalism provides for other protecting mechanisms.

of expressing one's individual autonomy in deliberative processes); second, communities promote the civic dynamics necessary to the effective individual participation in those common deliberative processes and public spaces;[18] third, communities enhance individual autonomy in that they constitute joint spaces of differentiation; in other words, the existence of different communities promotes a higher possible realm of individual choices even in contexts where collective action is necessary. National political communities provide therefore a framework to reconcile liberal and communitarian ideals (perhaps not, with regard to the latter, in a thick sense but in the republican sense of a community that promotes civic virtues).

Those ideals are themselves reflected in the tensions of constitutionalism to which national political communities provide a commonly agreed resolution. The political contract underlying national political communities guarantees, in this way, both the political and social viability of the normative project of constitutionalism.[19] Constitutionalism in this form requires loyalty and the latter requires some form of identity and long term commitment. The most benign form of providing such identity has been the political contract of the Constitutional Nation State.

The question now becomes whether such project can currently be transposed to the global level? If it is not, does that mean the end of any claim for constitutionalising global governance? And if such claim can survive in the absence of a political community a second question arises: how to relate this new form of global constitutionalism with the claims of national constitutionalism? In this sense to move constitutionalism to the arena of global governance is to move it beyond a normative theory of political communities to a normative theory of social decision-making. It is to have constitutionalism without a constitution. Even if such move is necessary (as argued before) and possible (as will be argued below) it does not mean that such form of constitutionalism can and ought to overcome the form of constitutionalism linked to national political communities, particularly absent a global political community.

CONSTITUTIONALISM AT THE GLOBAL LEVEL

How should the challenge to constitutionalism brought by global governance be addressed? Should such challenge be opposed or accepted in normative terms? And if can be legitimated in normative terms, when and how should that be the case? Normative conceptions of global governance tend to reflect a myriad of philosophical perspectives. There are

---

[18] Something that was highlighted by the Republican tradition.

[19] Refer and discuss difference with Habermas in the Postnational Constellation: Political Essays (Cambridge, MIT Press, 2001).

many theories and in the opposing extremes one can find either national-ist theories supported by communitarian ideals or cosmopolitan propos-als supported by liberal ideals. The perspectives on global governance tend therefore to intersect with general philosophical perspectives regard-ing individual autonomy and communities or with institutional perspec-tives and assumptions on political process versus the market for example. Constitutionalism is not absent from these discussions but is more fre-quently assumed than exposed. Constitutionalism appears in the context of global governance in two opposing senses: on the one hand, there are those that use it to legitimise the process of global governance; on the other hand, there are those that use it precisely to oppose the same process. Within each of these sides there are different versions of constitu-tionalism and its relation with global governance that I will briefly review next.

THE ALTERNATIVE PROGRAMMES OF GLOBAL
CONSTITUTIONALISM:

Rights Constitutionalism

Petersmann speaks of a developing international constitutionalism the contours of which are still unclear.[20] As in regional forms of integration, trade law is conceived as the engine of global integration and its emerg-ing constitutionalism.[21] The World Trade Organization and the agree-ments derived from the Uruguay Round are conceived as the primary tool for such global constitutionalism. He argues for a 'rights-based' con-stitutional development from the ground up, through individual litigants and courts (such as happen in the European Union).[22] Departing from a certain Kantian conception of the international community, Petersmann establishes a direct legitimating link between individuals and the new forms of global governance, mainly those based no human rights and international trade. The role of international trade law is that of guarantee-ing the freedom of individuals in the international arena so that they can fully enjoy their personal autonomy. The way to promote global con-stitutionalism is by extending the scope and application of international trade law, human rights documents and dispute-settlement mechanisms. For Petersman there is an emerging process of global constitutionalism where democracies will operate 'in a constitutional framework of national

---

[20] EU Petersmann, 'How to Reform the UN System? Constitutionalism, International Law and International Organizations', 10 Leiden Journal of International Laws (1997) 421, at 463.
[21] *Ibid* at 445.
[22] See n 27 at 423.

and international guarantees of freedom, non-discrimination, rule of law and institutional checks and balances'.[23]

This vision of Petersmann, shared by others, transfers to the global arena Hayek's[24] and the ordo-liberals conception of constitutionalism as a constraint on public power. A conception that has also influenced the discourse of European constitutionalism.[25] Under this view, international human rights and international trade law are not in opposition but, on the contrary, in the words of another author

> they are topologically similar: (b)oth international trade law and international human rights are largely deregulatory—they declare what the State should not do. In each regime, the problem to be solved is the overbearing State which wants to control voluntary activity.[26]

But, of course, this entails a particular notion of both human rights and international trade law which is not consensual. The content of human rights is not undisputed and they may also require strong government intervention. In the same way, international trade law may be developed by enacting international regulatory standards to which all economic operators would have to conform instead of focusing on the liberalisation of trade through the elimination of the different regulatory standards to which economic operators have to comply. As a consequence, the relevant question becomes whether the current processes of global governance hold the necessary legitimacy to enforce a particular conception of human rights or international trade.

The focus of such form of global constitutionalism is on a minimal notion of constitutionalism: non-discrimination, individual rights (mainly economic rights) and dispute-settlement mechanisms. The expectation is that these instances will develop into a set of individual constitutional rights protected at the global level from any form of power. The dynamics of international trade will fuel the development of an international rule of law through these economic rights and dispute-settlement mechanisms. Such dynamics will result however in a limited conception of the ideals of constitutionalism. The fundamental idea is that of constitutionalism as limited government. The fundamental fear is that of the many. The fundamental suspicion lies over the political process. In reality, behind such conception lies a deep distrust over the political process and the way it organises and exercises power. However, the alternative institutions to which power is transferred through general rules of a higher

---

[23] Op. cit., at 447 and 448.

[24] Friedrich A. Hayek, *The Road to Serfdom*, 50th Anniversary edn, Intro by Milton Friedman (Illinois, University of Chicago Press, 1994).

[25] Miguel Poiares Maduro, We The Court: The European Court of Justice and the European Economic Constitution (Oxford, Hart Publishing, 1998).

[26] Steve Charnovitz, 'The Globalization of Economic Human Rights', 25 *Brooklyn Journal of International Law* 1999, 113.

legal rank, embodied in such a particular set of human rights, are generally assumed in an idealised form. Those institutions tend to be either the courts or the market. But, as the analysis of the paradoxes and tensions of constitutionalism has hopefully highlighted, such institutions are themselves subject to other forms of constitutional suspicion and potential malfunctions.

Political Constitutionalism: The Cosmopolitan View

The other Kantian and liberal trend is that which focus on the ideal of a cosmopolis. Here the ambition is greater than in the previous case. The ambition is that of creating a global civil society that can reconstitute at that global level the political contract of the States (and not between the States). The existence of a global political community would make it possible to have democracy at that level. Such an ambition is supported on a liberal normative claim to higher inclusion and to bring down the national borders that restrict a full expression of the ideal of a society of free and equal individuals. In this light, the processes of global governance become a welcome scenario from which to build this global democracy. The proposals on how to do it vary[27] but they have both bottom-up elements (for example, promoting the creation of transnational political action) and top-down elements (promoting the democratic reform of international organisations such as the UN).

The first problem with such vision is how difficult it is to transform it into a viable programme for action. This result's not only in a pragmatic critique but also in a normative one: the gap between the basis for the legitimacy claim and its expression on global governance is such that the theory may serve to legitimate non-democratic processes. But there is a broader problem with this theory that transcends its viability problem. It is a theory that, again, focuses on a limited perspective of constitutionalism. It ignores that the problem with larger political communities and constitutionalism is not simply a problem of how difficult it is to achieve them. It is also a problem that regards the balance between scope and intensity of participation that I have mentioned above. The larger the political community the more inclusive it will be. But the more inclusive it is the lower the importance and relative weight of each individual participant and, with it, the higher it is also the risk of less individual autonomy. Smaller jurisdictions exist not only because large ones are not possible. They exist because, in some instances, they provide for better participation and allow for greater differentiation and individual autonomy.[28]

---

[27] See David Held, Democracy and the Global Order-From The State to Cosmopoliton Governance (Cambridge Polity Press, 1995) and Richard Falk, Revitalizing International Law (Anels, Iowa State University Press, 1989).

[28] They may also give rise to opposite fears, but that is something I will discuss below.

PROCEDURAL CONSTITUTIONALISM: ALTERNATIVE DELIBERATIVE PROCESSES

Here the focus is on overcoming the challenge of the State to the legitimacy of global governance by focusing on the quality of the deliberative processes adopted at the global level: they should be more inclusive of civil society (ONGs participation etc); they should promote access to the deliberative process; they should adopt higher standards than the State regarding transparency and access to information. The legitimacy generated by these alternative forms of participation from those of the classic representative model of the State would provide global governance with its value added vis à vis States and their forms of constitutionalism.

The basic shortcoming pointed to such visions is that the legitimacy that they promote does not appear to be sufficient to overcome the more traditional democratic legitimacy of the State. It may be true that they furnish global governance with some democratic insights but what happens when, as increasingly is the case, the exercises of power by the processes of global governance conflict with those democratically determined by a State? But there are also problems regarding the idealised assumptions of deliberative processes made by such theories. In some cases, more access to the decision-making processes and higher transparency may not solve but aggravate problems of participation. Such deliberative views tend to overlook the simple fact that participation is dependent on both the costs of participation and its benefits. If the individual benefits are low because quite disseminated (as it is often the case with dispersed groups and disseminated interests) then easier access and higher transparency may simple make the decision making processes even more susceptible to capture by concentrated interests. It will be the latter (due to their much higher stakes) to make predominant use of that easier access and higher transparency. In reality, in some cases, the move to a higher jurisdiction, such as some process of global governance, may improve constitutional ideals precisely because such process is less accessible and therefore it insulates the political process from the influence of concentrated interests. Again, no limited conception of constitutionalism will serve us.

THE REJECTION OF GLOBAL CONSTITUTIONALISM

The State View

A first argument against global constitutionalism can be encapsulated in a slogan: 'small is better'. The presumption is that small communities work better in processing the different affected interests. Transaction and information costs are lower, participation viable, more intense and more effective and with that also cooperation is easier. There is even, in some, a certain ideal view of small communities of deliberation where rational discourse is fully possible, the different perspectives are taken into account, and the decisions are often achieved through consensus. In some cases, the imaginary is not based on the State but on smaller communities but it, naturally, serves to criticise even larger jurisdictions. Of course, the dangers of exclusion and tyranny involved in small communities are also often acknowledged but States are assumed as having dominated those risks and, as a consequence, global governance is a step too far from the original ideal of small communities. There is also another common perception of democracy linked to this: that power should be as close as possible to the people. By moving power to a larger jurisdiction we are moving it further away from them with all its perceived negative consequences. As it moves from the city to the world, democracy appears to loose its quality and, in some sense, it is almost as if its great ambition (to include all) also becomes its greatest handicap.

Again we have a limited view of constitutionalism: small is not always better. And that is the case because of the exclusionary features of small jurisdictions and the frequent externalities of their decisions (lower inclusion) but also because, in other instances, they may be particularly prone to majoritarian bias (a minority may be easy to identify and insulate from the rest of the community).

Another aspect that can be found, in less or clear fashion, underlying some views opposing global constitutionalism to is the normative assumption that it cannot (and not simply that it currently does not) secure the necessary conditions of political loyalty. The latter would require some form of ethno, cultural or historical identity and not simply civic commitment. In this light, constitutionalism is not a producer of values but instead produced by them. It does not form a community of discourse for values deliberation but it embodies, instead, the values of a pre-existent community. This is a thicker communitarian view. This view is different from the above in that the latter does not require such pre-existent community of values. It simply argues that democracy works better in smaller jurisdictions. This is a view of constitutionalism that is also in opposition with the view of constitutionalism argued above that I dispense myself from repeating.

There is, however, a stronger argument in favour of the State as the single form of constitutionalism and, therefore, as constituting both the limit and the single form of legitimacy for global governance. It departs from the absence in the global society of some of the characteristics of national constitutions (such as the lack of an underlying political community that I have noted above). Koskenniemi has argued that, in spite of the generalised international agreement on a human rights discourse, the lack of a true international consensus on the number and content of human rights entails that these cannot form the basis for an alternative source of legitimacy of a new international social order.[29] For this author, the best form to prevent an authoritarian definition of what those rights and other principles of international law are is the intermediation of the State 'because its formal-bureaucratic rationality provides a safeguard against the totalitarianism inherent in a commitment to substantive values, which forces those values on people not sharing them'.[30] Following this view, the only legitimate form of global governance would be that limited to cooperation and institutionalised debate among States. They would remain the single source of the international society.[31] There are two problems in this: first, it ignores the reality that, as the same author recognises, international organisations more than simply enforcing pre-existing agreements, establish and define priorities and policies.[32] Even if we could still say that many of such priorities and policies are defined by deliberation where States representatives participate the question still arises: what kind of regime should govern those deliberations once they become an independent form of power (constitutionalism or traditional international law?); second, it makes a too broadaclaim of constitutional legitimacy for the State. As I will argue in more detail below Koskenniemi may be right if he is simply noting a presumption in favour of national constitutional processes but that presumption does not have to be absolute and there are even instances where a form of global constitutionalism can be legitimate precisely because of the role it plays in improving national constitutional processes.

THE STRUCTURAL BIAS VIEW

A final perspective over global governance notes its dangers not through opposition to the State but because of the particular character of the constitutionalism that global governance is seen as embodying. Global governance is conceived, for example, as determining not only a loss of State control but of political control in general. In this perspective, globalisation is presented as a more or less atomised form of power at the global level whose processes reflect a particular set of interests. It is not globalisation or global constitutionalism that is at stake but the particular set of values that it currently embodies. Global governance is illegitimate not because

---

[29] Martti Koskenniemi, 'The Future of Statehood', (1991) 32 *Harvard International Law Journal*, 397. For example, at 399: 'The protection of human rights, however, cannot form a meaningful basis for social order. If we are to define our polity in terms of human rights, we must ascertain the number and content of such rights'.

[30] *Ibid*, at 407.

[31] People still disagree about the political good. In normal circumstances, states still provide the means to direct substantive disagreement into institutionalised debate. *Ibid*, at 410.

[32] *Ibid*, at 403.

of its global character but because of its structural bias. Its processes are seen, at best, as empowering the market at the expense of the political processes, at worst, as empowering particular economic interests at the expense of the general community. In some cases, this is conceived as the product of a decentralised form of power.[33] In others, it is even traced back to a centralised authoritarian imposition of one power over all the others.

Concepts of international trade, for example, are seen as embedding particular moral and societal visions. This is criticised not only because it promotes what is seen as an illegitimate imposition of particular con- testable notions of societal values on all political communities but also because that application often entail the transposition of those values to totally different contexts without taking into account the particularities of those contexts. Moreover, it is also the case that those values are often exported in an ideal form that does not even correspond to the reality of their application in their home systems.[34]

This visions are more difficult to criticise, in the context of this paper, because they tend to be self-referential and to challenge many of the assumptions of constitutionalism with which I have worked. In some cases they deny the legitimacy of the outcomes of democratic deliberation because they deny that the conditions for such democratic deliberation can be fulfilled by current societies. In some other cases they deny broad- ly the potential for rational deliberation. Let me therefore be simple: if they are simply noting that current constitutional forms do not provide a full realisation of constitutional ideals they are right. As I have stated, the nature of constitutionalism is such that it never provides a perfect reflec- tion of all the involved interests and their intensity. It can only provide for approximations. Theories of structural bias can be useful in pointing to some constitutional malfunctions in the current institutions but that tell us nothing in terms of a normative program for the pursuit of constitu- tionalism and democracy. First, these theories are often short in terms of putting forward institutional alternatives. Second, even if those institu- tional alternatives where advanced we would still have to review whether they would not suffer from even more serious constitutional malfunc- tions.

The problem with all these different theories is that they adopt a single institutional perspective[35] or, perhaps better, a single constitutional view- point. Those that argue for a rights constitutionalism are, in effect, trusting the definition of those rights to either the market (economic competition

---

[33] Michael Hardt and Antonis Negri, *Empire* (Mass, Harvard University Press, 2001).
[34] David Kennedy *When Renewal Repeats Thinking Against the Box.*
[35] 2000 *New York Journal of International Law and Politics* 2, 335.

under free trade and non-discrimination) or international courts. They distrust national States and highlight the potential malfunctions in their political and judicial processes. But they forget the potential malfunctions in the transnational institutions which they empower. Their analysis of the latter normally takes place in a costless transaction world, contrary to their view of the former, normally assessed in real world contexts. Those that argue for cosmopolitan perspectives suffer from a similar shortcoming. They stress the gains in inclusion generated by democratic global institutions. But ignore the many democratic malfunctions that arise in the context of larger jurisdictions of participation. Champions of the State and its sovereign powers also adopt a single institutional perspective. They highlight the democratic deficiencies of global processes but ignore many of the current constitutional malfunctions of the State both in terms of inclusion of outside interests and participation of certain domestic interests. The same could be said of the sophisticated deliberative theories. They assume that those perfect deliberative conditions are easy to establish through the right procedures but ignore that in massive and complex societies of high transaction and information costs those procedures may actually increase some of the traditional political malfunctions. As discussed above, it is not even true that we can establish higher transparency and access to the political process and information as generalised principles of constitutional law to be applicable in all cases. So much for civil society as a solution for our problems. The higher participation of the so called actors of the civil society may, in some instances, be part of the solution but it may also be part of the problem. That depends on the specific context and the available institutional alternatives.

This is not to say that these theories have no normative value. On the contrary, they highlight the potential democratic and constitutional value of the different institutional alternatives. But, in doing so, they in effect prove that, in a costless transaction world, all these institutions would provide perfect participation. In the market, people would freely express their preferences through what they buy or in what jurisdiction they live. The aggregation of all the voluntary market transactions would bring about the most democratic decision (that most preferred by either the higher number of people or by the higher intensity of their different preferences). In States, national political processes would have no problem in collecting the necessary information to aggregate collective preferences, expressed according to the intensity of the stakes of the different affected interests (whose full participation was assured by the absence of information and transaction costs). Those States could latter fully coordinate their preferences with those of all other States in a costless transaction world of international relations. But in such a world, the same could be done by international organisations, capable of collecting all the necessary information and reflect the interests of all participating States. In such a costless transaction world, international organisations could even take localised decisions because they would have no problem in measuring the intensity of the different interests to design the appropriate localised decisions and then balance them with the benefits of possible harmonisation. Of course, such localised decisions could also be left to localised deliberative processes since, in such a costless transaction world, they could perfectly reflect all the local interests and internalise outside costs.[36] To sum up: in a world without transaction and information costs it would not matter what institutional choice one would make in the international order (absent of redistributive goals). Of course, we do not live in such a world and therefore any constitutional proposal that assumes, on the one hand, a certain constitutional malfunction, detected in 'real-life' circumstances, and, on the other hand, a certain constitutional ideal model, conceived in a world without transaction and information costs, may be insightful but not suitable.

In Search of an International Constitutional Framework for Comparative Institutional Analysis

I can now to move into briefly presenting a different approach for a normative project of constitutionalism in global governance. But do not expect a new constitutional model with a complete architecture of principles and institutions. My argument has been precisely that no such model can be found. Instead, what I try to put forward is much more modest: it is a methodology for constitutional choices in global governance that can make use of all the theories mentioned and, in doing so, reflects the paradoxes and tensions upon which constitutionalism is founded. This same genetic imprint of constitutionalism coupled with the high transaction and information costs of our world means that no choices are easy and that they can often be wrong. But it is by truly looking at them that we may get closer to being right.

A first conclusion from the previous analysis is that the usual approaches to global governance suffer from something that, for lack of a better name, I identified as single constitutionalism: they focus on a particular set of constitutional malfunctions and propose a constitutional alternative without taking into account the paradoxes and balances of constitutionalism and the potential constitutional malfunctions of the alternatives proposed in a world of high transaction and information costs. The normative project of constitutionalism cannot be pursued by the setting up of idealised institutions or processes. No single constitutional model is adequate. First, the transaction and information costs prevent constitutional institutions from being a perfect mirror of thier

---

[36] See H. Regan, Regulatory Purpose and "Like Products" In Article 111:4 of the GATT (with additional remarks an Árt. 11:2) Journal of World Trade, nn. 3–2002, pp. 443–78.

constitutional ideals. The existence of different constitutional institutions is a reflection of such reality and of the need to make institutional choices between increasingly imperfect institutional alternatives.[37] Any model which argues on the basis of an institutional ideal in comparison with an institution operating in a world of transaction and information costs is doomed from the start. Second, constitutionalism is inherently paradoxical and grounded on a permanent balance between opposing values. Any form of single constitutionalism, which advocates for a particular institutional model of constitutionalism, ignores those paradoxes of constitutionalism and how they require different institutional alternatives.

A second conclusion which I have made is that this same nature of constitutionalism allows us to see national constitutionalism as simply a contextual representation of constitutionalism and not as its single expression. There is nothing in constitutionalism that requires its limitation to the borders of the States. This does not mean, however, that national constitutionalism is both unnecessary and without normative authority. A third conclusion was precisely that national constitutionalism is still, nevertheless, the closer approximation we have to constitutional ideals. This is so because of the conditions created by the national political communities. They provide conditions of political and social loyalty (linked to a long-term political contract) that allow for the best contextual resolution of the tensions of constitutionalism. This recognition of the particular legitimate authority hold by national constitutionalism cannot, however, ignore that there is a claim for constitutionalism at the global level. This claim, as I argued before, derives from the character of power that the processes of global governance already entail. These phenomena requires more than a simple reference to the international commitment of the State; they require a constitutional form of controlling the extent of autonomous normative decisions that are left for global and regional institutions and of reviewing their impact on national constitutionalism; they also require a constitutional form of balancing the competing national constitutional claims that come into conflict through the mechanisms of interdependence (such as those of free trade).[38]

But what can be the character of global constitutionalism and how is it to be related to national constitutionalism? In other words, how can I reconcile the claim for a global constitutionalism with the recognition of the higher normative authority claimed by national constitutionalism? To solve this conundrum I first propose a distinction between constitutions and constitutionalism. Constitutions refer to constitutionalism linked to a long term political contract supported by or with a political community.

[37] See Niel Komesar, n 1 above.
[38] See Miguel Poiares Maduro, 'Is There Any Such Thing as Free or Fair Trade? A Constitutional Analysis of the Impact of International Trade on the European Social Model' in de Busca and Scoll (eds).

Constitutionalism, itself, is broader: it is a normative theory to allocate, discipline and govern power in such a way as to maximise the ideals of freedom and full participation and representation. Such a theory is applicable to larger and smaller jurisdictions of social decision-making, to political processes and to courts or markets. It is and ought to be applicable to any institution that exercises power. Its expression does not have to be the same of national constitutionalism. What it does require is the same burden of choices between institutional alternatives. Choices to be made in light of the substantive and procedural processes I have identified and the dynamics of participation linked to those institutional contexts. We cannot require global governance to be legitimated under the same conditions as those of national constitutional law. But we must require it to be legitimised in constitutional terms. Constitutionalism without a political community must focus on new and enhanced forms of participation without expecting a strong loyalty in the absence of a collective identity. It cannot therefore be based in the traditional democratic model of the State. But it must proceed to similar constitutional choices taking into the constant trade-offs between the constitutional values of inclusion and intensity of participation, the different stakes of potentially affected interests and the way the different global institutional alternatives interact with transaction and information costs. The fact is that global governance cannot aspire to reflect the democratic and constitutional model of the States but, instead, its normative value can be found in providing new institutional alternatives to correct some of the malfunctions of national political communities.

The conundrum I have presented is not however totally solved by recognising the existence of constitutionalism beyond the State. What happens when global constitutionalism collides with national constitutionalism? The conditions fulfilled by national constitutionalism as a proxy for constitutionalism do establish a presumption in its favour. It must be global governance to hold the burden of demonstrating its added constitutional value in certain settings to overcome that preference. Where (independent) power has been transferred towards the global level we must find a constitutional added value to legitimise the exercise of such power. The tendency here would be to say that when global constitutionalism provides for the inclusion of out-of-state interests it would overcome that burden. But that is not so: again, we would be forgetting that the paradoxes and balances of constitutionalism may require us to favour intensity or civic solidarity instead of inclusion and that could tilt the balance in favour of national constitutionalism (that's why we continue to often accept instances of national preference towards our own citizens). Moreover, the lack of long-term political contract makes it difficult, as we said, for global constitutionalism to realise some of the trade-offs that are related to less consensual modes of constitutional decision-making. This further reinforces the presumption in favour of national constitutionalism but does not make it insuperable.

There are instances where global governance and constitutionalism can prevail over national claims of constitutional self-determination even when it involves an exercise of power that cannot be traced back to an explicit State commitment. We can present some proxies that may help us in identify when we can apply the normative claims derived from global constitutionalism in its relation with the States:

> When States can be said to have made a broader commitment to a partial global constitutionalisation of certain areas or forms of action. In other words, where they have committed themselves to include out-of-state interests.

> When the international commitments of States bring their respective constitutional orders into collision. There is an inherent tension between the emergence of international inter-dependence (which presupposes impacting on the polities of the others) and the respect for the independent decisions of different polities (which can be argued both in terms of sovereignty and in terms of higher democratic claims). This must also be regulated by global constitutionalism.

> Where forms of global governance alter the constitutional balance of the States although the State may continue to have the dominant voice in the supra-national decision (in this case, the role of global constitutionalism will predominantly be that of re-installing the national constitutional balance at the global level).

> When global constitutionalism simply serves to reform national democracies from their own internal perspective. In other words, it does not replace the decision of the national political community but helps to correct domestic constitutional malfunctions in the way such decision is being taken.

This does not mean that the processes of global governance should prevail in all these circumstances but simply that it is more likely that the presumption in favour of national constitutionalism will be overcome. Whether or not that will be the case depends on the constitutional and comparative institutional analysis to be made in the specific cases. I cannot provide abstract constitutional choices but simply constitutional criteria on how concrete constitutional choices ought to be made.

There is a further aspect I would like to address and that helps identifying the viability of global constitutionalism even in the context of national constitutionalism. I would call it the dynamic of mirroring interests. It refers to the fact that in many instances the inclusion of out-of-state interests also.